THE LAST RIDE

of the

PONY EXPRESS

THE LAST RIDE

of the

PONY EXPRESS

MY 2,000-MILE HORSEBACK JOURNEY INTO THE OLD WEST

WILL GRANT

Little, Brown and Company
New York Boston London

Little, Brown and Company
Hachette Book Group
1290 Avenue of the Americas, New York, NY 10104
littlebrown.com

First Edition: June 2023

Little, Brown and Company is a division of Hachette Book Group, Inc. The Little, Brown name and logo are trademarks of Hachette Book Group, Inc.

The publisher is not responsible for websites (or their content) that are not owned by the publisher.

The Hachette Speakers Bureau provides a wide range of authors for speaking events. To find out more, go to hachettespeakersbureau.com or call (866) 376-6591.

Little, Brown and Company books may be purchased in bulk for business, educational, or promotional use. For information, please contact your local bookseller or the Hachette Book Group Special Markets Department at special.markets@hbgusa.com.

Map by Mike Reagan, www.mreaganmaps.com

Print interior design by Abby Reilly

ISBN 9780316422314
Library of Congress Control Number: 2023934894

10 9 8 7 6 5 4 3 2 1

MRQ-T

Printed in Canada

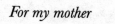
For my mother

Contents

CONTENTS

Author's Note

In May 2019, I set out from St. Joseph, Missouri, with two horses and a plan to ride to Sacramento, California, along the Pony Express Trail. This book is the story of what I saw, who I met, and what happened. I undertook the journey as a largescale exercise in horsemanship with the goal of achieving a boots-on-the-ground understanding of the famed Pony Express mail service. I also wanted to make a transect of the cultural West. I wanted to meet the people and learn about their lives in all the places that I'd never been to along the trail. I hope that I have portrayed those people with the same levels of respect and grace with which they treated me. I owe a debt of gratitude to everyone who helped and supported me during my summer on horseback. The journey would not have been possible without them.

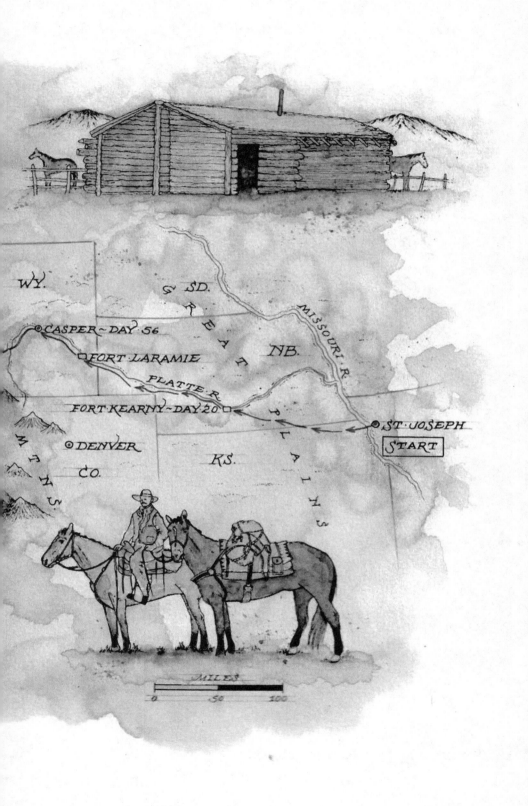

THE LAST RIDE

of the

PONY EXPRESS

PROLOGUE

I WATCHED THE roan horse wallow in a mudhole a mile below me. You wouldn't have thought that amid all that wind and sky and rock of Utah's West Desert there'd be water enough to make a mudhole, but there in front of me on a yellow plain that seared under a high sun, the dusky horse flopped from side to side, kicking its legs in the air like a dog scratching fleas. The horse's solitude told me it was a stallion. Four hundred wild horses, known as the Onaqui herd, summer in this valley, and the only ones that range alone are mares about to foal, old horses about to die, and stallions without harems of mares. This horse didn't look old and wild mares don't foal in August, so I assumed he was a stallion. He stood from rolling, and when he walked out of the mud, he appeared a much darker horse. He hadn't seen me and my two horses— Chicken Fry and Badger—enter the valley from the east, but I figured it was only a matter of time.

Chicken Fry and Badger showed no signs of agitation, but why would they? For the past three months, we'd been traveling west on rural roads, past farms and ranches and suburban subdivisions, and they'd seen many horses. But those horses posed no threat; they were domesticated. This one was different.

This was a wild horse, a mustang, a free-roaming member of feral equines that became part of the Western landscape after sixteenth-century Spanish conquistadors brought the first horses North America had seen since the last ice age, ten thousand years ago. The Spanish, and countless others since, lost horses that stampeded to freedom in the middle of the night or wandered off in search of fresh grass or otherwise untethered themselves from their owners. Those strays gathered in herds and became known as *mesteños* (Spanish for "escaped livestock"). The word was later anglicized into "mustang," and today it's a common term for a wild horse of the American West. Over the centuries, one enduring trait has been that they're apt to harass domestic horses. The roan mustang before me posed a problem because I wanted to camp at a corral beside the mudhole that he'd just rolled in. That corral was the only safe haven for my horses for a day's ride in any direction.

Wild stallions will kill a domestic gelding, a castrated horse, in the same way that wolves will kill a domestic dog. Chicken

Fry and Badger, therefore, were vulnerable. Mares may be absorbed into a harem, but geldings are a threat. And since domestic geldings rarely mature with the sparring and fighting that establishes social hierarchy within a wild herd, Chicken Fry and Badger would likely not last long. They'd also be wearing their saddles and carrying my gear—trappings of domestication that would hinder their survival. I was more than halfway up the Pony Express Trail—ninety-two days and more than a thousand miles out from its eastern terminus in St. Joseph, Missouri—and I hadn't come this far just to lose my horses in a running fight with a mustang stallion.

So I decided to take a nap. Better to do nothing and potentially avoid a wreck than walk right into one. I figured the situation might work itself out, that after an hour's doze the stallion would be gone. As I unlashed the panniers from the packsaddle, slid the bridle off Badger, and loosened the cinches on the saddles, both horses sighed with the prospect of a reprieve. I leaned against a tree, and ran the ropes under my legs so that I could feel any sudden movement they made. When I lifted my hat from my eyes an hour or so later, three mustangs stood on the plain. An old white horse with a swayed back, a black horse, beyond the white, that waved in mirage like a candleflame, and, nearest to us, the roan. The area around the mudhole had become a bachelor boneyard, and I could have listed things I would rather have seen.

I asked Chicken Fry and Badger if they had any ideas about scattering the congregation, but they only yawned and stretched like soldiers waking from a halt. So I came up with one: I would throw rocks. Rocks the size of lemons or base-balls. I'd wait to throw them until I could see the whites of the stallion's eyes. I carried a lightweight .357 revolver in case I needed to humanely put down one of my horses due to some catastrophic injury, and I took the pistol from my saddlebag and slid it into my vest pocket. I didn't know what I would do with the gun—maybe shoot the ground in front of the roan—but if I did that, Badger, sensitive as he was, would probably jerk the reins from my hands and take off across the desert. Which would leave me down a horse and in a world of trouble, assuming I could still hang on to Chicken Fry.

I readied my horses and hardened up the cinches on both saddles tighter than if there had been no mustangs in my future. I stepped onto Badger, and eased downhill into the furnace of an August afternoon. When I was halfway to the corral, the roan horse saw us. He jerked up his head from grazing, and I cursed him. He took a few halting steps, broke into a trot, and pretty soon headed our way at a run.

I slid from the saddle and informed Chicken Fry and Badger that we were about to have our first scrape with a mustang. The roan stallion made quick work of the distance between us, and when he was a hundred yards off, he vectored to the right, hammering over the dry plain on black hooves that looked and sounded as hard as the basalt cobbles beneath him. He arched his neck and swung his head in bold communication, and his posturing was not lost on me. He was a large horse, the color of rust, with a black mane and tail, and his head was dark and unrefined. Old scars on his flanks and along his back showed as gnarled lines and crescent moons—haired-over glyphs from that hierarchical herd sorting that betrayed him to be no colt, but a mature horse. The tops of his legs had the horizontal striping of ancient equine DNA, and though I knew he carried the distant pedigree of a domestic horse, he looked as raw and wild as the desert that made him.

He wheeled a full circle around us at a gallop. In one hand, I held the reins to Badger and the lead rope to Chicken Fry, and had a rock in the other as he came in front of us, some forty feet off. I missed with my first rock. The second hit him at the base of his neck, and he shied violently, leaping forward into the air and pawing at the rock that had just invaded his space. I landed another rock in his flank, and he bucked, kicked his hindquarters straight out with a snap of hooves and muscle that looked like he might kick the door off heaven, and then he took off at a flat run in the other direction.

He charged another circle around us, but this time he appeared frustrated. He stopped square in front of us, looking right at me with his head held high and his nostrils flaring, and I figured that this was my chance to put one between his eyes, but I missed. The rock flew wide to his left, and he dodged right and disengaged, quartering away from us at a walk. Chicken Fry and Badger were unfazed, had stood quietly behind me while I stood our ground. I filled my pockets with more rocks. Once the roan was about one hundred yards away, he lowered his head to graze. But he was not disinterested; I could see the insides of his ears. His ears turned toward us told me that we held his focus as I made for the corral afoot, leading Chicken Fry and Badger so that if the stallion made another run for us, I'd be ready.

I'd known there would be wild horses in western Utah. I'd known that wild horses would be a fixture of the range between the Rocky Mountains and Sierra Nevada. But I hadn't anticipated the acute threat they would pose to my horses. I might as well have been camped on the African savanna with lions and leopards. The mustangs felt just as dangerous.

For the past three months I'd seen the color of the West in shades of people and land and circumstance. I was passing through a continental theater where I found too little rainfall, too much of the original prairie broken up by the iron plow, too many old timers who remember heavy-snow winters like they don't get any more. I found too many invasive species, too much irrigation draining dwindling aquifers, too many small towns ready to fall off the map. But what I found at the mudhole three days into the desert was different, more unsettling. The roan stallion reminded me that the undiminished wildness of the West was dangerous—beautiful and intriguing, but dangerous—and that not everything had changed since the days of the Pony Express.

Chapter 1
The Making of the West

SAGEBRUSH IS AS good a way to define the American West as anything else. Other metrics may be used to delineate the high and dry Western midsection of North America, but few do so as fully as the woody, generally low-growing shrub of the *Artemisia* family commonly known as sagebrush. It's endemic to the North American West. You won't find it on the banks of the Mississippi River or in the forests of New England or anywhere else in the world. It prefers an open steppe-like environment with poor soil and plenty of wind. On a landscape scale, it covers rolling prairies with a greenish-gray hue that can only accurately be described as the color of sagebrush. An afternoon rain shower releases its sweet, unique aroma. Terpenoids give it its pungency and flammability. Indigenous peoples use it as a smoldering smudge, among many other things, and anyone who's ever camped on the plains has likely used it for fuel wood. More so than the pronghorn or the bison or the mounted cowboy, it is an icon of the American West. Which means that if you want to know the extent of the West, look at a map of the distribution of sagebrush.[1]

Technically, the American West includes portions of seventeen states. Border states foster the gradients of change. Kansas, Nebraska, Texas, and the Dakotas lie over the transition zone from the humid forestlands of the Midwest and South to the arid shortgrass prairies of the high plains. From farm country to rangeland. From muggy summers to monsoonal summers.[2] From a region where precipitation exceeds evaporation to where the opposite can be true: there are places in the West where more water returns to the atmosphere through evaporation than falls from the sky.[3] California, Oregon, and Washington are part of the West in their interior regions, but their coastal portions receive too much rain and are home to too many people, and sagebrush is found in only a few locations there.

That's the geography of the West. Academic authors of peer-reviewed journals and bureaucrats like those at the Bureau of Land Management sometimes call portions of it the Intermountain West. People who don't live there refer to it as Out West. It runs from the center of Nebraska to the Sierra Nevada. From the northern grasslands of Montana to the bootheel of New Mexico. It's the high, dry, and lonesome part of North America where you find prairie dogs and jackrabbits and vistas so long you can see into next week. It's prone to its romantic moments—if you don't mind the dust and the wind—but for all its spatial grandeur and wide-open freedom, one of the most important things to know about the West is its contribution to our national identity.

The first European American to put a number on where the West begins was the geologist and Grand Canyon explorer John Wesley Powell. In an 1879 report to the U.S. Congress, Powell identified an east-west rainfall gradient along the 100th meridian. He found that annual rainfall decreased from twenty-four inches of precipitation east of the 100th to eighteen inches west of it.[4] Powell's study of the West was largely scientific, but in 1931 the historian Walter Prescott Webb, in his seminal book *The Great Plains*, refined the observation to the 98th meridian and furthered it to include the cultural gradient between the East and West:

> As one contrasts the civilization of the Great Plains with that of the eastern timberland, one sees what may be called an institutional *fault* (comparable to a geological fault) running from middle Texas to Illinois or Dakota, roughly following the ninety-eighth meridian. At this *fault* the ways of life and of living changed.[5]

This is not a revelation. Where thin runs the fabric of civilization, the hand of the land bears heavily upon those who make from it what life they may. Before anthropogenic development deprives a landscape of its natural attributes—before sidewalks pave the red-dirt mud or city parks beat back the thorned vegetation or municipal water runs from household taps—the earthen qualities of that landscape may be seen in the crow's-foot folds of the eyes squinting into its sun. I know this to be true. That land arrests certain characteristics of its people—how they look, how they dress, what they build their houses with—to a degree proportional to their proximity to the land. I don't need an anthropologist to tell me that a Sámi reindeer herder is a product of the Scandinavian landscape. Or that a Maasai tribesman of East Africa reflects his environment. In the heart of the American West, I see three tangible factors that have shaped the cultures within it: a lack of timber, a scarcity of water, and a temperate, continental climate. But more so than any climatic or biological influence, the wide-open country is what has made the people. The miles between horizons produce a psyche that, like sagebrush, doesn't happen in the East. The psyche that the western frontier of the United States produced in the nineteenth century is significant because it affected the national psyche. One of the first people to recognize this was the historian Frederick Jackson Turner.

In 1893, Turner published an essay titled "The Significance of the Frontier in American History," in which he argues that the idea of a frontier was fundamental to the American character. Turner's essay reflects a dated perspective, and it's been widely criticized for its failure to address the expansion of the U.S. as the conquest of existing societies. But one thing that he articulated as well as anyone since was the roughshod psyche that developed in European Americans during the eighteenth and nineteenth centuries.

> From the conditions of frontier life came intellectual traits of profound importance... The result is that to the frontier the American intellect owes its striking charac- teristics. That coarseness and strength combined with acuteness and inquisitiveness; that practical, inventive turn of mind, quick to find expedients; that masterful grasp of material things, lacking in the artistic but pow- erful to effect great ends; that restless, nervous energy; that dominant individualism, working for good and for evil, and withal that buoyancy and exuberance which comes with freedom—these are traits of the frontier, or traits called out elsewhere because of the existence of the frontier.[6]

The West, therefore, becomes more than a region. It is a time and a place and a consciousness. Turner argues that when the census of 1890 declared that the frontier no longer existed, it was, in fact, the truth. Others have felt similarly. The scholar Charles Neider, who's best known for editing Mark Twain's autobiography, published in 1959, assembled contemporary articles, documents, and essays in the compen- dium *The Great West: A Treasure of Firsthand Accounts*, published in 1958. From the conquistador Francisco Vázquez de Coro- nado's own account of his expedition to the death warrant for Billy the Kid, Neider's coverage of the West is thorough, though it contains many excerpts rather than complete works. The first sentence of the introduction opens the book with its place-time parameters:

> For the purpose of this volume, I have regarded the American West as beginning geographically west of the Mississippi River and ending chronologically at the turn of the last century, approximately with the closing of the frontier.[7]

The chronological beginning of the West is not as clear as its ending. The current environment began to take shape when the last ice age ended ten thousand years ago. Indigenous peoples developed nomadic and seminomadic lifeways that followed the seasons, the wildlife, the water. A network of trade routes connected parts of the West with the rest of the Americas, and complex civilizations arose on the Great Plains and throughout the Southwest and wherever there were sufficient resources to support settlement. The biggest change to the cultural landscape, though, came with the arrival of Europeans. In 1519, the Spanish explorer Hernán Cortés landed at what would become Veracruz, Mexico. Twenty-one years later, in 1540, Francisco Coronado marched north as far as present-day Kansas with guns, germs, and 1,000 horses.[8] By 1790, Spain claimed sovereignty over most of western North America, from Mexico to Alaska. At the same time, British, French, and Anglo-American trappers looking for beaver hides made inroads to the Pacific Northwest. Indigenous peoples faced intrusion from all sides, and the end of their pre-European existence began in earnest when Spain ceded the massive territory of Louisiana to Napoleon Bonaparte in 1800, who took physical possession of it in November 1803 and quickly turned it over to President Thomas Jefferson in December of that year.

No one from Spain, France, or the United States knew the extent of Louisiana when it was handed over. Jefferson interpreted it to include land from the Mississippi River to the Continental Divide, but no one knew for sure the trace of the Continental Divide or how far north the region ran. The historian Stephen Ambrose makes this clear in his book about the Lewis and Clark Expedition, *Undaunted Courage*:

> Jefferson wanted land. He wanted empire. He reached out to seize what he wanted, first of all by continually expanding the boundaries of Louisiana.[9]

And then he sent Meriwether Lewis and William Clark to find a navigable waterway to the Pacific Ocean, what was optimistically referred to as the Northwest Passage. They found that no such waterway existed—"It was Lewis's unhappy task to tell the president that his hope for an all-water route linking the Atlantic and the Pacific was gone," Ambrose writes—but they laid the first tenuous trace of U.S. sovereignty in the West.[10] For the purpose of this book, that is the chronological beginning of the American West.

The West existed in two phases: the Old West and the Wild West. The Old West opened in the beginning of the nineteenth century with fur trappers wading in icy streams up and down the Rocky Mountains. They were known as "free trappers" because of their fickle allegiance to anything other than money, wild places, and the freedom to wander. They filled in much of the map, though, for the country behind them, and a handful were actually literate enough to draw maps for publication.

The beaver trade dried up about the time Oregon became an emigrant's destination. In the 1830s, the mountain man found new work as a guide, scout, *un vaqueano*—Spanish for "one who knows the way." By the late 1830s what beaver remained in the Rocky Mountain streams weren't worth the effort to trap, and though Oregon was claimed by both the United States and Great Britain, American settlers began arriving once the wagon road over the Rocky Mountains was established. When Oregon became a U.S. territory in 1846, emigration became more organized and consistent. The decorated historian Francis Parkman was there to see it. He's best known for his book *The Oregon Trail: Sketches of Prairie and Rocky-Mountain Life*. Like every other account of the trail, the book is filled with roadside graves and wagon accidents and failing livestock. It also depicts another aspect of the frontier: the diversity of people attracted it. Parkman's point of view reflects a dated prejudice of the time, though his tally of ethnicities present is informative. From a boat on the Missouri River, which was the jumping-off point for all the trails going west, he describes an array of characters assembled on the bank on a rainy evening in the spring of 1846: a group of Spaniards headed for Santa Fe, Mexican Indigenous peoples crouched over a fire, a few French hunters "with their long hair and buckskin dresses," and "sitting on a log close at hand were three men, with rifles lying across their knees."[11]

Emigration westward idled along through the 1840s. Brigham Young and his Mormon vanguard broke earth in the Salt Lake Valley in 1847, and in 1848, gold washed up in the tailrace at Sutter's Mill near Coloma, California, setting off the gold rush. California became a state two years later— the first state west of the Missouri River—and emigration westward soared over the next decade. Nearly three hundred thousand people left the East or a homeland abroad for the wide-open West between 1840 and 1860.[12] And yet, European-American inroads across the West were little more than that. The bison herds were intact. The U.S. government had not declared widespread war on Indigenous peoples in the West. The only sizable European-American settlement between California and the Missouri River was the Mormon outpost in Utah. Then, in April 1861, shots at Fort Sumter turned all attention to the East. The Civil War ended the Old West.

After the Civil War, the Wild West was born. The people who populated the Wild West lent their character to the time. They were party to the deflowerment of the landscape, and they affected the profound changes that forever altered the West as they had found it, as it had been for millennia. One such man was a buffalo hunter named Frank Mayer.

Mayer was born in Louisiana in 1850 and served as a bugler during the Civil War. He lived to be 104 years old. He came west in 1872 and first heard about bison hunting in Dodge City, Kansas. He dictated his experience as a commercial hunter to author Charles B. Roth. Roth published Mayer's account in *The Buffalo Harvest*, a thin book printed in 1958 that gives procedural detail to the wholesale slaughter of the bison. Mayer was part of the contingent of men who supplied the booming hide trade of the 1870s and '80s and who left in their wake millions of hideless carcasses to rot on the prairie. His story encapsulates what happened on the Great Plains from 1870 to 1890, and part of understanding that episode is understanding those people's reasons for being on the plains in the first place:

> At the close of any war there are bound to be thousands of young men who find peacetime pursuits too dull for their adventure-stirred lives. Maybe that was truer after the Civil War than at any other time. I know how I felt. I was restive. I wanted out. Fortunately for us then we had what you don't have now: we had a frontier to conquer. It was a very good substitute for war.[13]

Mayer and his colleagues made quick work of the bison. What had once been a population estimated at approximately

60 million was reduced to 541 by 1889. Mayer conceded that the removal of the bison was a condemnable act but argued, essentially, that no one knew any better. A detail he refers to is that they didn't call themselves hunters: "We professionals didn't run buffalo at all, but we called ourselves buffalo runners, never hunters." But it was clearly a commercial hunting venture, and it was done without regard for the long-term survival of the species:

> Maybe we runners served our purpose in helping abolish the buffalo; maybe it was our ruthless harvesting of him which telescoped the control of the Indian by a decade or maybe more. Or maybe I am just rationalizing. Maybe we were just a greedy lot who wanted to get ours, and to hell with posterity, the buffalo, and anyone else, just so we kept our scalps on and our money pouches filled. I think maybe that is the way it was.[14]

Mayer's statement approaches the great paradox of the Wild West. The subjugation of the Indigenous peoples and the near extinction of the bison are the ugliest aspects of the time—two points of no return that speak to the imperialistic, headlong expansion of the U.S.

The great Indigenous nations of the mountains and plains fell during the Wild West. Leaders like Geronimo, Sitting Bull, Crazy Horse, and Red Cloud saw the forced movement of their peoples onto U.S. government reservations while the guns of bison hunters cleared the ranges. What the historical record lacks, though, is the prairie ecosystem's response to the lack of its dominant ruminant. Nothing that I've read confronts the topic, but it's my speculation that those years, between the removal of the bison and the arrival of livestock, transformed the prairie into an abundance of grasses and wildflowers that may have never before occurred, so that when the first entrepreneurial cowmen arrived from Texas, they found a sea of pasture waiting for them. None was probably aware of the unique timing of his visit—that he was looking at grassland devoid of its keystone grazers—and none wasted time in stocking and overstocking the cool-grass ranges of the high plains. That was the genesis of the American cowboy. He was a mounted stockman who developed his own style: saddles, spurs, hats, bedrolls, and all the other gear that came with living on the range and tending cattle by horseback. The cowboy of the Wild West was usually uncouth, penniless, and unfit for civilization, but his life was full of excitement and danger, and though his personal effects usually amounted to only a saddle and a bedroll, he fixed himself as an American character.

If you want to read a good story about cowboys, read Larry McMurtry's *Lonesome Dove*. If want to read something that's less suitable as a children's bedtime story but more indicative of why the Wild West was wild, read the story of I. P. ("Print") Olive. The saga of Print Olive has been told and retold throughout the canon of Western literature and history. The most thorough is Harry Chrisman's book,

The Ladder of Rivers. All accounts note that Olive was one of three brothers from Texas who trailed cattle north, eventually settling in northwest Nebraska. A cowboy named E. C. "Teddy Blue" Abbott worked on one of the Olive drives, and included the experience in his book, *We Pointed Them North: Recollections of a Cowpuncher.* He wrote that all four of the Olive brothers "was dark, like so many Texas men of that early day, with them black eyes like a rattlesnake's and the temper to match."[15]

In 1878, the Olives suspected neighboring ranchers of stealing cattle, or rustling, as it's known in the West. This was before the time of barbed wire, and cattle herds wandered and mingled freely. Bob Olive confronted the neighbors, who shot and killed Bob in the front yard of their cabin. Print put a $700 bounty on their heads. Rather than fight, the two men turned themselves in to the Keith County sheriff, who turned over the two rustlers to Print on the premise that he would have them tried before a judge. The finer points of what happened next are argued over, but the end result was that the two men were hanged from a tree by lariats, the thin, coiled ropes that cowboys carry on their saddles. One of the prisoners had been shot in the arm. Both had been burned, charred black as coal. Some say that Print hanged the men and then poured coal oil over them. As they swung in front of him, he shot them with a rifle, and the powder blast from the gun ignited the oil, leaving the burned bodies.[16] Another version says that Print only hanged the men, that two of his drunk cowboys returned to the scene that night and poured whiskey on the hanging bodies and in their mouths, and then set them on fire.[17] Either way, the undertaker H. M. Hatch took photographs of the blackened, contorted corpses behind his facility in Kearney, Nebraska, which were then widely circulated. Print was tried before a jury and found guilty of the murders. Abbott went to see him in jail and wrote, "He was just like a caged lion, fit to tear himself to pieces."[18]

Such was the raucous adolescence of the American West. It was a wild, lawless time that inspired the national psyche through promoters like Buffalo Bill Cody and his Wild West show, through the dime novels of writers like Ned Buntline, and through Eastern journalists who came West and trotted home with tall tales of the frontier. By the turn of the century the dust had mostly settled. The bison were few, the Indian Wars had mostly ended, and the land grab was over. When the twentieth century rolled in, the conquering of the West was handed down as the growing pains of a nation. Modernization paved over the old trails, and the forts and battlefields and crude graveyards were designated as historical landmarks.

But the West did not become an anachronism. All is not lost. The land has retained its wild character. The new riders of the purple sage have no shortage of sage through which to ride. Montana winters are still cold. The state of Nevada remains larger than all of New England, and clean air blows over New Mexico. In the American West, we will never undo the fundamental changes to the landscape inflicted over the past two centuries, but I can tell you one thing: there are still a lot of ways to die out in the sagebrush.

———

I am a product of the West. My patrilineal family came west to Colorado in the 1860s, and my matrilineal family settled in Texas in the 1930s and '40s. I was born and raised south of Denver, Colorado. From an early age I was afflicted with a love for the cowboy way. The first photograph of me on a horse was taken in 1981. I was two years old, astride a palomino gelding named Buster at the family ranch near Steamboat Springs, Colorado. I never looked back. For all my parents' dissuasion from a life on horseback, I hardly wanted to be anywhere else.

I landed my first horse-training job after college. An outfit in Larkspur, Colorado, hired me to ride young horses for the wage of $15 per ride. Riding young horses that have not been previously ridden, sometimes called breaking horses or starting horses, is hard work. Individual horses handle the initial training phases differently, but nearly all experience some degree of discomfort as they learn to accept a saddle and rider. Young ones can be particularly physical in their responses. If a horse isn't fully convinced that trotting around with a rider on its back is a good deal, it may buck in an effort to dislodge the rider. Sometimes young horses kick or bite. Sometimes they get defensive, upset, frustrated, or sullen. Sometimes they panic. If you're riding a horse that's never been ridden and you inadvertently scare him with a wave of your hand or a sneeze, the level of kinetic energy beneath you can dramatically increase in a short period of time. One moment you're sitting in the saddle; a half second later you've been darted into the ground, heaped upon your twisted neck, wondering where your horse ran off to. Starting horses is an easy to job to do wrong, and in Larkspur I learned how to ride young horses because I grew tired of getting bucked off. But I lacked direction. I was twenty-three years old and needed someone to look up to.

In 2003, my boss, a woman named Bobbi, told me that a horse ranch in North Texas was looking for someone to start a bunch of young horses. An old man named Jack Brainard was overseeing the training. He was something of a legend, she told me, and had been inducted into both the American Quarter Horse Association Hall of Fame and the National Reining Horse Association Hall of Fame. Jack wanted to see a video of me riding, so Bobbi filmed me working with a young horse and mailed the VHS tape to Jack. Three weeks later I drove to the ranch for an interview. They put me on a few horses in the afternoon, and that evening, the ranch owners and Jack and his wife and I ate dinner at Jack's house. One of the owners asked what I wanted for my future with horses. I told her that I wasn't totally sure. Jack, though, had an answer: "It doesn't matter. Once I teach you how to train a horse, you can go do whatever you want."

A month later I moved to Texas. For five years, Jack and I got on like two burning houses. He taught me how to teach a horse to trot sideways, to spin like a dreidel, to stop when the rider says whoa. He taught me how a horse's skeletal structure, musculature, and psychology affect its movement, balance, and motivations. He taught me how to manipulate a horse's brain in coordination with its body, and he helped me see that riding horses is a unique human-animal relationship because the animal bears the rider. Which means that the human can communicate with and affect a horse with innumerable cues. Jack walked me through a thousand horses in terms that I could understand, and he changed the way I perceived them. But I never envisioned spending the rest of my life in Texas, and in 2008, I enrolled in journalism school at the University of Montana. Jack was not happy about it.

"Why in hell do you need to go to journalism school to write about the West?" he asked. "Paul Barrett wrote a book, and he's not even literate."

Paul Barrett was one of Jack's cronies who always seemed to be angling a horse deal. I wasn't aware of any book Paul Barrett had ever written. Jack, though, had written half a dozen books by that time, some of them memoirs, some of them how-to books on horse training, and eventually he came around to support me.

Over the next ten years, I tried to get magazine assignments linked to my horse expertise. I raced horses across Mongolia, looked for gold in Arizona, and rode 400 miles across Wyoming for *Outside* magazine. What I could not find was an avenue to describe the West as I knew it. I needed a focal point for all the elements of the land and its people that informed my psyche. Which is to say that I needed a way to explain my identity. It came on a December night at my home in Santa Fe, New Mexico. A friend and editor at *Outside*, Jonah Ogles, asked me what I knew about the Pony Express. Fast horses and young men, I told him. He encouraged me to look further.

So I did.

———

The Pony Express was a frontier mail service. It carried letter mail between the Missouri River, which was the end of the railroad from the East, and San Francisco. It launched in the spring of 1860 at the twilight of the Old West. It was an express service, a fast-horse mail relay in which riders changed horses at waystations spaced ten, fifteen, twenty miles apart for nearly 2,000 miles. The delivery time was ten days—a breakneck schedule that ruptured the hearts and tendons of more horses than we'll ever know. Each rider covered one hundred or so miles, riding day and night, before handing off the mail to the next rider so that the four bundles of tissue-thin letters, wrapped in oilcloth for protection from the elements, flew across the continent at the speed of a galloping horse.[19] That's nearly the way it happened.

Fast-horse mail relays have likely been in operation since the domestication of modern horses 4,200 years ago. One of the first was the Persian mail relay described by Herodotus in the fifth century BCE.[20] The Roman Empire used a similar service.[21] Perhaps the most famous and longest lasting was Genghis Khan's postal system, the *Yam*, which he set up in the thirteenth century. Under the Yam, riders carried a pass that allowed them to procure a fresh horse, food, water, whatever needed from stations spaced twenty to thirty miles apart. Marco Polo described the Yam in use under Genghis Khan's grandson Kublai. The Yam partly relied on the wide distribution of nomads, and, according to William Taylor, an assistant professor of archaeology at the University of Colorado, it was last used as recently as the 1940s, after roughly eight hundred years of service.[22]

Taylor, whose archaeological work has taken him to Mongolia, told me that he interviewed a man in northern Mongolia whose family was part of the Yam during the twentieth century. That man told Taylor that his grandparents, in lieu of paying taxes, were required to keep a horse saddled at all hours of the day to carry the mail when it arrived. Part of the Yam's success was the prevalence of nomads who kept horses. The Pony Express, on the other hand, ran through a sparsely populated country where horses were not so easy to come by, and, for a lot of reasons, it didn't last nearly as long.

The Pony Express was the greatest display of American horsemanship to ever color the pages of a history book—based on its mileage, number of horses, and rapid execution—but it was brief. It ran for slightly more than eighteen months, from April 3, 1860, to October 26, 1861. Its brevity is best explained by the fact that it was prohibitively expensive to

operate. It couldn't carry enough mail to pay its bills. Estimates say that its total receipts paid for one tenth of the cost
to run it.[23] And the reason that it was so costly was because
carrying the mail at an average speed of eleven miles per
hour for ten continuous days across so vast an area was too
tall a task to be sustainable. For an express service, it covered
a massive distance—like running horses between Madrid and
Moscow. Or across Australia from Sydney to Perth. The
American West is impressively expansive, and in 1860, it was
mostly devoid of horseflesh.

To gallop the mail across half a continent, hundreds,
perhaps a thousand or more horses were strung out along
the line. They were staged by the half dozen or so at each
waystation the proprietor of the Pony Express, a frontier
freighting firm by the name of Russell, Majors and Waddell,
had enlisted for the service.[24] The route ran from St. Joseph,
Missouri, northwest to the Platte River, where it joined the
Oregon Trail. It followed the Platte River to the Continental
Divide in what is today Central Wyoming. From there it ran
southwest along the Mormon Road to Salt Lake City, where
some 8,000 people lived. From Salt Lake City the mail went
straight west across the deserts of the Great Basin to cross
the Sierra Nevada in the vicinity of Lake Tahoe. It then ran
downhill to Sacramento, where the mail was transferred to a
steamship to San Francisco. The eastern portion of the route
along the Oregon Trail saw traffic in the summer months, but
the western portion of the route, from Salt Lake City to the
Sierra Nevada, never saw traffic and was as thinly populated

by either Indigenous peoples or white settlers as any other place in the conterminous U.S. It was remote, arid, and rough—the route crossed fourteen mountain ranges across what is today Nevada—and running a fast-horse mail relay over it proved difficult.

The number of waystations that connected the relays of the Pony Express is variously reported from 153 to 197, though some hardly passed for stations. One in Utah was a hole dug into the side of a hill. One station in Nevada was made of unmortared rock walls and had no roof. Another was no station at all, just a pole corral for the horses, with the men living out in the open.[25] Furniture was rare. Some stations had no usable water source; water had to be hauled in for the mail horses and the stock tenders. Some needed hay brought in where pasturage was thin or nonexistent. When the mail was running twice weekly in both directions, maintaining the service required a huge effort.

Hard data on what the Pony Express accomplished may be seen in the postal record. The study of stamps, also known as philately, has produced a legion of philatelists who have thoroughly tabulated the Pony Express. The most authoritative reference on the subject is *The Pony Express: A Postal History*, by Richard Frajola, George Kramer, and Steven Walske. The book lists what the authors believe to be a reference of every surviving Pony Express cover, what a non-philatelist calls an envelope. The book lists every trip made by the Pony Express: when it departed, when it arrived, and if any covers from the trip survive. The book documents the postage, the meterings, and the rates for delivery of a half-ounce letter, which varied from $1 initially—about $35 today—to $5, or about $160 today. Photographic plates of the covers show fine cursive penmanship not often seen these days, and most letters are marked "per Pony Express" in the way people used to mark letters to Europe with "Air Mail." The status of the senders and the recipients reflects the high cost of the postage: bankers, businessmen, entrepreneurs, and politicians. Reports from the British Navy at war with China were sent per Pony Express. The U.S. Consulate in Honolulu, Hawaii, sent two letters per Pony Express to the Fifth Auditor of the Treasury in Washington, D.C. Of all the covers and what they reveal about the transcontinental postal service, two of the most interesting were part of the lost mail.[26]

The Pony Express was a financial failure, but it mostly succeeded in getting the mail through. Only one delivery was lost. The mail traveled in a removable saddle skirting, a sort of over-saddle apron with four pouches sewn on it, called a mochila, Spanish for "packsaddle" or "knapsack," which could be transferred between horses. Only one mochila failed to make the journey. On or about July 28, 1860, a rider was crossing the North Platte River near present-day Casper, Wyoming, when he and his horse plunged off the bridge. The event is known as the Incident at Platte Bridge. According to Frajola, Kramer, and Walske, someone spooked the horse, and the horse, rider, and mochila went into the river. The horse was never seen again, the rider survived, and the mail turned up two years later. No documentation exists on its recovery, but Wells Fargo and Co., who would go on to become one of the great express institutions of the West, forwarded the mail for processing. Two covers survive from that trip, and both were received in New York in May 1862. One of the letters bears the inscription, "recovered from a mail stolen by the Indians in 1860." The other reads, "recovered from a mail stolen in 1860."[27]

What the two covers from the missing mail provide, and what the Pony Express severely lacks, is tangible evidence of what the actual job entailed. None of the Pony Express riders seem to have kept a journal. What we know about their experiences mostly comes from later recollections. A rider named Billy Fisher, who carried the mail in Nevada and Utah, recounted that he was lost in a blizzard for a full twenty hours. At some point, he dismounted his horse, and leaned against a tree to take a nap, which is a good way to freeze to death. A rabbit woke him. Fisher claimed that the rabbit jumped onto his legs, startled him awake, and saved his life.[28]

Rider J. G. Kelley said that his closest scrape with death was when some "fool emigrants" shot at him as he was running past because, they said, "We thought you was an Indian."[29] George Washington Thatcher claimed that he was leading his horse through deep snow when a wolverine attacked him.[30] Most of the riders, however, recall that the hardest part of the job was the toll of hard riding. Rider William Pridham points to the "long hours of severe toil and unspeakable loneliness, with no companionship but the faithful horses we rode."

Pridham went on to have a long career with Wells Fargo and said:

> In all my fifty years of continuous service with the express company, through all my graduation, the work on the pony was the least attractive...Much romance has been injected by some of the historians in the history of the Pony Express, but my own experience compels me to say it was a stern reality.[31]

That's not to say that the job was without its hairy moments. A rider who left Sacramento in the middle of the night collided with an ox sleeping in the road. In the collision, the horse fell on the rider, breaking his shoulder.[32] Another rider in California was thrown from his horse and broke his leg.[33] A Wells Fargo stagecoach—probably not unlike the ones the company uses in its logo—picked up the mail and carried it to the next station. A rider in Utah was shot through the hand by Paiutes. The shot killed the mule under him, and whoever killed the mule later cut off the its long ears, allegedly for souvenirs.[34] One rider said that getting caught in a bison stampede was what they most feared. A rider in Nebraska lost his horse while crossing the Platte River, and the horse drowned.[35] One rider was never seen again, presumed dead, after his horse trotted into a station with an empty saddle.[36] That's how the Pony Express shook out. It was a wild ride. But to what historical end this all contributed is not so clear.

The significance of the Pony Express is not as apparent as its execution is memorable. The value of what happened during those eighteen months has transgressed the tangible effects carried in the padlocked saddle bags. The Pony Express as a cultural symbol has enjoyed a lot of traction over the years, and among the many artists, authors, journalists, and historians to depict and describe it, few have been able to resist romanticizing it. The apocryphal horseman has galloped off into the sunset so many times that exaggeration has adulterated fact. One exception is the 1930 book *Six Horses*, written by Captain William Banning and George Hugh Banning. William's father was a transportation tycoon in California in the late 1800s. The book covers communication, freighting, and passenger conveyance in the West in the nineteenth century. Its title refers to a team of horses drawing a stagecoach. Banning dedicates two chapters to the Pony Express, and his observations are telling:

> It did not involve more than 150 round trips. It did not cover a full nineteen months. Like a belated fragment of a storm, it came and was gone. Yet the fact remains: a more glamorous contribution to our historic West than that of this ephemeral Pony would be difficult to name.[37]

Banning refers to the Pony Express as an "immortal Pegasus" that was "able to identify himself with the new empire as permanently as though he had come racing up from the gold rush to the last spike driven for the Pacific Railroad." History has lauded the Pony Express as a bold stroke of transcontinental progress, but Banning argues that the Pony Express "neither caused nor hastened the developments that followed his trail" and that "had he never existed, all must have been the same." It was an exciting drama while it lasted, but it was little more than a drama. Its contribution to our historic West, therefore, lies in the fabling that it inspired:

> Thus what benefits were born from the Pony Express is a question better left if the entertainment of a nation is not enough.[38]

Nearly one hundred years have passed since Banning wrote *Six Horses*. The Pony Express entertains the nation yet. But for all the investigation and discourse, questions remain unasked: Why has history been so kind to the Pony Express? What does that treatment say about how we interpret our recent past? How does the Pony Express inform our Western ideology?

———

The more I learned, the surer I became that I was bound to ride the trail. How else could I attain an encompassing grasp of the Pony Express without riding the old mail route? Anything short of doing so was shirking from the truth: that the only way for me to fully understand the breadth and nature of the

Pony Express was to horseback it from one end to the other. It emerged as a challenge, a pinnacle of horsemanship that was high and dangerous. But if I could pull it off, I'd land in rare company. Any horseman worth his salt would agree: the Pony Express is an apex of American horsemanship and to trace its course would be nothing short of transcendental. And so I talked myself into it. Some people look for answers in a library; I'd look for mine between the ears of a horse.

As I began to consider the scope and magnitude of the undertaking—that I'd have to ride every day all day all summer—I realized that the Pony Express Trail was my avenue to understanding the American West. I wanted to know who lived in southern Nebraska and western Nevada and all the places between that I'd never been to. I wanted to see the old Pony Express stations and camp along the trail and judge for myself the desolation of the deserts, but I also wanted to fill in my own demographic map of the West. I wanted to meet the farmers and ranchers and whoever else lived out there. I believe that the best way to interpret a landscape is through the lives of the people subject to that landscape, and so I wanted be a traveler in my own country. I wouldn't race across the West like the Pony Express riders. Instead, I'd walk across the West. I'd take my time, travel slowly, let the answers to my questions percolate with the miles.

With this resolution, I could hardly believe my luck—that I'd found a path to enlightenment between the 98th meridian and the golden shores of California—and in the honeymoon phase of having decided to ride the trail but not having thoroughly confronted the logistics of making it happen, the romance of it all ran pretty deep. It was invigorating and daunting. I didn't know what I didn't know, but for me, it was an honest approach to both the history of the Pony Express and the current landscape of the modern West. And that was reason enough.

CHAPTER 2
A Few Good Horses

THE FIRST THING I needed was a few good horses. The phrase "good horse" means a lot of different things to different people, but essentially, a good horse is one suited to the job being asked of it. Horses come in a lot of shapes and sizes; I wanted Pony Express horses. Long and lean, built to travel but with enough bulk to handle hard work, something like a marathon runner with the physique of a Navy SEAL. They had to be mature horses. A typical horse's working life begins at three or four years old and can last until the horse is twenty or thereabouts (the average lifespan of a domestic horse is twenty-five to thirty years). Young horses would lack the necessary muscle development for such a long trip. I was looking for horses between eight and fifteen years old.

At that time, in January 2019, my girlfriend, Claire, who works in a hospital emergency room, and I were renting a house on a small horse property outside Santa Fe, New Mexico. I owned two horses but neither was suited to a 2,000-mile journey. One was too young, the other too lazy. Coaxing a lazy horse across the West would be too much work, and a young horse might not hold up to the work, meaning it would experience some physical failure such as lameness. I needed horses with a lot of natural forward momentum. Just like humans, some horses are inclined toward idleness, while others are inclined to move, and I wanted horses that wanted to move. So I set about scanning horses-for-sale websites and rattling my network of horse people.

The first horse I bought was a mustang named Rio. He was a brown-and-white paint, small enough to be called a pony but pretty enough to have just trotted off the set of *Dances with Wolves*. He was born in the wild, on the dry ranges of southern New Mexico. His previous owner, a woman who used him mostly for trail rides, adopted him from the New Mexico Livestock Board. The Livestock Board had confiscated the horse from a man who trapped a herd of wild horses in a corral. Trapping wild horses can sometimes be easier than one might think. This man, whose property abutted the horse range, simply left a corral gate open with water available in the corral. In southern New Mexico, an available water source is not likely to be overlooked, and pretty soon the horses were coming to the corral regularly. The man closed the gate on the horses one day and then proceeded to neglect them, which led the Livestock Board to impound the horses and put them up for adoption. Rio was part of that group. His owner adopted him when he was three. I bought him when he was nine.

I brought Rio home, and the first time I rode him, he shied at a crow. The crow was sitting on a fence as we approached it. I was looking right at it, and so was Rio. When we were about forty feet from it, it took off from the fence with a squawk and big heaving motions of its wings, and Rio wheeled away from it so hard and fast that I was left clinging to his side, one arm over his neck, one leg over the saddle, and a thoroughly stretched groin as he bolted for the barn. I managed to stay aboard, but the incident was unsettling because, for one, if every crow we encountered between Missouri and California shot us back in the direction we'd come, it could be a long trip. Secondly, I thought it fair to assume that Rio's wild upbringing had acquainted him with crows, especially given that they are all over New Mexico. More concerning than his flightiness, as I learned over the next few days, was that he was nearly too small. I like small horses: they're easier to get on and off and when something goes wrong, you're closer to the ground if you have to make a crash landing. Rio's previous owner had assured me that whatever he lacked in size, he made up for in heart, but the packsaddle hardly fit him. I kept him as an alternate—a horse that I could have delivered to me mid-journey if another came up lame or was injured.

My next horse was Jackson. Jackson was a long-legged gray horse with ears that turned inward at their tips. A friend of mine, who I had queried about horses, had agreed to lend me

Jackson because she thought a long journey would be good for him. He "had some growing up to do," she told me. He had also done some long-distance racing, had covered one hundred miles in less than ten hours. That sounded like a good choice for the Pony Express Trail, so she sent him my way.

Jackson had a big motor. He felt like a racehorse. And he acted like one. Meaning that he was prone to dramatic bursts of energy. He was also fractious. One afternoon I was breezing him up a sandy arroyo, or dry creekbed, when Jackson decided we'd gone far enough. For whatever reason, the horse didn't want to go any farther. The more pressure I applied, by tapping him with my spurs, the more upset he became. In my head, I heard my old mentor, Jack Brainard, tell me to swat the horse on the butt with the long ends of my bridle reins, send him forward with authority. When I did that, Jackson ran straight sideways across the arroyo and plunged us into a shrubby juniper tree so that the horse nearly sat down amid the branches. My right leg was partially under him, and I was able to get my spur into his ribs to jump him out of the tree. Which sent Jackson ricocheting back across the arroyo, again at a sideways, mostly uncontrolled run. It being February in the high desert, the opposite bank shaded some ice and snow from a recent storm, and when Jackson hit the icy slope, all four feet shot out from under him and we went down in a heap. We were both left slightly limping, but I wasn't convinced the horse had learned anything.

I had originally planned to use three horses for the trip. I'd ride one and lead a packhorse, and the third horse would be tied to the packsaddle so that we would travel in a line. As I acquainted Rio, Jackson, and my lazy gelding, who I thought I might also need as an alternate, with this routine, it became clear none of them enjoyed being the packhorse. Some people consider the job of being a packhorse a demotion from saddle horse, and some horses feel the same. A week after Jackson's wipeout, I was using my lazy gelding as the packhorse, riding Jackson, when the horses became agitated and quickly separated. I was leading the gelding off my right side, until he spun around behind me to the left and twisted me from the saddle, stretching me out horizontally four feet over the prairie with the packhorse leaving to my left, Jackson leaving to my right, and nothing but dust between me and the earth.

Jackson's final tantrum came a few days later. He was loaded with the packs, two duffel bag–type panniers filled with a rough assortment of about fifty pounds of gear that I was combing through in an effort to finalize my kit. As I strapped the packs to the packsaddle, Jackson wore an ugly expression. When a horse cocks his ears back and hoods his eye with his eyelid, it means he's not happy. I told Jackson to soften up, that he'd seen the packsaddle rig nearly every day for the past month. As I stepped away from him, he flew into a violent fit of bucking. The panniers rocked and bounced until they finally came loose and went tumbling off through the dust. Once free of the packs, Jackson broke into a flat run, arcing away through the desert scrub, with sixty feet of lash ropes still tied to the packsaddle and flying in the air behind him like the cast-off marionette strings to some wild puppet. I found him wadded up in a cholla cactus with all that rope around him as if he'd been caught in a massive spider web. He was breathing hard and wearing a few cactus spines but otherwise appeared no worse for the incident. After that, though, Jackson went back to his owner.

Finally, I got a break. A cowboy and horse trainer named Jerry Speer from eastern New Mexico called me. He said he knew of a horse that might work for me. The horse had been born in Mexico, "where they use horses like pickup trucks," he told me. Jerry bought the horse as a young horse the day after he was trucked across the border in Columbus, New Mexico, which is about as far south as you can get in the state. Jerry had ridden the horse for many years, had used him for all types of cowboy work, had been in a thousand tight scrapes with the horse and was only alive today thanks to the horse's level head and clear thinking. His name was Chicken Fry.

"If I was going to do what you're about to do, there's two horses I'd use," Jerry told me. "One is dead. The other is Chicken Fry."

———

Jerry did not own Chicken Fry when I talked to him. A year or so prior, he'd sold the horse to a man named Brant Ward who lived outside San Angelo, Texas. Jerry said to call Brant, ask him if he'd sell me Chicken Fry. So I called Brant and told him that Jerry had given me his phone number.

"Jerry Speer? What kinda outlaws are you running with?" he asked.

I told him that I didn't really know Jerry, had only talked to him about a horse named Chicken Fry.

"Jerry is a very dear friend of mine. Him and I have known each other for a long time. When can you come look at Chicken Fry?"

Three days later, I blew into San Angelo on the heels of a blue norther that had been running cold air over the Llano Estacado and across the prairies of west Texas for the past week. San Angelo sits in west-central Texas, on the shore of a cactus-scrub rangeland that hums all summer with the buzz of rattlesnakes and turns gray and cold in the winter. And that's the shape I found the country: cold and gray, the sky flat and without depth or definition.

Brant lived a few miles northeast of town on an unprotected hilltop. I parked before his barn, a low, steel-sided building with corrals running off three sides of it. Brant rode up on a brown mare as I climbed out of the truck. He wore a duck-canvas chore coat over a hooded sweatshirt and a ball cap that said Cactus Ropes. He stepped off his horse, and I followed him and the brown mare through a gate, across a paddock of frozen mud to where, on the other side of a pipe fence, lay a buckskin horse with all four of his legs tucked under him and his head raised at our approach. Brant slapped the top rail of the fence with his bridle reins and said, "Git up, Chicken Fry."

Chicken Fry unfolded his legs and stood and stretched in a bow and then yawned and looked at me. He was the color of tanned deer hide. His legs were black to his knees, and he had a black muzzle and black ears and a black mane and tail.

"My girls come up here day 'fore yesterday, knocked some of the mud off him, but he ain't been rode in a month," Brant said.

Brant climbed on the brown mare as I saddled Chicken Fry beside my pickup. As I hardened up the cinch, he backed his ears in an unhappy expression and gave me a look that suggested he might just as soon buck my ass off and return to his nap as let me swing a leg over him. I looked at Brant and asked, six thousand dollars for a horse that acts like it wants to buck?

"Try him, he should be fine," Brant said.

Chicken Fry didn't buck. He stood like a rock as I climbed aboard, and that's exactly what a cowboy wants: a horse that even Grandma could get on. We angled across the driveway and made for a gate that Brant rode up to and was about to open when I asked him if I might handle it. Opening and closing a long pipe gate on horseback requires the horse to be easily controlled with one hand on the reins, one hand on the gate. Any honest cowboy would rather open and close a gate from the back of a horse than afoot, because, for one, cowboys can't wait to impress someone with their horsemanship, and, secondly, they're generally too lazy to get off a horse if the job can be done horseback. It's also a good test of a horse's training. Chicken Fry walked up to that pipe gate like a Toyota Prius on park-assist. I didn't do anything, just sat there in the saddle while he sidestepped on autopilot to the gate so that the latch was abreast of my knee, and he stood there waiting for me to open it. I leaned down and threw the latch, and Chicken Fry sidestepped through the gate, pushed it open, waited for Brant and the mare to walk through, and then swung around to the inside and sidestepped to where I could latch it closed.

Brant and I rode through a dry, hillocked pasture cobbled with blocks of limestone. Half a dozen Boer goats browsed the yellow grasses among the rubble. Chicken Fry walked with purpose. He looked over the goats as we passed them. He picked his way among the rocks, was careful with his feet, seemed to be aware of both the ground immediately under-foot and the setting sun over the western horizon. He felt quiet and intelligent. We circled the pasture back to the barn and unsaddled the horses in the thin, fading light of a winter evening. I threw my saddle in my pickup, and Brant said, "Let's go t' the house for a beer."

We walked through a mudroom full of cold-weather gear and into the kitchen. Brant opened the refrigerator and pulled out two Coors Lights and handed me one. He unzipped his chore coat, hooked his thumb in the pocket of his jeans, and took a long pull off the beer.

"What's this Pony Express stuff you're talking about?" he asked.

I told him my plan. He asked how long I thought the journey would take. One hundred days, I told him.

"Jesus Christ. You'll be one tired hombre, time you get done with that. Chicken Fry could do it, though."

I told him that $6,000 was more than I could give for the horse. Generally speaking, $6,000 will get you a good horse in the West. Prices of horses vary from free to six digits, but a trained, mostly reliable horse will cost about that. I'm among the world's worst hagglers, but I knew that my girlfriend, Claire, would have a fit if I didn't try to barter so I asked if he'd take $4,500 for Chicken Fry.

"I gotta have six for him. At six, I've already lost money on the horse."

I ate dinner that night at a Mexican restaurant in San Angelo and rented a room at a beltway motel. I lay on the dirty comforter of the bed, drinking a Modelo Negra, thinking about Chicken Fry. A meteorologist on TV droned on about the cold front. I was buying more of a partner than a horse, and I wondered if half an hour's time with him was enough to see what I needed to see. The biggest challenge of buying a horse for a 2,000-mile journey, I reckoned, is that the only proof a horse could make such a trip would be having made such a trip. Since people rarely travel that far with horses these days, all I had was my gut. I tried to imagine being in the Nevada desert with Chicken Fry, but I'd never been to the Nevada desert. Chicken Fry, though, had conveyed a sense of stability. I couldn't point to any particular behavior, but he inspired calmness. I swallowed a shot of Nyquil, turned off the TV, and figured I'd sleep on it.

A week later I was parked in front of the same motel with a horse trailer. I ate a chicken-fried steak for dinner and picked up Chicken Fry the next morning. I drove home to Santa

Fe through blowing snow and unloaded him under the flood-lights of the barn. Large snowflakes showed yellow against the night and fell in turning circles like autumn leaves. Inside the barn, I put Chicken Fry in a box stall, turned on the over-head lights, and threw him an armful of hay. The horse was muddy to his knees and had mud caked all down one side. His coat was dull, as though he could use a dose of wormer. He shivered from the cold as he ate the hay. I shrugged my shoulders and hoped he'd look better in a month.

My next horse was advertised as a "big, classy" gelding. "Brush, rocks, rough country, this horse can handle it all," the ad read. The horse had been bred in Nevada, foaled in east-ern Oregon, and passed among ranchers and horse trainers until he landed with a woman named Lydia, who managed a ranch an hour west of my home in Santa Fe. I called her on the phone and told her what I was looking for.

"Well, I don't know if you're for real about this Pony Express thing," she said. "But if you are, this is your horse."

The bay horse was standing in the aisle of an old stone barn, tied along one wall when I drove up to the ranch. Lydia walked into the aisle pushing a baby stroller with a tightly swaddled child in it. She told me that *Red Dawn* had been filmed at the ranch and that Patrick Swayze had owned the property for a while. She rocked the baby stroller while I looked over the horse. He was long-muscled and looked like a racehorse. He was dark brown with black legs, and he had a faint line of white hairs running down the center of his face. His back looked a little swayed. He was so lean I could just about count his ribs. Shallow nicks and scratches marked his chest and the fronts of his legs. I nodded at them.

"The cowboys here been chasing yearlings on him for the past month," Lydia said. "They're gonna be awful sorry to see him go."

I saddled the horse in the barn and rode out into a pasture that had only barely turned green with spring. After two minutes, I felt the right stuff. The horse was extremely sensitive to slight commands. He had the tight steering of a sports car, and he demanded the same careful handling. Too much throttle could leave you hanging in the air without a horse under you. If you hit the brakes, you better be ready to stop. The horse moved quickly with balanced footwork that belied his unremarkable body structure and shape. He didn't appear to have the mental stability that Chicken Fry had, but he could travel. He idled at a high RPM. I felt miles in his long stride. A week later he was in my corral with Chicken Fry, and I started calling him Badger for no other reason than it seemed like a good name for a horse. At that point, I abandoned the idea of traveling with three horses. I had my team for the Pony Express Trail: Chicken Fry and Badger.

———

The most important factor to ensure that I could ride across the West was having good horses. The second was ensuring that I didn't lose those horses, particularly at night. Losing horses while camping has a been consistent aspect of traveling with them for as long as people have been doing so. In 1859, Horace Greeley, editor of the *New-York Tribune* and a future presidential candidate, traveled across the West. Near Laramie, Wyoming, his party's mules ran off during the night and kept everyone awake until dawn trying regather them.[1] Author Rinker Buck, who drove a mule-drawn wagon up the Oregon Trail in 2012, lost his mules in Wyoming.[2] When I rode four hundred miles across Wyoming in 2017, we lost our horses on the banks of the Green River. Ask anyone who's ever camped with horses for more than a few days if he or she ever woke in the morning to find the livestock gone, and they'll tell you it's a common occurrence.

Of the several ways to restrain horses at night, none are fail-safe. The two most common methods are picketing and hobbling. Picketing a horse involves tying it to something. You can run a rope between two trees and tie the horse to the horizontal rope. This is a safe way to restrain a horse but does not allow the horse to graze or walk freely, and requires conveniently spaced trees. You can also picket a horse to a stake in the ground, tied by either its front foot or lead rope. This allows the horse to graze the area surrounding the stake, but it can be dangerous because the animal can get entangled in the rope. When horses become tangled in ropes, they usually panic and end up injured. Horses need to be properly trained to handle being picketed, and I didn't have the time to do it, nor did I want to take the risk.

To hobble a horse is to fetter it, or tie its feet together in such a way that the horse can take only small steps and therefore cannot travel quickly or easily. Eurasian nomads, who first domesticated horses, invented hobbles because they lived on the treeless steppe, where there was no easy place to tie a horse.[3] A leather strap or section of rope is used to tie the front feet together, sometimes including a back foot, as well. The effect is the same as if a person's shoelaces were tied together. Small steps are possible but running is not. The problem with hobbles, in my situation, was that they would not allow my horses to stretch or lie down.

As I mulled over the safest way to contain my horses while still allowing them to graze, I reached out to a mule packer who contracts with the U.S. Forest Service to haul freight into wilderness areas where motor vehicles are prohibited. His name is Chris Eyer. I learned about him through a *New Yorker* profile titled "Instagram's Most Famous Mules."[4] Sure enough, his Instagram account was filled with photos of pack trains—nine mules tied head to tail in a line—hauling massive bridge timbers, hay bales, lumber. I wrote to him, and we began a correspondence about how to restrain my two horses. He told me that the path to fewest accidents, in his experience, was a portable electric fence. The fence was a strand of three-eighths-inch rope with aluminum wire braided into it. A solar-powered charger electrifies the fence. Fiberglass corner posts support the rope, and each post is two pieces connected in the middle by a ferrule sleeve like those used on fishing rods so that the posts could come apart to fit on a packsaddle. The fence could be set up on a slope, over a creek, at a highway rest stop, anywhere over grass, and it could be made as big or small as necessary. I thanked Chris and put together the rope, posts, and solar charger for a fence that was sixty feet square, which would allow Chicken Fry and Badger plenty of space to graze, roll, and lie down.

By the end of April, I was ready to go. My gear was sorted. I'd carry a lightweight, one-person tent that was about the size of a coffin, so small my hat hardly fit through the door. I'd carry two small camping stoves, a small ultraviolet light to purify water, a basic med kit, a harness repair kit, a couple layers of insulation, a hard-shell rain jacket, an extra shirt, an extra pair of Wrangler jeans, and half a dozen new pairs of heavyweight wool socks. I decided to carry exactly one spare pair of underwear with no plan of how to clean it. I reckoned that's how a Pony Express rider would do it: one change of underwear. As far as using the bathroom, I was looking at a fairly uncomfortable situation, but figured I'd have to handle it on a case-by-case basis. I didn't know what my prospects were for showering or bathing—nor did I care—but I knew that I couldn't be bothered to shave my face. A toothbrush, a tube of toothpaste, and a bar of soap was my hygiene kit. I'd have a headlamp, a flashlight, half a dozen notebooks, and a pair of fencing pliers, which could serve as a hammer, wire cutter, horseshoe puller, and pliers. At each opportunity to resupply, I would lade eight days of food—canned beef stew, macaroni and cheese, canned chili and Fritos, a few dehydrated back-packer meals. My gear, including the electric fence and my bedroll, fit into two canvas panniers, which are like duffel bags without handles, that I sprayed with silicon water-repellent.

Each pannier would weigh about forty pounds and be lashed to one side of the packsaddle. I used a hanging scale to ensure that each pannier weighed the same because an unbalanced load is a good way to make a horse's back sore.

What I could not do was plan the entire trip. The lay of the Pony Express Trail, which is generally more of an auto-tour route rather than a single-track trail, determined my general course, though I'd vary from it to find the quietest, safest paths to travel, but I had no way of knowing when I would reach Nevada or when I would cross the Continental Divide or even how long it would take me to ride the breadth of Nebraska. The horses would determine my daily and weekly mileage, though I hoped to cover twenty to twenty-five miles per day. They would also determine where I camped because they needed grass and water. I would sleep beside them, roll out my bedroll under the fence. I would avoid sleeping in the tent so that I could see the horses without unzipping a screen door. I'd need permission to camp on private land; there was no question about that. A sure-enough mark of a tourist in the West is someone who isn't aware of private property lines. I wasn't concerned about trespassing on government-owned land, but I was not going to camp without permission on private land, mostly because of the damage it would do to my reliance on help from locals along the way. Neither was I going to sleep in a motel or anyone's house. I'd sleep with my horses.

I planned to travel four consecutive days before stopping for a day's rest. That schedule put me on the road for one hundred days, arriving in Sacramento in early August. It seemed unlikely for things to play out in that way, but it was the framework of a method. Some of the best travel advice I've ever received came from my former boss Robert Young Pelton, author of the offhand travel compendium *The World's Most Dangerous Places* and who had traveled extensively in dangerous places. He told me: be flexible, stay relaxed, and keep smiling. That advice, along with two good horses, a portable electric fence, and my cell phone for navigation, was my approach to riding across the West.

———

A quick look at the map of the Pony Express Trail reveals that for most of the route's eastern half, it's not the kind of place a guy could starve to death. In Kansas, it runs through densely developed farmland. For most of Nebraska, it follows U.S. and interstate highways. The Pony Express Trail doesn't run through large tracts of public land until halfway through Wyoming. While on the eastern half of the trail, the first half of my journey, I'd have no shortage of cell service or grocery stores and would be unlikely to get lost, but it was the people I was worried about—the population density, the towns, the highways, the Union Pacific Railroad. My plan to ride the Pony Express Trail was dangerous because I wanted to travel by horseback in places not designed for traveling by horseback. The risk extended beyond injury to myself. If you get bucked off your horse in a pasture, the horse runs back to the barn. If you get bucked off on the shoulder of an interstate highway, you're liable to have a traffic fatality to your name. And if you're traveling with two horses, rather than one, the potential for something to go wrong increases by an amount proportional to the ability of the handler, the horses' own good (or bad) sense, and whatever random factors providence may send forth over the course of a journey of who knows how many thousands of steps.

The danger that I faced on the Pony Express Trail was the inverse of the dangers the original riders faced. A phrase often associated with the Pony Express is "orphans preferred." Author Christopher Corbett used it for his 2003 book, *Orphans Preferred: The Twisted Truth and Lasting Legend of the Pony Express*. The phrase appears in the Pony Express National Museum and in countless histories of the mail service. All uses of it descend from a newspaper ad, allegedly taken out by Russell, Majors, and Waddell, that no one has been able to find. The advertisement purportedly read, "Wanted: Young, skinny, wiry fellows, not over eighteen. Must be expert riders, willing to risk death daily. Orphans preferred. Wages $25 per week." The original copy of this has never surfaced, but because it so succinctly conveys a few biographical details of the riders and their experience, it has become ingrained in the mythology.

The perhaps fictional ad implies that orphans were preferred so as to spare the firm being the bringer of bad news to a mother who'd consecrated her boy to the hurricane deck of a Pony Express horse. Because the possibility for an accident was inherent to the job. Galloping a horse is always dangerous—accidents happen even on the groomed footing of racetracks. Risking death daily came with the running of the horses. Forget the storms or dark nights or scrapes with hostile Indigenous peoples, delivering the mail was fundamentally dangerous.

If you've never been at full throttle on a horse, it can be hard to imagine the energy and interplay of muscles involved in propelling a thousand-pound animal and its rider to thirty or more miles per hour. When a horse's four legs are cycling through a footfall sequence so fast that the horse feels like it's vibrating, any misstep can lead to a crash. If the horse trips while galloping, his front legs and shoulders must catch him to recover from the stumble. When a horse stumbles, the rider's momentum is carried forward, loading the horse's front legs with extra weight and thereby offsetting the horse's balance and inhibiting the recovery. If the horse can't recover, the rider will have about a tenth of a second to eject from the saddle and kick free from the stirrups to avoid becoming entangled in the mess. If the rider gets hung up on the saddle, the horse can fall on him or her, and that can kill a person. If the rider ejects, he or she will have to find a soft spot to land on the prairie that's been flying by, and you don't want to use your face as a landing gear, as a cowboy would say.

The Pony Express riders had to be able horsemen because of the speed they traveled, the wilderness around them, and the distance of the relays. Each rider covered about one hundred miles in eight hours, swapping out horses several times at waystations spaced between the home stations where the riders slept. When the mail was running twice weekly service, riders would make four 100-mile relays per week, and that's a lot of riding and a lot of opportunity to have something bad happen at a gallop. Eight hours of running a horse is not like sitting at a desk for eight hours. It's exhausting. And for the riders of the Pony Express, it came with responsibility: the mail must get through.

As for me, I would travel at the pace of a walk. What took them ten days, I planned to cover in one hundred. Whereas the riders faced empty prairies, I faced Interstate 80. My first obstacle on the trail was a muti-lane bridge over the Missouri River. The river is a half mile wide. The bridge over it, called the Pony Express Bridge, is a mile long. As I looked at satellite images of the bridge, I thought that riding across it was unwise. In 1860, the Pony Express riders ferried their horses across the Missouri, and that seemed like a quieter prospect. A Google search turned up a barge company called Transport 360, based in St. Joseph. The website said it was "a full-service facility for all transportation needs including barge, rail and transloading." A newspaper story about the company quoted its CEO as saying one barge held enough grain to fill fifty-eight large semi-trucks.[5] Certainly room enough on deck for Chicken Fry and Badger, I thought, so I called the phone number listed.

The man who picked up said that ferrying horses across the Missouri River was pretty much not feasible. "Most everybody operates up and down the river, not across it," he said.

He seemed a little unwilling to think outside the box, but I could understand that he might not want to tie up company equipment on my behalf. I asked him if he knew anyone who owned a boat or something similar that might accommodate two horses and be available for hire.

"Do you know the river's at flood stage right now? Been that way for weeks," he said.

I told him that I'd seen news headlines about the flooding, but that I'd also seen what looked like a boat ramp on land owned by the Army Corps of Engineers directly opposite St. Joseph. Surely a flat-bottomed boat could pull up and deposit me and the horses in Kansas. I told him that if he could find someone to handle the boat, I could handle the horses.

"Look, what you're envisioning is basically not possible," he said.

I told him that my only other option was the highway, and highways are not good places to ride horses. I asked him what he would do in my shoes.

"Take the highway. I'm not a horse guy, but I think that's your best bet."

The safest way to take the highway was with a law enforcement escort, but I figured that the cops had better things to do than shadow some dude from New Mexico and his two horses over the bridge. I figured that they might even tell me that I couldn't do it, that horses were prohibited from the highway out of safety for the poor bastard ripping along in his sedan at fifty-five miles per hour not expecting to find horses trotting in the right lane. But I decided it was worth a try. I found the contact information for the patrol captain of the Buchanan

County Sheriff's Office, a man named Tiger Parsons, and I called the number listed.

A man picked up and said, "Capt'n Parsons."

I told Captain Parsons that I planned to ride the Pony Express Trail from St. Joseph to Sacramento and was wondering if it were possible to get a sheriff deputy escort over the bridge so that I could safely leave Missouri to begin my journey.

"I'm rarely at my desk; you're lucky to catch me," he said. "When are you thinking about doing this?"

I thought that Sunday morning would be the time of least traffic, and I told him that I was thinking of the morning of Sunday, May 5.

"I'll tell you what. I'll send one of my guys to the Pony Express Stables at 9 a.m. on Sunday morning to get you across the bridge. I'll give you my cell phone number, and if your schedule changes, text me."

With that, I locked in my departure for the Pony Express Trail.

———

What I most wanted from the Pony Express Trail was an education through people, mileage, and time. What I didn't want was to make a stupid mistake that resulted in injury to me or a horse. Traveling alone meant that I made all the decisions, could do as I pleased, wouldn't have to listen to someone complain about a bad camp or long day or anything else. But if something went wrong, it was on me. The hell of it all was that I didn't think it was possible to horseback it across the West without something going wrong. No way can anyone ride 2,000 miles without incident, privation, blood-shed of some degree—just not possible. A Wyoming rancher once told me that the greatest piece of safety equipment a guy has is his brain. Your head keeps you safe. You need to see the accident before it happens. You need to defuse a bad situation before it becomes one. The best horseman might be the one who stays out of trouble. If I could simply walk my horses from Missouri to California, that'd be enough. It wasn't a race; it was a test.

The night before Claire and I left Santa Fe to haul the horses to Missouri, I sat on the tailgate of the pickup, watching the sun set behind Chicken Fry and Badger as they ate hay. I was staring down the barrel of a long journey. So were Chicken Fry and Badger. A nicer pair of geldings would be hard to find. Their servitude was impressive. A horse will let you run it to the point of heart failure. It happens regularly to racehorses. I wondered if that was an evolutionary flaw in horses. A donkey would never let you do that. Chicken Fry and Badger would follow my lead, but what right did I have to involve these two in my plan for crossing the West? I reasoned that the best thing going for them was my sincere devotion to their well-being. I'd logged my hours horseback. I knew what an ailing, sore, or despondent horse looked like. I knew enough to recognize when a particular workload was too much for a particular horse. I didn't know who the hell lived in the center of Nebraska or how I was going to ride through the Salt Lake

City area, where more than a million people lived, but I did know that if my horses could do it, I could do it.

There's a saying about the outside of a horse being good for the inside of a man, which I think is true. And if the timing is right, a horse, or two, can elevate a person more than a few feet. From the back of a horse, you can see your way across half a continent. That's the magic of horsemanship. No one's born knowing it. You have to experience it to believe it, and good horses are the surest way to get there. Chicken Fry and Badger had become more than a pair of geldings: they had become the right and left hemispheres of the last ride of the Pony Express.

CHAPTER 3
A Fish out of History

St. Joseph, Missouri, lies nearly in the center of the conterminous United States. The city is technically about 200 miles east of the U.S. Geological Survey monument marking the official center point of the Lower 48, which is in northern Kansas, but St. Joseph is, essentially, in the center of the nation.[1] It sits on the east bank of the Missouri River, about fifty miles north of Kansas City and not far from the junction of Missouri, Kansas, Nebraska, and Iowa. Today it's a red-brick town of about 75,000 people, built on the low bluffs over the river. In this part of Missouri, the state line follows the river; the west bank is Kansas.

In 1860, St. Joseph had a population of 8,932, according the census of that year, which was the eighth U.S. Census.[2]

Like several other towns on the Missouri River, St. Joseph was a jumping off point for overland travel to the West. At that time there were thirty-three states in the U.S., and California, Oregon, and Texas were the only three in the West. The Missouri River was the frontier—both a geographical boundary and a cultural one. Its existence reflected a perspective. From the United States, the Missouri River was the end of organized settlement. The farthest west track of railroad from the East was the Hannibal and St. Joseph Railroad, completed in February 1859.[3] Hannibal, Missouri, the hometown of Mark Twain, lay on the bank of the Mississippi River and the border with Illinois. St. Joseph was slightly less than two hundred miles straight west of Hannibal, and it was the end of the telegraph and regular, reliable mail service. Which is why St. Joseph was the eastern terminus of the Pony Express.

From my perspective, St. Joseph was a place to leave. It felt like the Midwest: too green, too humid, somewhere the skies might be cloudy all day—no place for a cowboy to jingle his spurs. But it is effectively the home of the Pony Express. No other city or town in the country associates itself with the Pony Express as strongly as St. Joseph. The name Pony Express has been borrowed for many things in the city: a school district, a mobile home court, a warehousing company, a farmer's market, the U.S. Highway 36 bridge over the Missouri River, west of town. The image of a Pony Express rider—a rider leaning forward on a running horse, a whip in his free hand, the front of his hat upturned by the speed of his travel— appears on billboards, murals, even landscaped in colored rocks beside the highway. Evidence of the Pony Express is so prevalent in St. Joseph that I doubt if it's possible to live there without being aware of the city's connection to the old horseback mail line.

The Pony Express mochila—the leather saddle covering with four mail pouches that was passed between horses for 2,000 miles—began its journey at a small post office opposite a large rectangular brick building not far from the Missouri River, called the Patee House. In 1860, the Patee House was a mile south of the city center and known as the nicest hotel west of the Mississippi. Russell, Majors and Waddell set up an office for the Pony Express on the first floor of the hotel, and that office was the point of dispatch for westbound mail and the receiving point for eastbound mail.[4] The horses for the Pony Express were kept in a long, low barn two blocks west of the Patee House, and that barn, which is today the Pony Express National Museum, was my point of departure.

I liveried the horses at a horse motel a few miles from downtown. Horse motels are barns, ranches, stables, and training centers all over the nation that offer nightly stall rental for people traveling with horses. Claire, who agreed to shadow me for the first few days, and I put up the horses at Sunset Hill Stable and camped in the driveway for two nights. Those two nights were the brief acclimation period for Chicken Fry and Badger. Horses can be sensitive to changes in climate, pasturage, any number of environmental factors. Coming from the high desert of New Mexico, their feet were liable to swell with the moisture and humidity. Their digestive systems would have to adjust to the grasses of the Midwest. The insects, fungi, and all the microfauna of the new ecosystem were potential physiological challenges. Two days isn't enough time for a horse to make a large adjustment—to accommodate, say, a change of seven hundred miles northeast from Santa Fe to St. Joseph in a horse trailer—but it was better than nothing, and I had no interest in sticking around any longer than absolutely necessary.

The predawn morning of May 5 smelled like water. The sun broke the eastern horizon through a hazy veil of clouds. We trailered Chicken Fry and Badger to the Pony Express Museum and unloaded them in the gravel parking just before eight o'clock. The horses looked out of place. They still held vestiges of their winter coats, long hair held on by the memories of too many springtime snowstorms. In the West, the first week of May can be cold, snowy, deceptively winterlike. In the Midwest, the first week of May smells like magnolia trees. Chicken Fry and Badger, looking like two overdressed mustangs from some faraway country, stood out as equine anomalies in that urban environment. In 1860, there would have been a horse in every direction, horse manure in the streets, the sounds of horses mixing with the creaking of harnesses and the groaning of wagon axles. In 2019, it felt like the fading city center of a Midwestern town. The streets were mostly empty. I rode Chicken Fry and led Badger up the centerline of Penn Street to the Patee House and down South 10th Street, and I told the horses not to worry, that we'd be in a better place before long.

Half an hour later, a man named Lyle Ladner drove up in a black pickup truck. Lyle was president of the National Pony Express Association, an organization dedicated to preserving the history of the mail service and identifying the original route with signage. The association stages an annual reenactment of the Pony Express with a time-faithful relay that involves hundreds of riders and horses, all handled with impressive logistical coordination. Lyle had agreed to help me find suitable campsites through northeast Kansas and to provide any assistance I might need getting across the Highway 36 bridge. He climbed out of his pickup wearing clean jeans, a National Pony Express Association ball cap, and a brown, long-sleeved t-shirt that said "XP" on the breast. He had a gray moustache that furled at both ends into cotton-like boughs, and he spoke softly. He asked when the sheriff's deputy was going to arrive. Half an hour, I told him. He asked about my horses, and I gave him their histories.

"They say that's what you want if you can find them, those good-broke ranch horses from out West," he said.

The comment was a clear reminder that I was not yet in the West, that I wouldn't be in the West for another month or so of riding. Eventually a Buchanan County deputy sheriff drove up in an SUV K-9 unit. The deputy stopped beside Chicken Fry and rolled down his window. I told him that I'd trot the horses over the bridge, make the trip as quick as possible, but that if one of my horses slipped on the concrete or balked at the expansion joints, I'd slide out of the saddle and lead the horses on foot because it would be safer than riding. Once I'm across the bridge, I told him, I'll peel off through the grass borrow ditch and you can be on your way. He nodded and said, "Ready when you are."

I screwed down my hat, felt that my saddle cinch was tight, and wheeled Chicken Fry over his haunches to set off at a high trot with Badger in tow. "Pony rider up!" Lyle yelled as we passed him. We clicked across the gravel parking lot of the museum with the sheriff behind us and the cool morning air running through the horses' manes. As we trotted southbound down 9th Street for the Highway 36 onramp, I passed a dark midcentury house, and on the front steps of the house sat a grim-looking woman smoking a cigarette. She wore a white nightgown and had large white slippers on her feet. She sat with her knees pulled up to her chest, holding the cigarette close to her face, and she looked hungover. I raised my hand and hollered good morning with the footfalls of the horses ringing off the house behind her, but she didn't acknowledge me.

Chicken Fry hit the highway onramp with all the momentum of the Man from Snowy River. Badger followed Chicken Fry's lead and held tightly to his flank for security. We fell into traffic while the cop swung out behind us with his lights flashing red and blue. Trash littered the sides of the highway: a dirty black shoe, what looked like a sports bra, random articles of clothing, undistinguishable pieces of plastic, fast-food containers. What a nice place to ride a horse, I thought. The highway was elevated, running over rooftops and smaller roads, and at an interchange where a sign pointed to Interstate

229 South to Kansas City, a stoplight turned red. I saw no incoming traffic, and I thought I might just sail through the light—better to make haste over the bridge and be done with it—but I didn't know what my sheriff's office escort would think about that, so I pulled Chicken Fry to a stop beside a car also stopped at the light. I walked up next to it and kept my head down, looking askance at Badger because I didn't want to make eye contact with some Show-Me-State Missourian in the passenger seat, which would probably lead to him or her rolling down the window and asking me what I was doing, and I wasn't interested in answering that question at the moment. When the light turned green, I took off at a trot, and the car went south.

As we approached the river, the bridge passed over a yard of railroad sidings and a riverside industrial complex. Where it climbed to span the Missouri River, I ran my hand up Chicken Fry's neck and told him, take us to Kansas, buddy. I was fifty feet over the river when I saw water through the first big expansion joint in the bridge. Some horses (and cattle) won't cross expansion joints because the gaps in the footing upset their depth perception. Chicken Fry saw the first joint coming, shortened his stride by half to ensure he stepped over it, and then broke into a steady canter. Traffic had started accumulating behind the sheriff. The line of cars stretched toward the green hills of Missouri. The river was wide and the color of chocolate milk, and the currents turned in large, foamy folds. Running horses over concrete always carries the risk of a horse slipping, so I rode as squarely down the middle as I could because I had nightmarish visions of Chicken Fry stumbling and catapulting me over the bridge's guardrail. With Kansas in front of me, the river channel flanking me on either side, and the cop and all that traffic following me, I was officially hurtling past the first challenge of a big job: crossing the Missouri River.

Once I hit Kansas soil, I pulled off the highway, and waved my hat to the cop in thanks. I angled through the empty parking lots of an asphalt paving company and the Pony Express Community Bank. The adrenaline from the bridge crossing ebbed, and everything became quiet. A large sign read, "Welcome to Elwood. Founded 1856." That was one state behind me, seven more ahead.

———

Northeast Kansas is a hilly country that breaks to the Missouri River in narrow, wooded draws. The topography is a result of incision, the down-cutting of streams through periglacial sediment deposited during the last ice age. Farmland occupies the level hilltops between areas of drainage. From the floodplain of the river, I rode a limestone gravel road through a tight valley that smelled like lilacs. Sycamores, oaks, and maples formed a dense canopy that teemed with an avian community that was easier to hear than see. Small birds shot between limbs and branches, dark and unidentifiable to me. A few descended from the leafy heights. Eastern kingbirds, with their black caps and white breasts, leapfrogged down the fence line before the horses. An indigo bunting shot across my bow and lit in a shrub beside the road. It glowed electric blue for an instant before vanishing with a turn and flash of its wings. A Mississippi kite the color of a stormy sky winged noiselessly down the valley behind me. The first few hours of riding felt like a birding tour of Kansas.

I planned my first night's camp at the Doniphan County Fairgrounds in Troy, Kansas, seventeen miles west of St. Joseph. A week prior, I'd found an online announcement for a rodeo at the fairgrounds, and the announcement listed Norman Meng as the person to contact about the event. I ran Norman through Google and saw that he operated a dairy farm nearby. I called his number and told him what I was doing, asked him about camping at the fairgrounds. He told me that I was welcome to camp there, that there would be a corral full of grass for my horses, and that he would stop by to see me that afternoon.

I rode west for most of the day on the white gravel road under a clear blue sky. In the middle of the afternoon, I entered Troy, population 762, and found the fairgrounds and the corral full of grass for my horses. Claire had arrived several hours before me. Half an hour after I turned loose the horses in the corral, Norman drove up in a blue late-model Chevy pickup. He stopped before the corral, rocked the truck into park with an upward swing of the shifter, and stepped out of the truck with a wide smile on his face.

Norman was a big man with a bald head the size of a bowling ball. He wore a navy-blue t-shirt with the sleeves cut off and jeans frayed at the bottoms in a shade-tree hem job that suggested he might occasionally tailor his own clothes. Wide blue suspenders held up his jeans, and he wore heel-less leather boots with white carpenter soles of the type that can be cleaned on a doorway boot scraper before entering a house. After we shook hands, he walked over to the corral, rested both his big arms on the top rail of the fence, and whistled through his teeth. "Them are some nice horses," he said.

Norman Meng is the third generation of his family to milk cows on the shallow hilltop four miles north of the Pony Express Trail. He runs a small dairy farm in a time when small farms are disappearing. According to the U.S. Department of Agriculture, he's a dying breed. Between 1970 and 2020, the number of dairy farms in the U.S. fell from 648,000 to 32,000, a ninety-five percent decrease. Over the same period, total milk production increased.[5] Small farms are giving way to larger ones. The USDA uses three metrics to define a small dairy farm: the operation produces its own feed, usually hay and grain, for its cows; it raises its own cattle for milking, rather than buying them; and the operator and his family do most of the labor, rather than hiring help.[6] Small dairy farmers, like a lot of other farmers, are facing the consolidation of agriculture into large corporations. Big farms are getting bigger, buying up land and dominating markets by a game of margins that the small operator is finding increasingly difficult to compete with. The largest dairies in the nation milk more than 30,000 cows twice a day using highly automated systems. Norman operates near the other end of the spectrum. He, along with his sons, brother, and nephew, milks about 200 cows.

I had never been to a dairy farm, so I asked Norman if Claire and I could visit him at milking time. He agreed and gave me directions to the farm. A couple of hours later, we left the horses at the fairgrounds and drove to his place.

The Meng farm looks like what you would expect a Midwestern farm to look like: tidy white buildings with metal roofs, corrals, several barns, a half dozen cylindrical silos for storing feed, a two-story gabled house. At 4:30 p.m. Norman's two hundred or so black-and-white Holstein cows were lined up outside the milking barn like concertgoers waiting for a venue to open. The barn was clean and cool and smelled like washed concrete. A large stainless-steel cooling tank sat at the front of the barn, where a truck came to collect the milk every day. A lot of things at a dairy work on a daily schedule that provides little leeway. The twice-daily chore of cleaning the milking equipment is unavoidable. Milking the cows twice daily is also unavoidable. If the milk in a cow's bag is not released, the cow will stop lactating because her bag can only hold so much milk. If the cow stops producing milk, she's no longer contributing to the farm's bottom line, and instead costing money to feed. She won't produce milk again until she's been bred, goes through nine months of pregnancy, and gives birth to a calf. A dairy farmer might as well be married to cows and chores because the farm and its animals can't run without constant attention.

The space inside a dairy barn where the cows are milked

is called the milking parlor. It's designed so that the cows enter freely from a paddock through a gate, align themselves in the milking stalls, and then leave once milked. It's called a herringbone system because it's not like the old days where you had to tie up or hobble the cow to milk her. The inner space of the parlor, where the farmers work, is a few feet below floor level so that the udders of the cows are about chest height. When the gate from the paddock to the parlor opened, the first cow to walk in was a large mostly white cow with a big black nose, and she definitely knew the routine. She walked to the forwardmost milking stall, sidestepped into place, and Norman smiled and rubbed her hip.

"Just like some humans always want to be first, Daisy's always gotta be first in line," Norman said. "I name all my cows, and they're all named after my old girlfriends." He looked at me and laughed. "Maybe in twenty years I'll run out of names, I don't know."

The milking parlor had six stalls along two sides, and pretty soon twelve cows had sidestepped into place, waiting to be milked. Norman's nephew walked down the line spraying the feet and udders of each cow with a hose, and Norman followed with a red bucket in one hand and a rag in the other to clean the udders a second time. The cows stood over a grate so that the water drained out the bottom. Automatic milkers were attached to the udders, and milk flowed through clear hoses that ran to the ceiling where a network of exposed plumbing delivered the milk to the cooling tank at the front of the barn. The men moved with an efficiency that would be hard to improve, a refinement of technique that comes from doing something twice a day every day. When one row of six cows had been milked, the hoses were moved to the six cows waiting on the other side of the parlor. The cows that had been milked filed out of the barn, and the gate opened to let in six unmilked cows with heavy, swinging bags. An essential part of any livestock operation is the quiet handling of the animals. There's a saying: you can't take milk from a cow— she has to give it to you. Which means that if a cow isn't comfortable, you can't milk her. Norman's milking operation was smooth and methodical.

A working farm is not a petting zoo. The livestock is for production. Relationships with the animals may be made— like naming cows after old girlfriends—but the farm is a business, and most of the animals will eventually be slaughtered and consumed. Uphill from the milk barn, 150 or so red chickens lived in a whitewashed coop. Norman told us the chickens were Rhode Island reds. They were classic-looking, round chickens with scarlet combs. Four orange traffic cones hung on the side of the coop, and Norman asked me if I knew what the cones were for. I shook my head.

"You know that after you kill a chicken you have to put it in scalding water?" he asked. I shook my head again. "That makes them easy to pluck. Gotta dunk them in hot water so the feathers come off easy. But they have to die first. You have to let them die."

Chickens are slaughtered by cutting their heads off. Once beheaded, a chicken typically lives for a few minutes, and the reaction of its severed nervous system can produce enough movement to have inspired the phrase "run around like a chicken with its head cut off." They're also put in something to contain them, which prevents headless chickens from flopping around and bruising the meat.

"So one day we were using a cinder block, sticking the chickens in one of those cinder blocks with two holes in it to die, and we had a friend over here helping us with the slaughter. Well, he cuts the head off one and puts it in that cinder block and then when he looks at it a minute later, the chicken is gone. Where's the chicken? No one could find the chicken. How did the chicken just disappear?" Norman thought the story was very funny, and then he turned to me and said in a quieter tone as though divulging a secret, "We think the dog actually grabbed it. Now we use the cones." He waved his hand through the air as though he had solved that set of problems by using orange cones to contain the headless chickens and said, "Let's go see my heifers."

Heifers are female bovines that have not given birth to a calf. Once a heifer has a calf, she's a cow. First births are not always easy for cattle, and when heifers are calving, they need to be closely monitored. On a dairy, calving happens throughout the year, and Norman told us that his heifers were in the midst of it. The heifer paddock was muddy. Thirty or so of the black-and-white first-time mothers stood in mud to their knees, some with very small calves at their sides. At the far end of the pen, a large blaze-faced sorrel horse loafed among the heifers. The horse had large, dinner-plate-size feet that seemed to have a snowshoe effect, keeping it afloat over the mud. Most dairy farmers have as much use for a horse as they do a pair of spurs, and I was surprised to see the red gelding in with the cattle. I nodded at the horse, and Norman told me that it was his horse and that his brother wanted him to sell it but that he had no intention of doing so.

As Norman was looking over his heifers, walking among them, post-holing through the mud with a sucking sound in every step, he suddenly said, "Uh oh, this one's calving right now."

Two small, yellow cloven hooves had emerged at the back end of a female bovine that was about to make the transition from heifer to cow. She was having trouble with the birth, and Norman hollered that we needed to get her into a chute to help deliver the calf. He began hazing her uphill toward drier ground, hobbling awkwardly through the mud behind the cow who was fighting the quagmire as much as Norman. Once she entered the chute, he closed a partial door around her shoulders and a gate behind her. I've spent enough time on farms and ranches to know that standing around with your hands in your pockets when there's an urgent job unfolding is the wrong thing to do, so I rolled up my sleeves and did what obviously needed doing: pulling on the calf's legs.

Finding purchase on the small hooves was not easy. The heifer bawled and rocked in the chute, and we finally managed to pull the ankles free. Norman ran a canvas strap around the calf's ankles and hooked the strap to a come-along winch that was chained to the side of the barn. I pulled on the calf while he slowly ratcheted the winch, and the calf emerged long and warm and sheathed in a thick amniotic sac.

"Don't let it drop to the ground!" Norman yelled. "You don't want to drop it. Ease it to the ground. Easy, easy, easy!" I cradled the calf in my arms and lowered it to the ground, and Norman pulled the strap off its legs and moved it into the shade. The calf seemed exceptionally long-legged. It lay formless in the dirt, like a puddle of a calf, as though its skeletal structure had yet to solidify. It had a mostly black head with a white triangle on its forehead and a pink nose. The white patches of its hide were yellowed with amniotic fluid and slightly streaked with blood. Its hooves, having felt nothing but liquid inside the womb, were pale yellow and looked soft as boiled eggs. The small pink nose began to run air in and out, and it blinked its hazy, bluish eyes a few times. Norman opened the chute door to let the mother investigate her baby, but she didn't seem much inclined toward it.

"She doesn't know its hers," he said. "Let's get out of here and leave her to figure it out." We walked out of the corral and stepped back from the fence. The mother walked over to the calf and lowered her head until her wet, black nose was within a hair's breadth of the small pink nose of the calf. The cow worked her ears back and forth as she considered the baby, and then she turned away and walked to the other side of the pen. She was uninterested in her own calf, and the calf seemed dwindled by the scale of life surrounding it. Norman assured us that soon the calf would "mother-up," that with a little time the cow would accept her calf, and that the situation was nothing to worry about. We turned to leave.

"How many calves did the Pony Express riders pull back in the day?" Norman asked, smiling. He slapped my back as we walked toward the milking parlor, and said, "You can put that in your book. Your first day on the trail."

———

The next morning, I rode out of the Doniphan County Fairgrounds thinking about dairy farming. Part of the value of seeing Norman's operation was that farming mostly happens out of the public eye. You generally can't walk up to a dairy farm and watch the milking. You can't just walk onto a ranch to watch calves being castrated or lambs being docked. On pig farms, anyone other than the farmer is prohibited from entering a barn full of pigs for slaughter, called butcher hogs, because of the risk of disease transmission.[7] An organic vegetable farm will probably let you pick your own carrots, but livestock producers can be wary of the public. Some farmers assume that every person driving a Subaru must also be an animal-welfare fanatic. The discord is growing. My opinion is that, as a society, our connection to the animals that provide us food is weakening. As large corporations consolidate agriculture, livestock become numbers. At a dairy that milks 30,000 cows twice a day, there's no Daisy, probably no big sorrel horse in with the heifers. Instead, the cows are microchipped and can be scanned for information like date of birth. The efficiency is impressive—and the cost savings is passed on to the consumer—but the sterilization of the relationship between the producer and the livestock is unfortunate.

Another effect of the consolidation of agriculture is the depopulation of the rural countryside. It's happening all over the Midwest.[8] Farms are being sold to corporations, and people are moving to the cities and towns. I saw this in real time. As I angled west and south from Troy, I rode past one abandoned farmstead after another. Old clapboard houses built around central chimneys were now the haunts of barn owls and raccoons. Glassless windows gaped into dark interiors, the sills and sashes still mostly square but the mullions and panes long since gone. Doors hung askew on twisted hinges, and the shingled roofs had curled and split and caved in in places. Frail fences of old, rusty wire enclosed what were once front yards, barnyards, and stackyards for hay. The old homesites were dark and quiet and overgrown, and they harkened to a former American lifeway defined by Fourth of July picnics and glasses of lemonade on the front porch, a time that William Carlos Williams referred to when he wrote "The Red Wheelbarrow":

so much depends
upon

a red wheel
barrow

glazed with rain
　　water

beside the white
　　chickens

The new face of the country was visible as cellular phone towers on hilltops, windfarms on the horizon, crop rows so straight they looked like perfect corduroy over the black soil. The days of a small farm with its menagerie of animals, like that of *Charlotte's Web*, seemed to be gone. Nearly every barn I passed lacked corrals because no one keeps working livestock anymore. Tractors have replaced draft horses and oxen. A farm in northeast Kansas is more likely to have a shop for maintaining equipment than a manger for feeding horses. Today in the Midwest, most barns are for machinery, not livestock, and I camped at exactly such a place twenty-one miles west of Troy.

One tool for finding campsites is a phone app called onX Hunt. The app provides landowner information for every square foot of the U.S. I found the Bunck Seed Farms pasture at what I figured to be a day's ride from Troy, and when I called the number listed, Betty Bunck answered the phone. I told her what I was doing, asked if I might camp there with my two horses, and said that Claire would also be there with the horse trailer.

"There's no water or electricity, but, sure, you can camp there. I haven't met you, so I'll have to take you at your word that you're a good and honest man."

I assured her that I was and thanked her for accommo-
dating me.

The old white barn stood alone on a hilltop, like a church
without a steeple. Plowed fields ran unbroken and bare over
the country around the barn. The farmhouse had long ago
been bulldozed into an earthen heap that was now covered in
weeds and a few small volunteer trees. The barn had a metal
roof and was constructed in a board-and-batten style, and it
was in good shape, looking as though it had been repainted
in the past decade or so. A lean-to for storing equipment had
been built on the south side of it, but it contained no equipment. The barn was tall and stood square, without listing
downwind or losing its siding, and it appeared to have so far
weathered antiquity with integrity.

I set up the electric fence in a stand of brome grass
before the barn. Claire and I cooked dinner in the lean-to,
and by five o'clock, a cloud front had obscured the lowering
sun. An hour later, mammatus apples hung over the barn
in an ominous, cobbled ceiling. Our horse trailer had a tack
room for storing saddles and other gear, and that's where we
slept. With nightfall came the rain. It fell in acre-feet, and I
wondered if the whole country might just slough off into the
creek bottoms. Chicken Fry and Badger stood motionless with
lowered heads as lightning flashed in quick, successive bursts.
As I fell asleep, I wondered if my single-strand electric fence
would contain the horses in such a storm. I wondered if the
electric fence might attract lightning. I figured that if lightning
hit the fence—and didn't just kill the horses graveyard-dead

in an instant—they would bolt. If I lost the horses, I reckoned, at least the ground was soft so I'd be able to track them.

I woke to the sound of coyotes. The rain had ceased. Yips and barks came from the night, and when I looked out toward the horses, I saw two coyotes hurtling over the plowed ground on the far side of the horses. The coyotes appeared white, and they looked as big as wolves. They ran a wide arc with the porpoise-like motion of greyhounds, and they seemed to be running over an ethereal plane between the mud below and the sky above. They weren't a threat to my horses—because a coyote doesn't want to risk getting his teeth kicked in—but they reminded me of wilder times. Amid all that farmland and changed landscape, the two coyotes running through the night were a comforting vestige of a former country.

———

The next morning hardly broke at all but only lightened slightly, and everything was gray and wet. I put the saddle blankets over wet hair and rode from the abandoned barn at seven thirty, headed west for the Kickapoo Indian Reservation. There are four Indian reservations in Kansas— Kickapoo, Potawatomi, Iowa, and Sac and Fox—and at twenty-two miles wide and twelve miles long, the Kickapoo is the largest.

The Kickapoo are an Algonquian-derived people that arrived in Kansas relatively recently, in 1832, and who histor-ically lived in the Great Lakes area. The arrival of Europeans in the 1500s and early 1600s brought a century of conflict to the region. Those years of conflict, known as the Iroquois Wars or Beaver Wars, displaced the Kickapoo to present day Wisconsin, which was the territory of the Winnebago and Menominee nations. In the early 1700s, the Kickapoo moved again, this time into present-day Illinois and Indiana, and they remained there until the era of the U.S. government's disingenuous treaty-making with Indigenous peoples in the 1800s. The existing Kickapoo Reservation in Kansas was established by an 1854 treaty, the same year that the Kansas-Nebraska Act established the two territories and granted them popular sovereignty over the issue of slavery, which ushered in a dark episode, known as Bleeding Kansas, on the prairies.[9]

In 1859, Horace Greeley traveled through eastern Kansas on the same route the Pony Express would use the following year. He reported crossing several Indian reservations. At that time, the Indigenous peoples of the plains and the European Americans from the United States were on mostly amicable terms. Several of the waystations where Greeley's wagon changed horses or mules were frequented by Native Americans. The British traveler Sir Richard Burton would make similar observations a year later.[10] As Greeley traveled through Kansas, he wrote extensively about the prospects of farming in the area, as well as the costs of establishing a settlement and what that settlement might produce. Of the Indigenous peoples' land, he speculated that the timbered valleys and fertile bottomlands of the reservations would likely fall to the United States:

The soil is a river deposit four to six feet deep; the timber is large and choice—oak, elm, bass, black walnut, sycamore, etc., with wild grape vines four to six inches through and a thick undergrowth of shrubbery and annuals. I begin to comprehend, though I do not excuse, the covetous impatience wherewith Indian reservations are regarded by their white neighbors.[11]

The Pony Express ran through Kickapoo land, but there is little mention of the Kickapoo presence within the history of the mail service. There was a Kickapoo Station, as well as a Kennekuk Station, and both were used by mail wagons, stagecoaches, and the Pony Express as places to exchange livestock. Frank Root, who drove a freight wagon over the plains in the 1860s, described the Kickapoo Reservation as "undoubtedly one of the finest bodies of land in Kansas" and "one of the garden spots of northern Kansas."[12]

I crossed the north end of Kickapoo land under a cold rain. I rode down the shoulder of the highway, and at the intersection with a small, dirt road from the north met a big Lincoln sedan. It was a long, wide car with a hood large enough to set up a tent on, and it was the color of a battleship. A pair of three-foot-wide horns off a longhorn steer had been wired to the center of the hood above the grill. Red, white, and blue ribbons had been tied to the center of the horns but the ribbons had frayed to short ends. The car had two plates on the front bumper: one was green and yellow and said John Deere, and the other was pink and white and black and read,

"I support Mothers Against Drunk Driving." A handicap parking permit hung from the rearview mirror.

I pulled up Chicken Fry to let the car pass, but instead the driver's side window slowly rolled down to reveal a woman with thick curls of jet-black hair couched over her shoulders. She wore sunglasses and was smiling as she looked me over so I asked her how she was doing. "Oh, I'm doing just fine," she said and then looked both ways on the road, pulled through the stop sign, and parked on the shoulder of the highway.

She climbed out of the Lincoln wearing a white t-shirt, gray sweatpants, and clean, white sneakers. I was wearing a full-length rain slicker, thermal base layers under my jeans and shirt, and a silk scarf wrapped twice around my neck. Water had begun to seep through the crown of my felt hat. She was clearly happy to see the horses. There was another woman in the passenger seat, but she remained in the car.

The woman walked up to Chicken Fry and said that she grew up with horses but that she hadn't ridden one in many years. She asked if she could pet him, and I nodded. She ran her hand down his wet face, and he softly pushed his black nose into her shirt. She turned to the woman in the car and said, "This one likes me."

I nodded when she asked if she could take a photo of the horses, and I asked if she lived nearby. She took a photo of me and the horses beside her car with the horns on the hood and said she lived only a few miles from where we stood, pointing east. She asked me where I was headed, and I pointed west. She turned to leave and thanked me, and I told her not to and tipped my hat to her. I watched as she swung the big Lincoln around and drove east.

An hour later, she pulled up beside me and rolled down the passenger-side window, grinning. The second woman was not in the car. I kept the horses walking and she drove slowly beside me in the oncoming lane. She lowered her head to better see me out the window, and I leaned forward on Chicken Fry's neck to better see in the car.

"Everything, okay?" she asked.

All good, I told her.

"Just checking on you," she said.

I gave her the thumbs-up sign, and she smiled and drove ahead and pulled over on the shoulder. She asked if she could pet Chicken Fry again. Also another photo, this time a close-up of Chicken Fry's hazel eye, and he looked like he might just go to sleep as she stroked him.

"I used to love riding horses," she said looking up at me. "That was so many years ago."

She thanked me again and drove off.

Of course she rode horses growing up. Fifty years ago, the whole country was filled with livestock. I suspected that for her, seeing and petting Chicken Fry was happy nostalgia, and I turned to Badger and told him, well we got a second career for our buddy: therapy horse. After he finishes the Pony Express, he can stand around and let people pet him. Would be a lot easier than hoofing it across the West, that's for sure. We walked along in the rain under a low sky, and after a while, I had a revelation to share with them: the value of a horse has no hard lines. You never know what effect a horse will have on someone. It's something heftier than what happens with dogs because no one ever conquered the world on the back of a dog. Horses, I told Chicken Fry and Badger, must be the most heroic of all animals. Maybe I'm biased, but it seemed to me that even though we buy and sell horses, we may never know the limits of their worth. Either way, I told them, you guys are not for sale.

———

As I crossed northern Kansas, the tenor of the country was slow change. Small towns were withering communities. The abandoned farmsteads were a depressing expression of the landscape. The productivity of the land was higher than ever before—as a result of increasingly efficient farming methods, as well as new technologies like windfarms—but I bemoaned the hands-off relationship that seemed to be the future of agriculture. I reckoned that no one wanted dirt under their fingernails anymore, that the younger generations of the work-force, the ones who would be assuming control of the family operations, would rather live in St. Joseph or Kansas City where they can eat take-out food for dinner and enjoy morn-ings without chores. I talked about this with a man named Roy Winkler, who let me camp in his pasture one night. We talked about the modernization of farming, about old trends giving way to new ones, about how the lack of family-held livestock has reduced the biodiversity on farms and on the land. Roy knew about modern farming. He'd managed barns of pigs and held a patent for a piglet feeder. Piglets are raised in groups of around three thousand. All three thousand share a barn together in what's called indoor confinement feeding until they're ready for slaughter. As in dairy farming, cleanliness is a top priority, and Roy's piglet feeder improved cleanliness and provided a better, more efficient way to feed more piglets. But he, too, bemoaned the change that he had seen unfold in his lifetime.

"I don't know," he said, "sometimes I think the Amish are the ones who got it figured out."

The Amish are generally seen as traditional farmers. The Amish faith grew out of the Protestant Reformation in the sixteenth century, and the first Amish immigrated to the United States in the early eighteenth century to escape religious persecution. The Pennsylvania Dutch Country became the center of the U.S. Amish presence, and today 596 Amish settlements are scattered throughout thirty-two states, including Kansas, and exist only in the U.S., Canada, and South America. The most recognizable sign that you're in Amish country is a black buggy hitched to a horse trotting down the road. All Amish groups adhere to a code of conduct dictated by the Ordnung—the word is German for "order" (the Amish still speak German during Sunday services). There are many subgroups within the Amish faith, and each subgroup determines its own version of the Ordnung, though there is little variance. All groups prohibit owning cars, radios, or televisions. Internet use is rare. Some allow washing machines, chainsaws, and indoor plumbing. A few allow the use of rototillers; fewer allow tractors.[13] Most Amish shun modern technology, wear plain clothing, and use horses instead of machinery. Which is to say that the Amish operate a farm in the ways of a bygone era, which Roy Winkler referred to when he said they might have it "figured out."

In northern Kansas, a small Amish community exists near the town of Axtell. Lyle Ladner, the former president of the National Pony Express Association who I had met at the Pony Express Museum, had arranged for me to camp in the yard of an Amish one-room schoolhouse outside Axtell. It was May 11, but Lyle told me that the school was closed and I'd find the place empty. "The kids get out for summer vacation early so they can help out on the farm," he said.

Just after five o'clock in the afternoon, I was half a mile from the Amish schoolhouse when I crested a low hill to see a small farm on the north side of the county road. A young girl in a long white dress stood beside a row of large round hay bales. The bales were a foot taller than the girl, and the low-angle sun lit up her dress with a diaphanous glow. At the end of the row of bales and just beyond the girl was a John Deere tractor with a large round-bale hay baler attached to it. When the girl saw me, she ducked behind the last bale. Out stepped a man wearing a wide-brimmed straw hat and what looked like dark gabardine trousers held up by thin suspenders. He had a long, dark beard, and he wore a white shirt. He held a wrench in one hand. The girl and a young boy emerged beside the man, and the boy was dressed the same as the man: floppy hat, white shirt, dark trousers held up by suspenders.

The three of them stood looking at me, and I waved, and both children waved back but the man did not. He stood holding the wrench, and I knew he was wondering what a man riding a horse and leading a packhorse was doing in front of his farm. I could see several barns beyond the tractor. A black Amish-style cart was parked with its traces lying on the ground. Half a dozen or so dark horses stood in a muddy corral downhill of the barns, and the horses raised their heads as we passed. The man and two children stood as they were until my movement put the bales between us.

After we were out of earshot, I asked Chicken Fry if he noticed that the young boy had a beard, same as his father. Even young Amish boys have beards. By the time an Amish boy can look over the top of a hay bale, he'll have a full-grown beard just like his dad. Chicken Fry, obviously, appreciated the remark. There's no better audience for a joke than two horses and a strong wind. I asked Chicken Fry what he thought about the lack of light-colored horses among the Amish. Except for their draft horses, Amish use only dark horses. Just as their carts are always black, their horses are always dark. I wasn't sure if dark horses were part of the Ordnung, but I told Chicken Fry that I didn't think you could free-and-clear give a buckskin horse to an Amish man. I looked at Badger, nice bay horse that he was. Badger and I agreed: ain't no place for a horse the color of Chicken Fry on an Amish farm. Going to be a long summer, I told the horses, just us three all day together without any company and me doing all the talking.

The Amish schoolhouse was a small white rectangular building with a small bell tower at one end with a bell hanging inside it. Behind the building sat a motorhome with its wheels covered and undersides walled in with sheet metal for insulation. I figured it to be the teacher's bunkhouse. A simple steel-pole swing set looked like the recess-time activity. A charred fifty-five-gallon burn barrel looked like the trash service. A plastic yellow portable toilet looked like it would be cold in the winter. A small steel-sided loafing shed provided a place to tie horses, and inside the shed, old dried manure ran a foot deep up the sides, betraying plenty of use.

I penned the horses in the overgrown baseball diamond. Claire met me there, and we camped in the gravel lot. At dusk, a child on a dark horse appeared on the road. His wide, light-colored straw hat stood out in the failing light. The kid rode the horse bareback, without a saddle, and with only a halter on the horse's head and the lead rope tied around the neck into a hackamore rein. He came into view where a tree line ended at the road, and he stopped his horse, looking at me. He sat the horse comfortably, in a way that conveyed many hours horseback, as though he might ride to school. His legs hung freely under him, his ankles barely dangling below the horse's belly, and he sat upright with squared shoulders and both hands folded in front of him over the horse's withers. He was looking right at me so I waved, but he didn't return the gesture.

Chicken Fry and Badger had seen him ride into view. I stood from where I had been sitting and walked over to Chicken Fry, crossed my arms over his back, and told the horses: yonder rides your Pony Expresser. I wondered if the Amish used electric fences. I wondered if there was one guy in every Amish community who made all the hats to look the same. I suspected that the boy was riding a carthorse, and I told Chicken Fry and Badger so. Probably one of those strange, uniquely American breeds of the Midwest, like standardbreds, that have no business chasing a cow through the sagebrush but will sure as hell drag a buggy all over town. Chicken Fry and Badger and I were looking at the young rider and his horse when he turned in the road and disappeared behind the tree line.

The kid was the first person I'd seen on horseback since New Mexico. In the fading twilight, he recalled a time when all the now-abandoned farms had been occupied and functioning. He provided some relief to a country that otherwise appeared to have become a ghost of its former self. In that way, he punctuated half a century's worth of change. I was sensitive to this because I had a foot in both worlds. I was traveling in an antiquated fashion. My daily necessities included grass and water for my horses, the same priorities for anyone who's ever traveled by horseback. I was hearing the same four-beat footfalls of horses at the walk, smelling the same sweet smell of horse sweat, watching for soreness in my horses' backs and legs no differently than the ancient nomads of Eurasia or the Spanish conquistadors or the first pioneers to cross the plains. At the same time, I was using satellite images on my phone to assess campsites before I arrived. I could see the boundaries and owner information of the Amish farm I rode past and that the owner of the farm also owned the school. I had an electric fence with a solar-powered charger to contain my horses, and I slept on an inflatable mattress that was three inches thick, weighed less than a pound, and was fully made of petroleum products.

The Amish boy on horseback brought this into focus. He was a middleman on the continuum of change, somewhere between the Pony Express and the massive wind turbines that slowly turned on the horizon northwest of the schoolhouse. He used a horse to check on the transient neighbors camped near his farm, yet his father baled hay with a John Deere tractor. The biggest change over the past century and a half is that the land doesn't look the same. It's all been farmed. There's no open range in northern Kansas. At the same time, the only thing that hasn't changed is the land. The only tangible remnants of the past are the tree lines and the creeks and the overgrown areas where the tractors can't reach— that's where you find the genetic offspring of the country that existed when the Pony Express came through. But as far as the old grassland prairies that stretched as far north as the boreal forest, as far south at the Gulf Coast, forget it, they're gone from this part of the world.

———

It took me ten days to ride the Pony Express Trail through northern Kansas. When I passed through the town of

Marysville, I turned the odometer one hundred miles. That same distance was one eight-hour relay for a Pony Express rider. I wasn't exactly on schedule, but at least I had a hundred miles behind me. Claire had been with me to ensure that the horses adjusted to the climate and the work, and she left me after a night camped at the Hollenberg Pony Express Station. The break-in period was over. I was twenty miles from Nebraska, nearly out of Kansas. It was a tenuous momentum. My morale rode on the premise of mileage westward, and there was no other litmus for progress. I needed bigger vistas, fewer trees, less rain. The soundness, health, and comfort of my horses was my priority, but moving was the only effective advancement of the job before me. Finally, I was traveling. Finally, I had something to lose. The beginning had ended.

CHAPTER 4

"You'll always need the farmer out there"

MY FIRST DAY in Nebraska was going great until Chicken Fry wrapped his lead rope around Badger's tail. It was 4:30 in the afternoon. We'd come twenty-four miles in eight hours. I had just looked at the map and was telling the horses that we had two more miles to camp, forty minutes of walking. I'm not exactly sure what happened—because I was facing forward like most people on horseback—but I suspect that Chicken Fry had been shooing flies with Badger's tail. The packhorse would often walk with its head in the tail of the horse I was riding to keep the flies off its eyes and face. Chicken Fry must have raised his rope up under Badger's tail, which is, not surprisingly, a sensitive area on a horse, because Badger sucked his butt under him and whiplashed me forward so hard that the back of the saddle rammed my tailbone, and we were off at a dead run. The section of the lead rope that I was holding ran through my right hand as we left Chicken Fry in the dust and Badger lit the afterburners headed straight for the flooded borrow ditch of the county road. The ditch was nearly as wide as the road, and it was veneered in bright green duckweed-type moss so that it looked like it was covered in sod but for its dark muddy edges.

I had too much slack in the reins. I couldn't pull Badger to a stop. It's like the driver's seat being too far back to fully depress the brake pedal on a car running downhill. So I ejected. I vaulted straight up out of the saddle, dropped the right rein, held on to the left, and landed on my feet. When I hit the ground, I set up hard on the left rein, and that spun Badger in a half turn and stopped him cold in his tracks. He stood looking at me with his eyes full of white, his front legs spread in a wide stance, and his muscles quivering like he might jump again. We'd stopped ten feet from the borrow ditch swamp. Chicken Fry stood in the middle of the road some thirty feet behind us with his head raised as though asking, "Why the sudden commotion?" Good question, Chicken Fry, I said aloud. I turned to Badger, who looked like a cocked pistol ready to go off, and I told him that he was going to have to mellow out a bit if we were going to make it to California in one piece.

The incident was a clear reminder of safety. After eight hours of riding, I was too easy in the saddle, too comfortable, too relaxed. If Badger had hit the borrow ditch, it would have been a splash landing. He might have tried to jump it, but I'm not sure he could have cleared it, and the ground on the other side of it looked so soft and saturated that he probably would have sunk to his stomach in the mud. Ditching a horse into a mudhole or a bog usually results in a lot of flailing and struggling, and it's easy to lose control of the horse. If I lost Badger, he and Chicken Fry would probably run back in the direction we'd just come from, and I'd be left to beg some farmer for help recovering them.

More worrying than losing my horses, though, was an injury. If I wasn't ready to pay out six feet of lead rope in an instant, I could be dragged from the saddle. If I tangled or wrapped the lead rope in my fingers I could break a finger. And if I broke a finger, I'd be done riding. You can't saddle a horse with one arm. You can't handle two horses with only one good hand. I could minimize—though not eliminate—the inherent dangers of handling horses, but the stakes were too high for unforced errors.

The thing I most wanted to avoid was looking like I wasn't in control. I didn't want people to think that I was one step away from a wreck because no one on a farm or ranch ever wants a guest camping with horses if that guest looks like a liability. My shirt and jeans were about as clean as my saddle blankets—there wasn't much I could do about being dirty or smelling like a horse—but I was adamant that my camp and horse gear were as dialed in as that of any horseman to pass through that country since the Pony Express hung up its spurs in the fall of 1861. That was the goal. I didn't want to give the impression that I was ever hungry, tired, hot, cold, sore, disorganized, lost, depressed, or otherwise put out. Because, I reckoned, my clear passage rode on my reputation. People had to know that I was unobtrusive, safe, and competent. I called the passing of my reputation the moccasin telegraph, which is originally Canadian slang for an informal communication network. I first heard the phrase at journalism school at the University of Montana, and I adopted it as the word-of-mouth news of my approach.

I'd be surprised if you could ride a horse and lead a pack-horse through any rural area in the world and not have people know you're coming their way. I also believe that any visitor should be compliant, polite, and nonconfrontational with the locals they encounter. I didn't want to argue with people about politics or water rights or anything else. The only impression I wanted to give was that I was riding the Pony Express Trail. But that got a bit complicated, during the morning of my third day in Nebraska, when a dog trotted out from a farmhouse to join me as I rode up the Little Blue River.

The dog was medium sized, short haired, and the color of dark chocolate. It had white toes and a white spot on its chest. It was a large dog with a broad head, like it was part pit bull, and it was overweight, weighing probably one hundred pounds. It looked friendly, but not intelligent, and when it trotted right in front of Chicken Fry and was nearly stepped on, I figured the dog didn't have much experience with horses. It circled us a few times and then trotted beside me with its mouth open and tail wagging like it wanted to go for a walk. I kept the horses steady in high gear, and I told the dog to go home, but it didn't respond. The horses were annoyed. They pinned their ears and glared at it with a lot of equine communication that the dog clearly didn't understand. As the dog dangled behind Chicken Fry's hocks, walking too close to the cycling hind legs, I thought maybe a soft kick would do the trick, so I told Chicken Fry to see if he couldn't just trim a little hide off old Chocolate's nose, turn it for home. But Chicken Fry didn't kick the dog, and it kept apace with us.

I didn't want the dog to follow us because I didn't want someone to think that I'd stolen their dog. The dog had created a problem for both of us. It had put itself in a tough situation because I wasn't turning around, and with the miles that we put behind us, its situation worsened. I stopped every car that passed me by riding out into the center of the road, so that the driver had no choice but to slow and I could ask him or her about the dog. No one seemed to know its owner or where it lived, and every time we stopped, the dog splashed into the muddy borrow ditch to lap up water and roll in the grass and mud.

After two hours, the dog was tired. Its tongue hung out the side of its mouth. It had walked about six miles from its house. I wasn't sure how I was going to find the dog a ride home when a large, dark blue Ford pickup passed us, turned around, and then stopped in the middle of the road in front of me. A broad-shouldered woman wearing a black t-shirt, jeans, and white high-top sneakers climbed out of the truck and stood in the road with her hands on her hips and a serious expression on her face.

I said howdy to her and asked her if she was missing a dog.

"I been getting calls and text messages about this dumb dog all morning," she said.

I asked her if it was her dog.

"Hell, no. It's my dumb in-laws' dog." She grabbed his collar, which wasn't hard because the muddy, panting dog was happy to stand still. "Jesus Christ, this dog is a mess," she said. Her expression told me she didn't like that the dog smelled like a borrow ditch, and she didn't seem quite sure about how to handle getting the dog home. "Why don't you ride on, and we'll see if maybe he loses interest in you."

I told her that I reckoned that the easiest way to contain the dog was to probably to just load him up in the cab of that nice, blue truck. She didn't seem to think my comment was funny. "That's the last thing I'm gonna do." Then she looked up at me and nodded up the road and said, "Go on now."

I touched the brim of my hat and told her that I was much obliged to her, but she didn't say anything. She seemed as annoyed with my being there as with the dog. So I put the horses in gear and thanked her one last time for her trouble.

———

My passage through southern Nebraska was characterized by corn, storms, and the approach to the 98th meridian. As the established beginning of the West, the 98th was a milepost that I was eager to pass. It was about a day and a half's ride to cross it, roughly thirty miles of the Pony Express Trail from where I handed off the muddy dog to the woman, but it took me longer than that because prairie storms are nothing to trifle with. Traveling by horseback necessitates certain priorities, and one of them is to avoid being caught in the open during severe weather. It was May 17, and that night thirteen tornadoes would touch down on the plains of Nebraska. It sparked a two-week period of thunderstorms that meteorologists would later call the tornado outbreak sequence of May 2019.[1]Unlike the early pioneers or the riders of the Pony Express, detailed forecasting allowed me to see weather patterns unfolding, and on that night, I was camped in a farm shop south of Shickley, Nebraska.

A man named Darrel Mosier owned the farm. He ran the operation with his son, his brother, and a hired man. I found Darrel through a farmer in Kansas, and he agreed to let me wait out the weather at his place. When I met him, he was wearing a gray t-shirt, jeans, and lace-up leather boots, and I had the impression that he dressed just about the same way every day. He had the lean muscling of someone who had worked hard most of his life. His face was tanned in such a way that I suspected he worked without the shade of a hat, and he was hatless when I met him.

Darrel led me to a corral for Chicken Fry and Badger that offered no shelter but was far more secure than my single-strand electric fence. The corral sat beside a large red barn with white trim and a cupola in the center of the roofline.

Darrel told me that he sheathed the old wooden barn in metal siding a few years prior to preserve the original framing that his grandfather raised around 1900. The barn's interior reflected changes that have since transpired. Long dowels hammered into the ceiling beams would have held the dark ribbons of leather harness for the teams of draft horses. Several feeder stalls—wooden U-shaped stalls with hay mangers at their fronts where horses are groomed and fed before and after work—were covered in decades' worth of dust and looked like they hadn't seen a horse in years. Opposite the feeder stalls, Darrel climbed a wooden ladder framed into the wall. He disappeared through a bay in the ceiling, and a second later a bale of hay came sailing down through the open space and hit the floor of the barn aisle with a cloud of dust. Down came another bale, and Darrel slid down the ladder and said, "Help yourself to as much of that hay there in the mow as you want."

A haymow is a place for storing hay, and it's an old term that, like barn architecture, came west with New England farmers and before that from the farming cultures of England and Europe. Before Darrel mentioned it to me, I wasn't sure I'd ever heard the term, and was only familiar with it through Eric Sloane's book *An Age of Barns*. I was glad to hear remnants of the old lexicon among the modernization that has so permeated farming today.

After we threw some hay to my horses, Darrel told me that the night before, he and his wife, Caroline, had thrown a graduation party for their youngest daughter, who was about to finish high school. "The house is still a bit of a mess," he said, "but we got a room ready for you."

I hadn't seen the inside of a shower in ten days. Everything I had on and with me smelled like a wet horse, and I had no interest in hauling my truck of gear into someone's guest bedroom so I told Darrel that I'd just sleep in his shop if that worked for him. "You sure?" he asked. I nodded. "Caroline's not going to like that at all."

Darrel's shop was large enough to park a semi-truck inside. A dozen or so dodgy cats had the run of the place. Among the welders and tools and countless buckets of oil, hydraulic fluid, and fuel additives, the cats slinked and darted and watched me like leopards. A mother with a litter of eight very small kittens lived on an old wool blanket canvased over the top of an empty fifty-five-gallon fuel drum. There was a dusty futon-type couch opposite one of the work benches, and I flattened the couch and rolled out my bedroll on top of the stained pink bedsheet covering it. That night the rain came down in iron sheets and lightning flashed in the windows of the shop, but the tornadoes missed us.

Two nights and a day of rest at Darrel's gave me a primer in modern corn farming. Corn is big business. The U.S. produces far more corn than any country in the world, and most of it comes from Illinois, Indiana, Iowa, and Nebraska. Darrel, like a lot of corn farmers, also produces soybeans because, although the beans bring a lower price, they fix nitrogen in the soil and are used rotationally with corn, every few years, to promote soil health.

Darrel's farm is a family-run operation, but it is not small. The yard was filled with enough equipment to make me think that a farmer also needed to be a mechanic. Semi-trucks, dump trucks, feed trucks, bobtailed trucks, and pickup trucks. Stock trailers, belly-dump semi-trailers, trailers for carrying large round bales of hay, flatbed trailers for hauling equipment, and trailers that are federally regulated to carry not more than 1,000 bushels of corn. Some of the equipment was under repair and some it was used every day, but nearly all of it was covered with the black mud of that rich Nebraska soil.

Darrel can produce about 250 bushels of corn per acre, and that's about as high of a yield as you can find. The average corn yield in the U.S. is 177 bushels per acre.[2] Darrel's able to harvest a higher yield because of, among other factors, the rich soil and a shallow aquifer, known as the Ogallala Aquifer, that allows him to irrigate the corn with groundwater. Like nearly every other farmer, he also fertilizes the corn, and on the afternoon of May 18, I was laid out on my bedroll reading maps when Darrel asked if I wanted to ride along with him in the field.

Darrel's John Deere 8330 tractor is a $300,000 piece of equipment with four rear tires that are six feet in diameter. To fertilize the corn, the tractor pulled an implement that ran sixteen iron discs in the soil to fertilize sixteen rows, and behind each disc was a sickle-like blade that applied the fertilizer a few inches underground within easy reach of the plants' roots. The cab of the tractor was spacious and comfortable. Because operator fatigue is one of the leading causes of farm accidents, the cab incorporates many ergonomic features to help a tired farmer avoid getting into a wreck.[3] Heating and air conditioning are standard. Nearly all tractors have satellite radio. Many have Wi-Fi, Bluetooth, an onboard Dual Core Intel processor, and an accelerometer to prevent theft. The air-ride seat adjusts in ways a car seat never does: firmness, armrest height, lateral adjustment. There's also a jump seat for a passenger, which is where I sat.

With three full tanks of fertilizer, Darrel drove the tractor into the field and stopped it near as he could to the twenty or so inches between crop rows. He threw a switch and engaged autopilot, which moved the tractor about two inches to the right. Autopilot turned the steering wheel. The tractor knew where the crop lines were. It knew where Darrel last applied fertilizer and where to begin the next. Autopilot drove the tractor via the network of data conveyed by satellite, which is why modern crop rows are as straight as latitude lines. As autopilot took over, Darrel pulled a Coors Light from his soft-sided cooler, popped it open, and asked me how my ride had been so far.

We were humming along under autopilot, talking about crossing the West, when Darrel said he needed to call his brother, Matt, to bring a wrench to make some adjustments to the implement. He was on the phone, listening to Matt, when he cupped his hand over the phone and looked at me.

"Sounds like the cats got into your food," he whispered. "Don't worry, I'll buy you more food."

That night was Caroline's birthday party, so Darrel and his family and I met a few friends at a nearby steakhouse. Caroline told me that every small town used to have a steakhouse but that most of them were gone. We found the place nearly empty. Several of Caroline and Darrel's friends showed up. The conversation centered around corn and soybeans and cattle prices. A ruddy-cheeked friend of Darrel's said that earlier that day he'd seen a video on Twitter of the first fully autonomous tractor harvesting corn.

"How'd it go?" Darrel asked.

"It went good. You know, they try to confuse it, give it problems, see if they can make it screw up, but they say it did good. Video looked good. Same as any other harvest—except there's no one inside the tractor."

Automation is the next big step for farming. Tractors became widespread in the 1930s and '40s, and a lot of working livestock found an easier life.[4] Artificial fertilizer became widespread after World War II, and per-acre production increased dramatically.[5] At the end of the twentieth century, tractors began communicating with overhead satellites. Darrel first started using tractors equipped with computers around 2005. There was a learning curve. Mechanical adjustments were increasingly made electronically. Software technicians from John Deere came to the farm every year to update the tractors. Technology progressed in other parts of the operation at the same time, and by the time I met Darrel, he had weather stations in his fields sending him text messages telling him how much rain the field received, the soil temperature, and the humidity. From this data he calculated the best times to plant or fertilize or harvest.

One effect of automation is further depopulation of the countryside. One person in an office remotely driving half a dozen tractors saves the farmer from hiring additional help. Farmhands will be needed, though not as many as before. But if no one is inside the tractor, I asked Darrel, how will the operator know if the implement needs adjusting?

The short answer is sensors. Automated tractors are equipped with an array of sensors to detect everything from a driveshaft that's about to fail to a leaking hydraulic hose.

"But you'll always need the farmer out there," Darrel said. "We won't ever fully get away from needing someone in the field."

———

Of all that I heard and saw about the cultivation of crops, a story about a man who drowned in corn affected me the most. John and Lynn Greer, who farmed two days' ride west of Darrel's place, told me the story over dinner. I was waiting out yet another storm while camped in their maintenance shop. Nearly every farm in Nebraska has a few tall, cylindrical silos, called grain bins, for storing corn and soybeans, and I had remarked how the top of one of John's bins looked like a bad place to be during severe weather. When I said that, I felt that I'd breached some kind of sensitive topic. John didn't even look up, just kept eating. Lynn set down her fork and looked at me and said, "Those bins are dangerous."

One evening during the fall harvest several years ago, their neighbor was emptying a bin full of corn into a truck. To remove corn from a bin, a large, corkscrew-type auger attaches to the base of the bin and runs the corn onto a conveyor belt that dumps the grain into a semi-truck. As the grain is being emptied from the bottom of the bin, it sometimes fails to uniformly settle. If the grain is damp, it can clump and stick to the side of the bin. Or it can form a crust that needs to be broken. Inside a fifty-five-foot-tall grain bin, corn can form cliffs, couloirs, sinkholes, or any number of formations that require someone to enter the bin from the top to help the grain properly settle and feed through the auger. Lynn and John's neighbor was augering corn with his son. The father climbed in the bin while the auger was running

"He went in there with a pole or something to help the corn go down," Lynn said.

Fifteen or so minutes after the man entered the bin, his son called to him but received no answer. The son climbed the ladder, looked inside the hatch, and saw only corn. His father had been buried.

"You think that if the corn's up to your knees you can pull your leg out, but you can't. It packs so tightly that you can't pull your leg out," Lynn said. "I was the one who called 9-1-1."

One foot of packed grain can create three hundred pounds of pressure on a person's leg. At two feet deep, the person will need mechanical advantage to be freed. If a farmer is standing on corn that is actively being drained, entrapment can occur in four seconds. Full engulfment can occur in twenty-two seconds.[6] This has been well researched by the Occupational Safety and Health Administration (OSHA) and universities, such as Purdue University, which has been tracking confined-space accidents on farms for the past forty years.[7] Purdue also holds annual training events that show farmers how to use harnesses, rigging, and other equipment to safely operate in grain bins. According to OSHA, if there's corn flowing beneath your feet, you have two seconds to react.

After Lynn called 9-1-1, she called every nearby farmer that she knew. By the time rescue operations were underway, the sun had set, and the farmers parked their trucks in a circle around the bin with their headlights shining inward on it. The men dug with shovels inside the bin like they were searching for an avalanche victim. They used tractors to tear a large hole in the bin. The corn spilled and ran from the hole. John was there that night trying to help dig out his neighbor.

"It had been so long since he'd been in there that I was worried about the men working too hard—everybody was working so hard, just covered in sweat," John said. "My feeling is that he had already passed by the time they loaded him onto the helicopter."

The next morning brought a depressing scene of the bin with a gaping hole in it.

"All the farmers met out there and cleaned up the mess," John said. "We called the elevator [which is the facility that purchases corn from farmers] and told them what happened, and they were really good to us—because the corn had a lot of mud in it and pieces of metal in it—and they bought it all."

Grain bin accidents aren't common, but they happen regularly. In 2019, twenty-three farmers died in grain bins. A lot of aspects of farming make it one of the most dangerous occupations in the country, but, Lynn said, grain bins deserve extra caution.

"I made John promise me that he'd never go in there when they're running corn," she said.

I knew that farming was dangerous. Being a devout horseman, I've tried to limit my time watering vegetables or tending crops, but I know that even everyday tasks like attaching a front-end loader to a tractor carry risk. But I didn't ever think that drowning in corn was a possibility. The more I learned about farming, the more mysterious it seemed. The economy of it all was beyond me. The radio reports of prices and futures for cattle, goats, grains, and whatever else might as well have been in French. I don't know how many ways there are to sell a pig, but you can hear about it every morning on radio stations all across the Midwest. And after ten days of it, I'd had enough.

———

Somewhere amid all those cornstalks and all that rain, I crossed the 98th meridian. Once I entered the West, the first thing I wanted to do was rest my horses. The opportunity arrived on

Memorial Day weekend at Fort Kearny State Historical Park. The park is the site of a U.S. Army fort built in the 1840s to protect emigrants on the Oregon Trail. It was also the location of a Pony Express station. Today it features a visitors' center, a log stockade, a parade ground, and a few buildings reconstructed according to historical aesthetics. A day's ride out from Fort Kearny, I called the park superintendent, Gene Hunt, to ask if I might be able to camp there.

"We'd love to have you," Gene said. "It's Living History weekend. You'll fit right in."

A living history weekend usually means some kind of re-enactment. Frontier soldiers, prairie settlers, a sheriff wearing a star badge on his vest and a gun loaded with blanks on his hip—when I was young, I'd seen living history groups at places like Dodge City, Kansas, and Old Tucson, Arizona. I wasn't sure what kind of program Gene ran, but I figured it'd be fun to watch whatever show they put on.

I rode up to the entrance to Fort Kearny on May 25. A handful of soldiers without guns wearing navy blue, Civil War–era uniforms and a woman in a long, Victorian-looking dress were standing under a large spruce tree as I approached. When they saw me, they put away their phones and walked out to greet us. I asked about Gene, and they pointed to an inbound golf cart. Gene pulled up with a big smile on his face.

"Here's our Pony Express rider! Welcome to Fort Kearny," he said as he stepped out of the golf cart. He was dressed in the typical drab uniform of a state park employee: khaki shirt, olive-green trousers, a ball cap that read "Parks Nebraska."

He walked toward the horses, and I slid out of the saddle. "No, no, get back on your horse. We need some photos," Gene said.

Gene took photos of me shaking hands with a soldier in front of the entrance sign to the park and in front of the replica stockade fort, posing me and the horses one way and another. Patting my leg, he told me I was earning my keep. Gene was quick to smile. He told me that he was flat-out tickled to have us as his guests for the weekend, and he said, "You can sleep in the powder magazine. We got a corral for your horses right behind it."

As we crossed the fort's parade grounds, Gene pointed to a line of elm trees and said that the site of the Pony Express station was just beyond the tree line, in the farmed ground beyond. He pointed to a massive cottonwood tree, probably five feet in diameter and faded white, that had fallen down some years before, and he said that the tree had likely been standing when the Pony Express ran.

"It was a witness tree," he said, and looked at me as though he were proud of the fact. He showed me the corral for my horses and opened the door to the powder magazine. "Dinner's at seven. Spaghetti. I always make dinner for the reenactors, and tonight we're having spaghetti, so come on over to the shop at seven," he said.

The original Fort Kearny was a collection of whitewashed buildings surrounding a parade ground and a central flagpole made of short logs lashed together, and like a lot of military installations, it had a powder magazine for storing gun powder, explosives, firearms, and other ordnance. A magazine, which was any ordnance storage facility, was either dug into the ground like a bunker, covered with earth like a tornado shelter, or made of stone—the idea being impregnable storage.

The magazine at Fort Kearny was an earthed-over conical structure, twenty feet high. The interior was floored in rough-cut lumber, walled in pine boards. The four walls came together in an apex. Empty wooden crates labeled for Sharps rifles, Springfield muskets, and howitzer rounds sat stacked against the walls. There were no windows, and it smelled dank, like a root cellar, but it was dry, and none of the boards showed watermarks.

For three weekends a year, the reenactors of the C Battery 3rd U.S. Artillery Living History Group stay in white canvas Civil War–style tents near the rebuilt blacksmith shop. The tents, a dozen of varying sizes and configurations and all guyed out with rope, were arranged in rows, not quite in military fashion but organized. Several tents had awnings run off the front for shade and cover from rain. Everyone was dressed in clothing of the period, and at seven o'clock, they all walked over to the fort's maintenance shop for dinner.

Gene had set up long tables and a buffet of spaghetti and tomato sauce and slices of white bread and butter. Half a dozen cell phones were plugged into wall sockets along a work bench because the reenactors had no electricity in their tents. One of the soldiers who had greeted me at the gate told me that he and his wife were just married. He was a young man, and he wore a blue wool uniform with brass buttons and a hat of the same color and material that slouched forward on his head. His wife stood beside him. She wore a pink dress and a bonnet. We stood in the door of the shop, looking out at a thin rain that had begun to fall. Meteorologists had predicted two inches in the next forty-eight hours. The young man told me that instead of sleeping at the fort, he and his wife were staying at the Holiday Inn.

"My first year not camping out," he said with a grim face. "Oh, well, there's always next year, I guess."

The reenactment was a family affair. Most of them were kin or might as well have been. The youngest was one year old, the third generation of his family to wear old-style clothes at the fort. A handful of young girls looking like they were cast for *Little House on the Prairie* sat at the end of one table, eating ice cream from Styrofoam bowls. Some of the men were dressed as soldiers, and some in nineteenth-century civilian garb. They were there to enrich the tourist experience, to talk about the historical role of the fort, to tinker with forge and anvil in the blacksmith shop, and to bring to life what history they could. But what they seemed most excited about was shooting the cannon.

The leader of the troop was a man named Terry Hendrickson, and he was in charge of the cannon firing. Terry was a tall, skinny man who looked like a cross between a chimney sweep and a Harley biker. His salt-and-pepper beard came to a wispy point just above the top button of his navy blue vest. He wore wire-rimmed, Ben Franklin–style glasses, smudged with soot, that sat low on his nose so that when he talked to someone he sometimes looked up over the top of his glasses. I stood beside Terry while he ate spaghetti and told me about his cannons.

"With the twenty-four pounder I can shoot just about a mile at five degrees elevation," he said. He slightly inclined his outstretched arm at the horizon, while holding his plate in his other hand, and then looked at me over the top of his glasses, and said, "Five degrees. That's not very much."

The comment made me wonder where Terry found a mile-long range to safely shoot a cannonball, but it also struck me as perhaps no different than the way a frontier cannon chief would have told a Pony Express rider about his work. I had assumed a historical persona—not by design, but also not by accident—through riding the trail. Talking to Terry in the Fort Kearny maintenance shop revealed an unlikely crossroads of the historical and the modern West. He was shooting a real cannon, albeit with blanks. He was using black powder, loading the cannon with a ramrod in more or less the same fashion as it was originally done. For Terry, it seemed to me, the cannon operations provided a direct connection to history. He enjoyed some level of authenticity.

As Terry forked spaghetti into his mouth, I wondered what he did for a living, but I didn't want to adulterate the fugitive nostalgia that I reckoned must be the inspiration for stripes of reenactors everywhere: that the tents and the period dress are a welcome reprieve from their everyday lives. And that's why the freshly married young man didn't want to sleep in the Holiday Inn. Because he only had three chances a year to escape reality through reenacting history.

Fort Kearny deepened my relationship with the Pony Express in a way that I did not anticipate. At Fort Kearny, all of the old trails convened. The Oregon, California, and Mormon trails, as well as all their various branches that began at the Missouri River, converged at the fort. The fort was the beginning of the heavily trafficked road to the Rocky Mountains, called the Great Platte River Road. Today, an archway over Interstate 80 in Kearney, a town of 30,000 people across the river from the fort, is a monument to the Platte River as an ancient and modern thoroughfare. Before I reached Fort Kearny, the Pony Express dominated the historical landscape. But at the fort, I began hearing about wagon trains and emigrants and families with a lot of children and baggage.

After three restful days of mostly rain, I said adios to Gene and the reenactors, and pointed Chicken Fry and Badger west on the Platte River Road. Thirty-five miles west of Fort Kearny, I passed a historical marker for the Plum Creek Historical Trail Ruts, where a shallow depression marks the trace of the old wagon road. The Pony Express used the same road, and the last thing you'd want to see if you were running the mail would be a wagon train blocking your way. The riders of the Pony Express were the fastest men on the frontier. They were a breed different than the emigrants. As I thought about the trail traffic on the Great Platte River Road, the distinction between those who were new to the West and those who were part of the West became clearer, and the defining personality for my entrenchment as a horseman of the Pony Express—rather than an emigrant—was a man named Rinker Buck.

Rinker Buck and his brother, Nick, drove a mule-drawn wagon up the Oregon Trail in 2012. I had read his 2015 book about the experience. Two days out from Fort Kearny, a few miles west of the site of the Plum Creek Pony Express Station, I crossed Rinker's tracks for the first time. Today the site is part of the Robb Ranch, which was established in 1874 and is now owned by Joe and Dianne Jeffrey. I rode up to the front gate of the ranch on the afternoon of May 30. Dianne met me at the end of the driveway. I said howdy and she did the same. As I rode past her, she said, "I like your buckskin," and nodded at Chicken Fry. "You might not leave here with him."

Here was an old woman wearing a denim shirt and pressed jeans and who looked like she used a blow-dryer on her hair every morning. When I turned in the saddle and looked back at her, she was smirking like a horse trader, looking over Chicken Fry's legs as though evaluating him for soundness, and I immediately liked her. I smiled and told her that the horse was not for sale.

Joe and Dianne are amiable people. Joe has had a variety of occupations—veterinarian, rancher, county commissioner—and hobbies. He collects bicycles, showed me his garage full of old bikes, couldn't help but to roll out one called a penny-farthing and show me how to ride it. Joe once made a music box that looked like a fence post and played "Don't Fence Me In," by Cole Porter. He's since sold more than seven hundred of them to people in five different countries, he said proudly.

That evening we sat on Joe and Dianne's back deck enjoying Joe's choice of drink: a Cuba libre, which is coke and rum and lime juice.

"Rinker and Nick stayed a few days with us," Joe said. "Boy, we really enjoyed their company."

"Stacked up the empty wine bottles, is what they did," Dianne said. "But they sure had nice mules."

"Really nice mules," Joe said. "Big mules. Big dark mules. So tall they could hardly walk through the doorway of that barn there." He pointed across the yard to a tall red and white wooden barn that had the ranch brand painted on the gable. The brand, which is a cauterized marking used to identify livestock, was the letter *J* with two stick-figure legs, called a walking *J*. Beyond the barn was a hay meadow, and Joe said that the meadow had been a popular campsite for emigrants heading West. The ford across Plum Creek, on the far side of the meadow, was still visible where the steep banks had been graded to accommodate a wagon.

"They say there's an average of one grave per mile on the Oregon Trail," Joe said. "No telling how many people are buried in that meadow. One afternoon, Rinker went out there to just sit for a while, take it all in."

The thing that Rinker never wrote about was his similarity to the original actors of his reenactment. He left the East with expectations of a transformation. Once in the West, he didn't always know what he was looking at. He thought he had altitude sickness on the plains of Wyoming after a one-month acclimation period (at three miles per hour) to a relatively low altitude (about five thousand six hundred feet above sea level). He called the sagebrush steppe of Wyoming "hilly but featureless scrublands." He came West with preconceived notions about the Mormons, and he nearly got in trouble with a landowner when he failed to recognize private property boundaries. But between the lines of his narrative is an allegory for the emigrant experience in the nineteenth century.[8]

As this came into focus, I realized two things. One, that I could never spend all summer in a wagon looking at the back end of a mule. And two, that, just as the Buck brothers were like those wagon-train emigrants, I was like the ghost of a Pony Express rider. The idea that I could reincarnate a time and a place and a persona was empowering. It gave me momentum. I was running a tight, autonomous operation. Chicken Fry and Badger had turned out in such gloss and muscle tone that I worried about them being stolen. Badger looked like he had just stepped off the track at Churchill Downs, and Chicken Fry had become so attuned to our daily routine that I half expected him to load the panniers in the morning. You couldn't ask for two better horses. I'd come about three hundred miles from St. Joseph, Missouri, and as far as I was concerned, the West was my oyster.

———

And then things turned south. Badger started limping. A day and a half's ride from the Jeffreys' ranch, Badger developed soreness in his right front foot. I was riding him that day. The unevenness in his gait knocked the air out of me. So I got off and led both horses by foot. I walked nine miles in my high-heeled, leather-soled riding boots, and if you've never hiked in riding boots, what most people would call cowboy boots, you're not missing anything. It was hot, I was upset, and Badger was hurting.

To make matters worse, I rode into the worst tick infesta-tion I'd ever seen in my life. Sleeping on the ground made interacting with them inevitable, and certainly uncomfortable. The ticks of the Platte River Valley, though, were more than uncomfortable; they were demoralizing. My tan canvas vest seemed to attract the ticks. I wondered if the deer-like colora-tion drew them. I found ticks inside my shirt, in the waistband of my underwear, and in my socks. They were so numerous that when I felt the urge to itch, I would immediately open my shirt or drop my jeans and find the tick with my Leatherman pliers. I woke to the tickling of a tick walking across my stom-ach. The horses suffered the same. I pulled ticks off their legs and from the underside of their bellies, and I swabbed their ears with a cone of toilet paper doused with the same insect repellent I used on myself, one hundred percent DEET Jungle Juice. When I pulled the toilet paper swab from their ears, it was bloody and spotted with ticks and fragments of ticks.

I rested for two days at an empty rental house south of the town of North Platte, hoping that Badger was only temporar-ily sore. For two days, I sat under a shade tree looking for ticks, drinking coffee, and watching the horses graze. I decided not to kill any ticks because there were too many and I thought doing so might erode my karma. Halfway through my second day of rest, a car pulled in the driveway of the house. It was a gray sedan, and three women sat in it. I had my boots and socks off and walked up to the car in my bare feet. The woman in the driver's seat rolled down the window and greeted me. She asked if I lived there, and I told her my story, that I was on the move and only stopped now and then to rest. She asked if she could give me a prayer, and I told her, sure, that I needed all the help I could get. She opened a Bible, rested it on the steering wheel, and read:

Look! The tent of God is with mankind, and he will reside with them, and they will be his people. And God himself will be with them. And he will wipe out every tear from their eyes, and death will be no more, neither will mourning nor outcry nor pain be any more. The former things have passed away.

When she finished, I took a photo of the passage, which was Revelation 21:3–4, and I thanked her. The other two women in the car said nothing. I wondered if they were missionaries in training. I nodded to each, the driver wished me luck, and when she drove off, I walked over to Badger and said, there ya go, may the word of God give us four wheels under you.

I left the next morning with the rising sun, and three miles down the road, just south of the town of North Platte, Badger was back to gimping along. We were walking slowly down a dirt road, when a red pickup truck passed us and then stopped on the shoulder of the road. A man wearing a straw cowboy hat and a pearl-snap shirt climbed out of the truck. He looked like a rancher. He leaned against his truck, folded his arms across his chest, and waited for me to approach. I was in a sour mood over Badger's soreness, and I aimed to just ride on past him, but he stopped me.

"How ya doing?" he asked.

I told him that I had a lame horse. He asked which horse. I nodded at Badger.

"Let's see him walk."

After I walked the horses a few feet forward so the man could see Badger limp, he walked over and picked up Badger's foot, and looked at the bottom of it. He rubbed his chin, set down the foot, and said that he didn't have any tools with him to test Badger's sole for soreness. I was about to be done with the old man who had touched one of my horses without my permission, when he said, "There's a place you can stay just over the hill."

Which hill? I asked.

He pointed down the road and said, "A quarter mile from here."

I told him that I'd ridden a long way to get there and that I might need to camp a day or two to see about a farrier or a vet.

"I know who you are. I'm Bob Majors."

I had talked to Bob on the phone a few days prior to ask about camping at his ranch. Bob is a descendant of Alexander Majors of Russell, Majors and Waddell, the freighting firm that established and operated the Pony Express. I'd thought it might be nice to talk to him about his pedigree and the Pony Express, but he'd told me over the phone that he had eight horses at his place and didn't have room for me. That'd been the end of that, and I planned on camping at a tract of public land seven miles farther up the road. But Bob had also told me that a man named Steve Sward was training a young horse for him, and that he lived just over the hill.

Anyone in the world would know that Steve Sward was a cowboy. He didn't look like a rancher; he looked like a cowboy. He was bandy-legged, long-muscled, and skinny enough to hide behind a fence post. His white shirt was tucked tight into his jeans, and he wore a bone-handled knife on his belt. The knife had a short blade and was carried in a horizontal sheath so that it was easily accessible but wouldn't interfere with sitting in a saddle. Cowboys are the only people I've seen carry knives in that kind of sheath.

But he was in a hurry when I met him. His wife, Holly, had a dentist appointment in town. "Bob said you got a hot-wire for your horses," he said.

I nodded.

"Throw it up yonder by that tractor. I'll be back in a few hours. There's alfalfa in the barn. My son, Dylan, is in there, he'll show ya where it's at."

Dylan was sixteen, the product of Steve's previous marriage. He had blond hair and a skinny, angular frame. His step-sister, Shyann, was the daughter of Holly's previous marriage, and the two teenagers periodically helped Steve during the summer, mucking stalls, feeding horses, doing whatever needed to be done for the twenty or so horses that Steve was working with.

The three of us hung out in the cool shade of the barn, drinking Dr Peppers while my horses ate alfalfa in the sun. Hawk, a one-year-old black-and-white barred rooster with a scarlet comb, strutted between the bridle racks and feed sacks. A cat named Turbo slept on a stack of saddle pads and occasionally stretched and yawned while we talked. Dylan said that Shyann was a good student and made good grades.

"Really good grades," she said with a nod of her head. "I see school as a way for me to travel, so I make good grades so that I can go see cool places. Next summer I'm going to Peru with my Spanish class. Pretty excited about that."

This was a refreshing conversation to be having with a sixteen-year-old girl in the middle of Nebraska. All that I'd been thinking, hearing, and talking about for the past month was farming, land, and livestock. Shyann said that she wanted to go to Japan someday and that travel was an education.

"The coolest part is that you never know what you're going to learn," she said. I told her that I had learned something from every person I'd met since leaving Missouri.

"For sure," she said, as though she already knew that. "Have you learned anything from us?"

I'd been there about an hour, and I had learned something. As I was sorting my gear after I arrived, Shyann and Dylan had been talking about eggs. One of Dylan's friends had found an egg laid in his barn and wasn't sure if the egg was edible or about to hatch into a chick. Shyann told him that an egg needs twenty-one days under a hen to make a chick. I told Shyann that I didn't know an egg could be a chick in twenty-one days.

After a couple of hours, Steve and Holly drove up. Steve had earned his spurs as a horse trainer through a series of competitions in which people train formerly wild mustangs to be saddle horses in a short amount of time, typically ninety days. It takes a good hand to make a straight-out-of-the-sagebrush mustang into a horse suitable for an obstacle-course competition, and Steve's good at it. These days, though, he spends part of his time training horses to handle adversity quietly and with more confidence, and part of his time training people who ride horses to do the same.

Like a lot of horse-training facilities, Steve's barn was a hub of quiet activity. During the two days I was there, a handful of people trickled in and out. A farrier came to look at Badger, but couldn't find any reason for the soreness, which had waned. Because I was about to cross into Colorado, I needed to renew the horses' health certificates. An equine health certificate is a voucher, good for thirty days, that says a veterinarian has evaluated the animal as healthy. Some state-line ports of entry are known to check entering livestock for health papers, so a veterinarian from Stockman's Veterinary Clinic drove out to write up a couple for Chicken Fry and Badger.

The vet was old. He had white hair, and he wore narrow black leather suspenders over a nearly see-through white shirt. He wore a cowboy hat and jeans and low-heeled leather boots. He walked stiffly, a little stove-up, like he might have been kicked by a horse a few times. He didn't bother to look at the horses, just got out of his pickup, went inside the barn, and wrote out two health certificates. I asked if he wanted to see the horses.

"Nah, I don't need to see 'em," he said. "If you made it this far and don't have any problems, your horses are healthy."

He asked how my ride had been. I told him Badger had been sore for a few days but appeared sound again. The ticks, though, had been irritating. I was pulling them off myself and the horses all day every day. I told him that I had places on my ankles and my waist where I'd pulled off ticks, and the places were raw, wouldn't heal.

"My aunt died of Rocky Mountain spotted fever," he said. "She'd been sick for a while, and they couldn't figure out why. Then she died, and when the mortician was preparing the body for the casket, he found a tick on her scalp." He looked at me and tilted his head slightly to the side, and said, "They say that tick killed her."

I asked him if she had lived in North Platte.

"All her life," he said.

I couldn't do anything about the ticks or the rain, but I could keep going. And so with two sound horses and a new health certificate for each, I made plans to leave the following day.

That night Steve, Holly, Dylan, Shyann, and I grilled bratwursts at the barn. Steve and I shared a six-pack of beer. He showed me leatherwork that he'd done over the past few years—a braided whip, a pair of chaps, bridles, hackamores, reins. He does his leatherwork in the winter, he said, when the days are shorter and he spends more time indoors. We sat in folding chairs outside the barn, and he asked about my progress so far. I told him that I was about 375 miles from St. Joseph and that I'd been riding for one month and three days. The mail of the Pony Express would have been to the same place in about 37 hours. We talked about my road ahead, and Steve told me to call him if I needed anything as I made my way toward Colorado.

"South of you will be the Wildcat Hills," he said. "Nothing but rattlesnakes in the Wildcats. Trust me, I've cowboyed in that country all my life. But north of you will be the Sandhills. And the Sandhills—well, that's the prettiest country on earth."

CHAPTER 5
A Short History of the Great Plains

GRASSLANDS ARE THE most threatened biome on earth. They've also seen the least amount of conservation and the highest degree of conversion to something other than a native state. Which means they're rare. Mostly because the fertile soil that grasslands produce makes good farmland, and that's why nearly every acre of tallgrass prairie between Central Nebraska and Lake Michigan has been broken up by the iron plow and converted to cropland.[1] The Sandhills, though, are a vestige of the old ecosystem. If you look at a map of Nebraska showing the levels of human modification of the landscape— by development, roads, agriculture—most of the state has suffered some degree of ecological loss, and little of the state has retained its original biology, except for the Sandhills.

They show up as an oval of undisturbed land, a holdout of the Great Plains ecosystem.[2] A recent paper published in the journal *Conservation Science and Practice* identifies seven tracts of grasslands that are the only remaining large-scale continuous expanses of the biome remaining on earth, and one of those was the Sandhills of Nebraska.[3]

I didn't want to ride to the Sandhills because I didn't want to detour the horses from the trail. But I did want to see them, so I arranged for a rangeland specialist with the USDA to take me out there. I met Nadine Bishop through a friend of mine whose father also worked for the USDA. Nadine had been with the Nebraska Natural Resources Conservation Service for the past forty years when I met her on the morning of June 11. I left Chicken Fry and Badger at a small farm outside the town of Ogallala, and as we left the river bottom in Nadine's car, the prairie took on the form of an ocean. The hills stood like waves frozen in motion. They were so covered in green grass that the country looked like Ireland. In the Sandhills there is no clear erosional cohesion between valley and hill. Most of the precipitation percolates through the soil rather than running on the surface. So the landscape is bowls and cups and dune-shaped hills. Sandhills, Nadine told me, are sand dunes covered in grass, and they make up the largest dune field, or erg, in North America.

Erg is a geological term for a sea of sand, and it's derived from the Arabic word *arq*, meaning dune field. The dune field began forming during the last Ice Age from sediment eroded from the Rocky Mountains.[4] Since its formation, the Sandhills erg has been periodically covered with vegetation and period-ically a Sahara-like desert. As recently as the medieval warm period, from 900 to 1300, the dunes were bare and wind-blown.[5] Even early settlers to the area reported large areas of sand, Nadine told me. Comparatively, though, very little sand is visible today.

"The dunes are now fully vegetated," she said. "But they say the Sandhills are always an inch or so from being a desert."

The poor soil—it's all sand—supports only a thin veneer, an inch or so in most places, of vegetation. Most of that vegetation is forbs, or wildflowers, and grasses, and if it's overgrazed the plants will die off and the country will look like an erg. Alternatively, if the range isn't grazed, the dead plant material that would otherwise have been carried away by ungulates will form a mat that will choke out the root system, and the vegetation will then die and the sand will blow again. Historically, bison maintained the health of the Sandhills through grazing. Today, Nadine said, cattle do.

Nadine pulled off the highway at a pasture gate and drove over the prairie for a half mile before stopping on the top of a green hill carpeted with flowers. She retrieved a short-handled shovel out of the trunk of the car and began to walk slowly in no particular direction, looking at the ground, carrying the shovel at its midpoint. When she saw an interesting plant, she stooped to feel the leaves. She had to feel the plants. I asked her to tell me what she was looking at, and out rolled the taxonomy of the Sandhills: little bluestem grass, western wheatgrass, six weeks fescue grass. Lamb's quarters, sand milkweed, wavyleafed thistle, silky prairie clover. She used the shovel to turn over a clump of grass. The roots were all shallow and ran horizontally, and they formed a tightly woven sod that was the veneer of grass over the sand.

At the top of a steep hill, she identified more of the plants around us. Western wallflower, shaggy dwarf morning glory, Princess Caroline larkspur. The biodiversity, nearly all of it living below knee height, was impressive. From the highway, little of it was visible. But kneeling among the grasses and flowers with Nadine was like seeing the landscape under a microscope. She said that invasive species, like the eastern red cedar, are starting to become a problem in the Sandhills, and it's something she and her colleagues worry more about every year. She slid her hand under a small red-and-white mottled seed pod that looked like an elaborately painted oriental vase the size of a jelly bean.

"Painted milkvetch. Some people call it painted bird's egg vetch," she said.

She pointed out brittle prickly pear and bigroot prickly pear and plains phlox and a prairie rose, whose flower color—white to pink to deep red—is determined by the chemical composition of the soil. She held a clump of prairie sandreed and said that the root system of the prairie sandreed is the backbone of the Sandhills ecosystem, what's keeping all the sand in one place. She pointed to ragweed, which is an early successional species, one of the first plants to germinate after a disturbance. It's mostly an undesirable plant, a weed.

"People get all freaked out about ragweed, but I consider it a soil stabilizer," she said.

One of the few endangered plants in Nebraska is the blowout penstemon, also known as Hayden's penstemon. A blowout is a barren sand area between vegetated dunes. They look like sand-trap bunkers big enough to drop a house in, or several houses in. Large blowouts can be several acres in area. The constant wind of the Sandhills will make a blowout from any gap in the vegetated cover, and once started, the blowouts increase in size until a plant suited to an eolian life in sand, like the blowout penstemon, finds purchase and stabilizes a microcommunity where other plants will do the same. Eventually the dispersed microcommunities will join to break the erosional cycle and revegetate the blowout.

"The blowout penstemon is having a hard time because people have been so successful at stabilizing the soil," Nadine said.

The biggest ecological characteristic of the pre-Columbian prairies that's missing today, Nadine said, is fire. Nadine and others at the USDA are trying to find a way to restore fire to the prairies without burning up any homes, livestock, windmills, or fences. Prescribed burns have proven successful, she said, but since very little public land exists in Nebraska—97 percent of the state is privately owned—management is a cooperative process between landowners and rangeland managers, and that process can take time. But, Nadine said, Sandhills ranchers have proven a responsible bunch.

"They're taking care of the land," she said, looking up from the blades of grass to the sea of green stretching away in every direction. "You can see it in the health of the prairie."

As far as ranching, the Sandhills is one of the best places in the country for it. Or so I've heard more than once. Water is the reason. There's a lot of it in the Sandhills. It's one of only two places in the Great Plains where natural lakes occur, and there are about 2,000 of them.[6] Between grass-covered dunes, the water pools into treeless, shallow oases fed mostly by ground water. In the Sandhills, the water table breaches the surface. And that water table, the Ogallala Aquifer, is one of the largest underground reservoirs in the world.

Stretching from Texas to South Dakota, it's also known as the High Plains Aquifer System, and it contains about as much water as Lake Huron—though recent reports show that the aquifer is being drained by irrigation faster than it can recharge. The water is held in solution between loosely consolidated sediments not unlike the sand of the dunes. The bottom of the aquifer is fairly uniform, averaging about 2,000 feet below sea level, or a mile below the surface, but the lateral and upper margins of the water body are irregular, at places 300 feet below the surface, at others pooling into lakes.[7]

"The water table is at about fifty feet right here," Nadine said, "but you can find water at five feet."

This was a boon for the prairie settlers. Water at five feet, hidden merely by the loose sand of the dune field, meant that digging a well was easy. A settler who put up a derrick and a windmill pump could have enough water for livestock, garden, kitchen, and laundry. With neither trees nor landforms to block the interminable wind, water could be pumped nearly at will. The windmill was a critical component to European-American settlement on the prairies. To populate the vast grasslands, settlers needed water. And that act of bringing groundwater to the surface marked a profound cultural development. Prior to that, the long distances between surface water—especially at places other than the Sandhills—prohibited any permanent habitation on the empty, rolling hills of grass.

—•—

Many of the original Great Plains cultures were nomadic. Indigenous peoples moved over the landscape in cyclical patterns, and no vestige of those patterns remains today. Nomadism is becoming rarer all over the world, but I saw it in Mongolia. In the fall of 2013, I helped a Mongolian family move camp. They lived in a valley a day-and-a-half drive southwest of the capital, Ulaanbaatar. The area was called Tsagaan Nuur, which means white lake. We loaded three yurts and three families' possessions onto two Korean trucks. Bed frames, tables, stoves—everything was packed up and stowed for the short fifteen-kilometer drive. Two other horsemen and I herded the livestock: roughly thirty sheep and thirty goats, a few lop-eared cows, and about two hundred horses. The two impressions that I came away with from three months on the steppe was, one, that a nomad's home is a region, a valley, an area like Tsagaan Nuur. Home was not described by pinpoint coordinates of latitude and longitude, because the nomadic families occupied four or five camps throughout the year, each one fifteen or so kilometers from the previous. And, two, that the nomadic perception of home does not include ownership of the land. It does include rights and privileges, but the straight lines of land patents or real estate surveys do not jibe with cyclical nomadism.

That is, of course, one of the fundamental reasons that the sedentary life on reservations presented such challenges to peoples of the Great Plains. Because their previous lifeways had developed over thousands of years. Their technologies, their spirituality, and their role within the ecosystem were products of a life on the move. One of the clearest descriptions of an Indigenous community moving camp comes from Sir Richard Burton's book *The City of the Saints: Among the Mormons and Across the Rocky Mountains to California.* Somewhere west of Fort Kearny, his wagon passed a long column of Pawnee on August 10, 1860.[8]

In a lot of ways, Burton's account is a timestamp. The Pawnee had horses, guns, and government-issued blankets, all signs of the past 250 years of European influence. It's also a peaceful encounter. In 1860, white settlers and Indigenous peoples along this section of the Platte were on mostly friendly terms. Relations later worsened in 1864, when the Sioux, Cheyenne, and Arapaho allied themselves in an effort to stanch the tide of white men from the East. In that way, Burton's description of a "shifting scene" of men, women, children, ponies, and dogs is a glimpse into the Plains culture before the Old West ended.

The men rode at the front of the column. They carried tomahawks and spears and bows and quivers of arrows, and a few carried rifles sheathed in buckskin covers that were fringed and beaded. Most wore pantaloons that ended at the upper thigh and were girdled to a leather belt, and all wore loincloths made of buckskin. Some rode with U.S. government–issued blankets wrapped about their torsos, others wore "sleeved waistcoats of dark drugget, over an American cotton shirt," Burton wrote. Most controlled their horses through a leather thong tied around the horse's lower jaw and knotted to its neck as a single, fixed rein.

Behind the men came the baggage of the village, and most of it was hauled by travois. *Travois* is a French-Canadian word originally meaning "cart shaft," and it was used to describe the method for rigging two poles A-frame style over the back of a dog to make a sledge for transporting cargo. The travois poles, usually made of softwood like cottonwood or aspen, were crossed over the dog's back and lashed together at an angle so that the splayed ends of the poles dragged on the ground. Cross members were fitted into a burden platform on the poles behind the dog. The elasticity of the thin poles absorbed some of the shock as the party moved the village or hauled buffalo meat back to camp or who knows what because very little archaeological evidence of early travois use remains. When horses arrived on the Plains, the travois were rigged with longer poles.

On one travois pulled by a dog, Burton reported, rode a tethered hawk. Burton comments, "Yet falconry has never, I believe, been practiced by the Indian." Atop a few horse-drawn travois were wicker-type cages that the elderly or very young could ride in, bouncing along in the shade of a blanket draped over the top of a frame. Among the travois-bearing animals were horses carrying the teepee poles, four or five poles bundled to each side of a horse, crossed and lashed over the top of a packsaddle, and like the travois poles, dragging the ground. The parallel ruts of all those poles dragging the ground clearly marked the course of travel, and at the end of the column, walking among the ruts and the constant dust, came the women and children.

To Burton's eye it appeared that the wealthy women rode and the less fortunate walked. Cradleboards were strapped to saddles so that the swaddled babies rocked all day with the swinging gait of the horses. All of the women wore shawls or blankets wrapped about their shoulders. Throughout Burton's extensive travels in the late nineteenth century, he hardly failed to concern himself with the local women—he even allegedly kidnapped a young woman in India—and in keeping with his personality, he shared gratuitous thoughts on the Pawnee women.[9]

Burton reported that the community was moving to find fresh pasturage for the horses. He described it as a "picture of Bedouin or gipsy life." In fact, what he was seeing was the twilight of the Indigenous nomadic cultures. Like the bison, those cultures would hardly see their cyclic way of life through the 1860s. Once the Civil War ended, white men poured west in unprecedented numbers. The railroad followed. Gunfire boomed over the buffalo ranges, and the hide men and the tongue-harvesters left the prairies scattered with rotting bison carcasses for the wolves and ravens to pick clean. The plains peoples watched their lifeblood disappear, and that was the end of the cultural landscape of the American West as first observed by Europeans.

The night after Nadine showed me the Sandhills, I camped on a hilltop above the floodplain two miles south of the river. The river was visible as a dark green stripe of cottonwood trees before soft hills of a lighter green. I was sitting on my saddle blankets cutting my toenails with the scissors of my Leatherman multi-tool, congratulating myself on a moment of personal hygiene and thinking about the nomads of the American West. I wondered what the movement of a Pawnee camp sounded like—horses blowing and snorting in the dust, babies crying in their cradleboards, the whispered skidding of all those poles dragging the prairie, and over the whole procession the ancient chants of the nomadic act. The image of a tethered hawk perched on a dog-drawn travois seemed as old as the continent. The sun had just dipped below the horizon, and when I looked up, a coyote emerged from the folds of prairie below me.

His ears showed as two small triangles that rose and fell with his pace. As he trotted toward me, he looked over his left shoulder and then over his right shoulder, as though he'd just left some kind of scene or incident. He sneezed like a dog, with a twist of his head, never breaking stride. He paid no mind to my horses, and I sat motionless leaning against my saddle. He came to within one hundred feet of the corrals where I sat, and then he stopped and turned a half circle to look back from where he'd come. Again he looked to his left, then to his right. He was thinking about something, weighing options. And then he left. He trotted downhill over his same tracks to return where I did not know. I told the horses, yonder trots your Pawnee dog, and I wondered how long it would take to train a coyote to drag a travois.

———

On June 12, I rode across the Colorado state line. The Pony Express Trail makes a short pass through the northeast corner of the state. The town of Julesburg was originally the site of a Pony Express station, and I camped at a pasture just outside town for two nights. A woman named Linda Dolezal had secured permission for me to camp there. Linda ran a hair salon in Julesburg, and when she called it a beauty shop, I thought that a little beautification was just what I needed. So I asked if she'd cut my hair, and she agreed.

There were four other women in the shop when I walked in the front door at 10:30 in the morning. One woman sat in front of a mirror and wore a smock and had folded strips of tinfoil and white paste in her hair. Another sat under a salad-bowl-type contraption that covered her head. The two others appeared to be loafers, there to gossip and read magazines. As

Linda was cutting my hair, she told me that a local historian, Gordy Wilkins, had a keen interest in the Pony Express, that he lived in Lodgepole, Nebraska, twenty miles down the road, and that he would probably let me camp at his place. After she finished cutting my hair, she gave me Gordy's phone number.

I never reached Gordy, but he found me himself, ten miles out from Julesburg. I was riding on the left shoulder, facing oncoming traffic. A silver Volkswagen beetle stopped on the opposite side of the highway ahead of me. Country music blared from the open window. The door opened and out stepped a man that looked about half like a mountain man. He wore a black felt hat with an uneven braided leather hat band that looked homemade. His collarless red shirt was decorated with Western-style zigzags down both sides of the front. He wore jeans and low-heeled leather boots. I slid out of the saddle as he approached.

"Gordy Wilkins, regional historian of Western Nebraska," he said and reached out to shake my hand. I told him what I was doing, and he said that he already knew about me, that he'd just come from Linda's shop. I asked him if he knew of a place near Lodgepole where I might camp for the night with my horses.

"Well, you can stay at the homestead if you like."

I asked him if it was his homestead.

"My late wife's great-grandfather's. It dates to 1883. It's a special place. Ten miles from where we're standing right now," he said. I thanked him and told him I'd meet him there.

The house was set back from the road a quarter mile. I found Gordy sitting in a lawn chair in the front yard. The yard was cluttered with items that appeared to be half serviceable. A section of kitchen cabinetry sat on the grass beside a tattered black office chair that was losing its foam upholstery to the wind. Flies crawled over the remains of a watermelon that sat on a small plastic table beside a blackened cinder-block hearth that had been heavily used. A large plastic water jug sat on another table. A child's red wagon lay overturned at the base of a sprawling cottonwood tree, and ten feet off the ground, a splitting maul with a yellow plastic handle was embedded in the tree. The folds of bark grown over the maul head suggested it had been there for many years. Gordy told me to pen my horses wherever I wanted, and I found a patch of grass under an elm tree.

As soon as I had turned up my sweaty saddle blankets to dry in the sun, Gordy walked over to say that we should go into Lodgepole to see the Pony Express Museum. Small museums that are either dedicated to the Pony Express or include information about it occur throughout the trail, and I wanted to see every one that I could, but at that moment I'd been in the saddle for nine hours and could have used a minute to air up. Gordy, though, wouldn't have it. "We might as well go right now," he said and turned to get the car. He pulled up to my bedroll in the silver Volkswagen with the music blaring, and when I climbed in, he said that he was hard of hearing and apologized for the high volume.

Lodgepole, population 314, was a quiet town when we

drove through it. It had a bank, a post office, a bar, and a few churches. The historical museum sat just off the main street. It had one wall and corner dedicated to the Pony Express, and Gordy was responsible for many of the items on display.

"I want to make Lodgepole the Pony Express capital of Nebraska," he said. "I keep telling them I want to make the exhibit bigger, but they're trying to rein me in and keep saying they have enough stuff already. Trying to cut me out of it, what they're really trying to do."

The exhibit included Pony Express movie posters, descriptions of the saddles and saddlebags used by the mail service, bronze and silver Pony Express coins minted at the U.S. Mint in Philadelphia, and highway signs of the major thoroughfares that run over the old trail today. The exhibit had more information than artifacts, and front and center in the display was a brown and beige Ford Bronco II with Pony Express decals on both doors that showed a rider on a galloping horse. The phrase "In Search of the Pony Express" was also painted on both doors and on the tailgate. The Bronco belonged to Joe Nardone, a longtime Pony Express historian who donated the vehicle to the museum. Nardone's name and signature were above the front wheel wells. Medallion-size stickers ran down both sides of the Bronco, one for each full journey along the Pony Express Trail, and Gordy told me there were thirty-seven stickers. On the right side was painted "This Bronco has traveled 761,327 miles dedicated to Pony Express history." A map of the trail was painted on the back window. The spare-tire cover was decorated with the Pony

Express Association logo. The California license plate, last tagged in August 2010, read "PE TRAIL."

"The Bronco's worth about $30,000," Gordy said. He was sitting on an old church pew, watching me look over the car. I asked him who the hell would give $30,000 for a Bronco that's been driven more than seven hundred thousand miles and is covered in stickers.

"It's a collector's item," he said. "Joe has done more for the Pony Express than anyone else in the world."

After locking up the museum, Gordy said he'd drive us to the site of the Texas Pony Express Station. A few miles outside town we stopped at a pull-off where a four-foot-tall slab of polished granite described the station as being a quarter mile east of the monument. No footprint or vestige of the old station could be seen from where we stood. Lodgepole Creek ran a mile to the north of us, and the trace of it was visible for the trees along its banks. The floodplain had been planted with corn, and the crop stood only a few inches tall.

"See, they put the station here away from the creek because of wolves and Indians," Gordy said. "Easier to see them coming, avoid ambushes that way. It still amazes me, what they went through."

If I had to wager, I'd say that the station was built a mile from the creek to avoid insects. I've heard that homesteads all over the West were often removed from a water source to avoid the mosquitoes, and I suspected that in 1860 the mosquitoes would be more problematic wolves or anyone else.

There's no record of the Pony Express having trouble with indigenous peoples along this stretch of the Platte River, and I don't think they were fearful of being ambushed by wolves. The historian Arthur Chapman, who published his book *Pony Express: The Record of a Romantic Adventure in Business* in 1932, was one of the few writers to record correspondences with riders. He quotes rider William Campbell, who was nineteen years old when he rode for the Pony Express, as saying that several Sioux men worked at the relay stations. The riders weren't scared of Sioux or Pawnee or anyone else; they were scared of bison, Campbell told Chapman:

The greatest danger I faced on the trail was buffaloes. They were along the trail in western Nebraska by thousands. If a rider ran into a herd, he was gone. Wolves were numerous—big fellows. One winter night I saw some fifteen or twenty of them around a crippled horse which they had killed. They followed me for fifteen miles to the next station. The next day I went back and doctored up that carcass of the horse with strychnine. Twelve dead wolves were lying around the bait the next time I went back. I got some Indians to prepare the hides and had twelve beautiful pelts, two of them white, which I had no trouble in selling at a good price.[10]

That doesn't sound to me like the voice of someone fearful of wolves. But no one really knows why Texas Station was built a mile south of Lodgepole Creek or if William Campbell or any of the other Pony Express riders feared wolves. We know that they ate them: Richard Burton reported that station keepers in Utah were eating wolf mutton.[11] I had my own opinion, but at that moment it was Gordy who was deep in thought. As we stood there in front of the granite monument with the country music ringing through the still evening air, I could just about feel Gordy thinking about the Pony Express. He loved the history. He put that museum together, helped put in the granite marker for the station, wanted to make Lodgepole the Pony Express capital of Nebraska. There, a quarter mile from the old station site, he was breathing the same air as the Pony Express riders, standing over the same soil and under the same sky, and I sensed that Gordy took great pleasure from this.

Gordy drove us back to his house and said that he'd cook a couple of steaks for us for dinner. His front yard had become his summertime living space, and the large cinder-block hearth was where he did most of his cooking. He heaped an armful of split firewood into the hearth, poured some diesel fuel on it from a yellow jerry can, and threw a match into the heap of wood. A minute later, a fire roared under the cottonwood tree with the splitting maul buried in it.

He opened a large can of Van Camp's pork and beans, crimped the lid backward, and set the can on an iron grate over the fire. He used a fork to lay the steaks in the flames, and he jerked his hand back as he did so because the flames were licking a foot above the cooking surface. He poured water from a plastic jug into a charred, stainless-steel percolator coffee pot that was missing its percolator, and he emptied grounds from a Folgers can into the pot.

"The grounds settle out," he said. "Cowboy coffee. Anymore, this is the only kind of coffee I can drink."

By then the beans were boiling in the can, and he told me to stir them quickly. He reached into the flames to flip our steaks. The top sides were raw and the grilled sides looked like they'd been smeared with fresh asphalt. We were both wearing leather gloves because the prairie fire he had made was hardly contained within the hearth. The coffee pot steamed and jumped on the grill. The label on the can of beans had burned off, and the aluminum had tempered into a spectrum of blues and purples. I wasn't sure if Gordy cooked every dinner in the same way, but ours was a quick and hot affair.

The fire finally smoldered down by the time we finished dinner. Gordy poured himself another cup of coffee. We sat in lawn chairs and watched horizontal rays of gold light riffle through the cottonwood trees along Lodgepole Creek.

After dark, I unrolled my bedroll beside Chicken Fry and Badger. As I was spitting toothpaste into the weeds, the door opened and Gordy hollered for me to come over, that he had something to show me.

His house was filled with artifacts and Western memorabilia. The couches and chairs were heaped with old blankets and dusty boxes. The shelves were stacked with old books and old and modern knives, a cavalry saber, a few old felt hats, and a lot of Native American paraphernalia. At the center of the crowded living room was the fireplace, and to its left, as though thrown from the open doorway, a toma-hawk-type hatchet was buried into the wood of the mantel. A Navy-style revolver leaned against an antique clock, and another pistol of the same style hung by a leather thong. Over the top of the mantle, an old-style flintlock rifle hung upside down with a coonskin cap draped over the end of the stock.

"Here you go, look at this," he said. He held a large black revolver. The barrel was the thickness of a garden hose and a foot long. I could see the brass bases of five rounds in the cylinder. He turned the gun in his right hand and then tossed it from hand to hand several times so that for a moment the loaded gun floated through the air. He handed me the gun and told me to be careful because it was loaded. I saw that it was a Smith and Wesson .50-caliber revolver, and handed it back to him.

———

Gordy helped me understand the broad spectrum of meaning that the Pony Express entails. For him, it was a source of iden-tity. By drinking cowboy coffee and cooking over a fire in the front yard, he appeared to be living out the history personally. The dialogue over whether Texas Station was located a mile from Lodgepole Creek to avoid insects, Indians, or wolves is inconsequential. The details don't matter; the immutable essence of the Pony Express is what matters. The spanning of the West by horseback couriers as a bold expression of the frontier psyche is what matters. Because that's what's on the landscape today.

In western Nebraska, Gordy is a preservationist of the nineteenth-century American West. On the other hand, one of Gordy's friends, a man named Ray Robinson, who lived seventeen miles west, was a preservationist of the twentieth century.

I rode into Ray Robinson's place in the middle of the afternoon. He walked out of his house wearing a clean straw cowboy hat, a white A-shirt that looked like an undershirt, and black cowboy boots that had been recently polished. Ray had only one arm. Gordy'd told me that Ray had lost it in some kind of accident. Under what remained of his left arm, which extended to just above the elbow, he clamped the barrel of a yellow and black pistol so that the grip pointed toward me. I nodded at the gun after we shook hands.

"Trying not to let my grandson shoot me with it," he said. "It's an air gun, shoots pellets."

I penned my horses in a small lot behind Ray's house, where two old Cadillacs sat with the grass growing up around them to the door handles. After I unloaded my gear, he invited me to his porch for a cup of coffee. Ray had been a truck driver for most of his working life. For half a century, he drove all over the West. His face was creased with wrinkles, and his hair was white as snow. He told me that he'd lost his arm when he wrecked his truck "on a winter run to

Minnesota." That was all he said about it, and I didn't want to pry. We sat drinking coffee, talking about trucking. He seemed to be a holdover from an earlier era of the West, in the style of *Smokey and the Bandit*. He harkened to a time when a trucker's log book was spiral bound, back before Route 66 was absorbed into the interstate highway system, back when truckers chatted on their C.B. radios with the breaker breaker–type lingo that has been all but lost among over-the-road long-haulers. Ray had watched the modernization of freighting on the roadways and had a perspective on not only time, but also space. He was more aware of the geography of my route than anyone I had met until that point.

"How you getting through Nevada?" he asked.

I told him that I'd enter Nevada in the wide-open range country north of Ely, and then ride through Austin and on to Carson City along U.S. Highway 50.

"They call that the Loneliest Road in America. Not a lot of anything out there," he said.

We talked about finding feed and water for my horses in the desert and about riding at night to beat the heat and about all that empty country between Salt Lake City and the Sierra Nevada.

"You plan to ride through Salt Lake City?" he asked.

I told him that my plan was to ride through the city on Sunday morning, when most of the population is in church. I thought this was an adroitly strategic move, and I told him that traffic shouldn't be a problem if my timing was right.

"Well, maybe, but I wouldn't count on it. We call that the

Mormon 500, and let me tell you, two and half million people live in that valley, and there's always traffic."

He asked if I had a target date to finish, and I told him that I didn't want to be in the Sierra Nevada when the snow flew. Late August, early September at the latest, I told him.

"This year?" he asked.

Damn right, I said. He canted his head slightly to one side and raised his eyebrows, looking right at me.

"Might be time to find another gear, partner. You know what I'm saying?"

That rattled me. But right after he said it, his daughter and two grandkids walked out of the house with a bag of carrots and asked if they might feed the horses. I said of course, and stood up, thanked Ray, and walked with the three of them out to Chicken Fry and Badger.

That night I marked campsites and dates on the large-scale map of the Pony Express Trail between Ray's house and St. Joseph. I tried to visualize the mileage behind me in the context of the mileage ahead. I'd spent forty-two days making about five hundred miles of the total 2,000 miles. At this rate, I'd be on the trail for a total of six months, which would put me into Sacramento just in time for Thanksgiving dinner.

I spent the next day resting at Ray's because a heavy storm blew in at noon. Ray and his daughter and grandkids went to lunch in nearby Sidney, Nebraska, and when they returned, I walked over to see Ray. I carried my notebook and annotated map. He stepped out of his cream-colored Cadillac and stretched his back by standing tall. He wore a black cow-boy hat, a black pearl-snap shirt, black Western slacks, and the same polished black boots. He looked like Johnny Cash. He told me that he was headed to Denver for back surgery the following day. I asked if he might have a minute to take a look at the map with me. He nodded, so I spread out the map on the trunk of his Cadillac. I opened my notebook and made ready to take notes. He traced the route of the trail with his index finger up the Plains and over the Rocky Mountains and across the Great Basin, and he seemed to be computing time and distances. I felt slightly helpless standing next to him, waiting for him to bestow on me the wise words of a traveling man.

"I don't know that I can be much help to you," he said. "No one knows your system except you, but I got a feeling the bad weather's part of why it's taken you so long to get this far."

He looked at the map, and I looked at him, and I let the silence hang between us. Ray was a man of integrity. He had broad, square shoulders and a frame like an old barn—it'd burn down before it fell over. He stretched his back again by standing tall.

"Yes sir, you still have a helluva long way to go," he said. "I envy you. I've always liked to be on the move." Then he tapped the map twice with his index finger, made a clicking sound with his tongue, and said his back was hurting and that he needed to lie down.

The problem with spending two nights camped in Ray's backyard was that I couldn't go to the bathroom. His house was small, and with his daughter and two grandkids in there, I had the feeling it was plenty crowded. And he never invited me in. I didn't want to go inside, but I did want to use the bathroom. Which wasn't an option. And he had so impressed me as a last living relic of the Golden West that I didn't want to soil his property with my feces. I thought that if he looked out his kitchen window to see me with my pants around my ankles, he'd probably shoot me with something more powerful than his grandson's pellet gun. So I was feeling pretty uncomfortable when I finally rode out his driveway under a thin rain on the morning of June 18. And at the first tree line out of sight from the road and Ray's house, I dropped my jeans while holding the horses.

———

I rode north into the panhandle of Nebraska. I crossed from the South Platte River Valley to the North Platte Valley, and rain fell the entire time. I camped at the site of the Mud Springs Pony Express Station in a pasture where a rock monument marked the site of the station. A fence around it prevented horses or cattle from rubbing on it. Under a massive cottonwood tree, I strung two tarps for shelter. Everything was muddy and wet, and rainwater pooled all around me. The gloomy weather exacerbated the fact that I felt like I would probably never see Ray Robinson again. I admired him for reasons that were hard for me to define. After dark, he sent me a text message saying that he had a comfortable hospital room, that he hoped I was staying dry, and that I shouldn't camp under a cottonwood tree because the trees are notoriously dangerous for losing limbs in a storm. Too late, I wrote back, and said that I'd check in with him in a few days.

Ray had planted the unfortunate seed in my head that I was behind schedule. This was troubling because I couldn't see a way to "find another gear," as he had said. There was no other gear. I couldn't trot my horses. People do trot packhorses, but not for very long, and usually it results in a loosening of the packs or soreness to the horse. I didn't know how to travel any faster than I was. I didn't want to ride more hours of the day or longer distances because I didn't want to wear out my horses when we still had most of the West yet to cover. I had to preserve and nurture the condition of the horses while maintaining progress. It was a balancing act, and I didn't feel as though I had achieved it, though Badger had improved and was no longer sore.

I had originally planned to spend one hundred days riding the Pony Express Trail. But there I was at day forty-four having covered about one quarter of the total distance. I was, in fact, behind the projected schedule. That schedule, though, had been cast in speculation, laid out on a yellow legal pad as camps conveniently spaced every twenty-five miles with a day of rest after every four days of travel. The execution was not as clean. I could not set the rhythm. The horses set the rhythm, and I had to find it, recognize it, sync with it, and not vary from it. It was a new form of horsemanship to me, and sitting there in the mud at Mud Springs, it felt like a hard lesson. I was ready to be finished with the saturated farm country. I was ready for the high plains and the Rocky Mountains and the deserts beyond. Give me a prairie wind over the humid East for the effort of six weeks' horsebacking it westward, but I couldn't hurry. I needed patience, not another gear.

CHAPTER 6

No Country for Old Ways

THE BIGGEST DIFFERENCES between Wyoming and Nebraska lie in the climate and topography. Wyoming can be cold any day of the year. There are places in the state that reliably experience winter weather nine months of the year. Part of the reason for that is the Rocky Mountains, which cover the western two-thirds of the state, including the Greater Yellowstone Area. The Wind River Range, a finger of rugged mountains running a hundred miles southeast from the Yellowstone area, ends just north of the Pony Express Trail, and that area is arguably one of the coldest stretches of the mail route. Nebraska has the Platte River Valley and the Sandhills dune field and the fertile bottomland of the Missouri River, but it's flat compared to Wyoming. It also has a population nearly four times that of Wyoming.

Wyoming is the least populated state in the nation, with slightly fewer than 580,000 people. With six people per square mile, it's also the least densely populated of the Lower 48 (Alaska has lower population density). Wyoming is cold and high, and it's also windy. In 2001, a rancher north of Cheyenne told me that one day the wind quit blowing and every chicken in the state fell over. It was a joke. The chickens, he explained, spend their lives leaning into the wind that never lays. What's not a joke, he said, is that your hat can blow off your head and if it doesn't hang up in a barbed wire fence in the first mile or two, it'll be gone forever.

These factors—the inhospitable climate, the lack of people, and the Rocky Mountains—produce a persona that you won't find in Nebraska. There are no mountains in Nebraska, and therefore no mountain men. The definition of a mountain man has evolved over the past two centuries, but its earliest personifications were a breed of hardy adventurers who combed the Rocky Mountain streams for beavers in the early nineteenth century. Those were the free trappers, and their image—fringed buckskin clothing, a long rifle, a grizzly beard, a homemade hat made from some small, fur-bearing animal— conveyed certain characteristics, mostly a reliance on one's own faculties for survival in a hard land. The most enduring psychological character trait of the mountain men is independence. They're an independent lot, and they're still around today, but they don't often wear fringed buckskin. I met my first two mountain men eighty miles inside the Wyoming state line on the north bank of the North Platte River.

Roy Dougherty was eighty-six years old when I rode into his driveway on the afternoon of June 29. He was working in his garden between rows of dark, leafy plants, leaning into a yellow gas-powered rototiller. The job didn't look like any fun, and after I penned my horses, Roy left the tiller, what he called "the god-damnedest thing," to decamp on the back deck of his house for a glass of iced tea. He had broad shoulders and big hands. He wore a maroon golf shirt and black shorts and black Velcro sneakers. His legs were pale and varicosed, but his face showed the bark and redness of eighty-six Rocky Mountain winters.

Roy and his wife, Mary, lived in a house that Roy built. It was a log house, long and low, with a straightforward, rectangular floorplan that someone without professional building expertise could handle. The house had a green tin roof and white trim around the windows, and the deck off the back was shady and made of cedar boards. A dozen flowerpots that looked like they'd been getting watered every day were arranged on the railing of the deck and beside the house. With a tall glass of tea in his hand, Roy sat in one of two rocking chairs, and pretty soon his pal Bill Sinnard showed up.

Bill was younger than Roy, but not by much. He drove up in an old flatbed ranch truck that rattled in the particular way that ranch trucks rattle: loose tools, chains, creaky axles, above it all the general moaning of an abused vehicle. He wore jeans and a pearl-snap shirt, and just the same as Roy, his hide was weather-beaten and creased, and it made me wonder if sunscreen arrived in Wyoming about the same time as the internet.

Bill nodded at Roy and asked, "What's the news?"

"Don't know it," said Roy. "Glass of tea?"

"No, thank you, Roy."

Bill eased himself into the chair beside Roy, and the two men sat slowly rocking, listening to the late afternoon. Minutes of silence hung between them in a comfortable way; neither seemed to feel the need to say anything. The only sounds were the clinking of ice cubes in Roy's glass, the creaking of boards under the rockers, and the wind riffling through the cotton-wood trees above us. As we sat there, I sensed that this same scene of these two old buzzards sitting beside each other had unfolded about a thousand times before I ever saw it, and after a while, Bill asked me where'd I camped the night before.

A set of corrals at Twin Springs, I told him, twenty miles south of Roy's house.

"I know the place," he said. "Good water there."

Twin Springs is named for two ice-cold springs that emerge from the ground into tractor tires placed over them to form water troughs and maintain the integrity of the springs. I told him that the posted regulations at the corrals prohibited camping.

"That's the biggest crock of shit in the world," Bill said. "Of course you can camp there. It's public land."

No good mountain man will pass up a chance to bash the federal government, usually the Bureau of Land Management, the Fish and Wildlife Service, or the Forest Service. Along with independence, resourcefulness, and an aversion to the elements, a consistent trait among mountain men is the freedom to choose which laws to obey and which to shrug aside as bureaucratic nonsense. But of all the topics covered between the two men on that back deck, Western history and heritage was what they most loved talking about. The West officially begins in Nebraska, Bill said, but the real West begins in Wyoming.

"You know that scene in *Butch Cassidy and the Sundance Kid* when they blow up the train and all the money's floating down through the air?" he asked. "That happened just south of here, and they say that the money really did that, came floating down that-a-way," and he made a fanning motion with his arms. "This is outlaw country. Doc Middleton owned a saloon just up the road from here."

Doc Middleton was a notorious horse thief, lawman, and participant in Buffalo Bill's Wild West show who died in the nearby town of Douglas after a knife fight. Roy and Bill agreed that ever since white settlers arrived, the area had recorded some tumultuous history. Bill said that a bend in the river not far from Twin Springs, called Bulls Bend, was the site of a Lakota Sioux camp after a skirmish with a mail coach in 1869. We talked about the movement of the Plains peoples up and down the Rocky Mountain front and about how the cultural landscape shifted with horses and firearms and then cholera and smallpox. The 1870s, we agreed, were a dark hour on the plains. Bill said that Roy had a gun from exactly that time period, which was "picked up off the Custer battlefield."

"Well, the guy who gave it to me said the guy he got it from told him that it was found at Little Bighorn," Roy said.

"Go get it, Roy, let's show it to him," Bill said.

Roy walked in the house and came back with a very old revolver.

"It's old all right," he said and handed me the gun. "But who really knows its story."

The gun was dark gray, almost black. It had weathered into a solid mass of iron so that it felt like it was filled with sand. The metal grips had been replaced with authentic grips for the same model gun but were in significantly better shape than the rest of the gun, having not sat on the open prairie for however long. Each side of the handle had an emblem showing the old Colt's manufacturing logo of a rearing horse with two lances embedded in its chest. The trigger guard and most of the front sight had long since rusted away.

"It's still loaded if you can believe that," Bill said, as though one might assume that given the wholesale slaughter of General George Custer and his 7th Cavalry, all live ammunition would have been used up. But the gun's provenance, of course, was unknown.

From a conversation that was mostly quiet, I felt Bill and Roy were pretty savvy men, the kind of companions you'd want for a hunting trip or a few nights in the mountains or anywhere where you might need someone to save your ass. So I asked them a question that had begun to vex me: What do I do if a wild stallion tries to run off my horses in the Nevada desert?

"You carrying some kind of firearm?" Roy asked.

I told him that I carried a lightweight, short-barreled .357 magnum.

"Where?" he asked.

In my saddlebags, I told him.

"I might keep that in my pocket if I was you."

I told him that I was worried about using a gun around the wild horses because, one, I didn't really want to shoot a horse, and, two, I'd probably be in a world of trouble if a Bureau of Land Management agent saw me shoot at a mustang.

"You've a right to protect your personal property. And, who knows, maybe if that BLM guy saw you do it, he might be proud of you."

———

Roy and Bill marked my crossing of a cultural fault line not unlike what Walter Prescott Webb described at the 98th meridian, some three hundred miles behind me. In central Wyoming, I was a lot deeper westward than the 98th. The nights were cooler, the sagebrush more prevalent, and the distances between towns longer. One of the biggest changes to the landscape, though, was open range. Open range is the lack of fences on the sides of roads so that livestock, mostly cattle, can wander freely to graze. It's usually marked by a yellow road sign with a black cow on it, but there are many roads in the West without such signage, where it's possible to come around a corner and find a group of steers blocking the way. Where a fence crosses the road, a cattleguard maintains the barrier. For me, open range meant that I'd have to open and close a gate every time I met a fence (cattleguards nearly always have some sort of gate beside them), but it allowed me plenty of room to ride off the road, away from traffic.

West of Fort Laramie, I was able to ride down the original trace of the Platte River Road. It was a shallow depression in the prairie, and though it's most commonly referred to as the Oregon Trail, anyone going east or west along the Platte, including the Pony Express, used the same road. Wagon ruts in the soft bedrock near the town of Guernsey have been preserved as the Oregon Trail Ruts State Historic Site, managed by the National Park Service, but I didn't see them because I didn't want to detour the horses or deal with the Fourth of July weekend crowds.

I was in Glenrock, Wyoming, for the Fourth of July. Claire drove up to spend the holiday with me. She brought our two dogs, an ice chest full of prepared dinners, and our horse trailer. We camped in the yard of former president of the National Pony Express Association Les Bennington. Les put up my horses in one of his pastures so that Claire and I could drive into the nearby town of Casper, population 58,656, to buy me a pair of spare boots, some new underwear, and a decent meal. We hauled the horses around Casper in the horse trailer because I didn't want to navigate the dangerous urban congestion. We spent two restful days at the site of the Willow Springs Pony Express Station, and on the morning of July 7, Claire left to drive home. I turned to the Sweetwater

River Valley, my path up to the Continental Divide, and for the first time, I was on large tracts of public land.

Public land in the West is land that's government owned. The land is most often managed by the BLM or the Forest Service, and it's usually designated as multiple-use land. Multiple-use means that you can camp, hunt, cut firewood, mountain bike, target shoot, or walk your dog. It also means that natural resource extraction companies can obtain permits to work there—drill for oil or mine coal, for instance—and that ranchers can remotely graze livestock on it, also with a permit. Nearly all public land in the West can be grazed. The most common system of doing so is that of a rancher who owns a tract of deeded acreage where the animals spend the winter; in the summer, the rancher drives the cattle to public land for the grazing season. Typically, the deeded acreage is along a valley bottom where there's water, and the permitted, public-land range is higher, though there are variations of this across the West. This cyclical system of grazing high ranges in the summer and spending the winter at lower elevations is called transhumance. In Wyoming, transhumance has been going on since the nineteenth century. But it wasn't until the Wyoming Cattle Boom from 1868 to 1886 that the surge of livestock into the state established the foundation for the ranching industry that pervades the rural West today. The cattle boom created the ranching industry and established the cowboy.

Along with the abundance of grass and ungoverned land, one of the most prominent drivers of the boom was the British demand for beef. English and Scottish investors poured millions of pounds sterling into American beef between 1865 and 1886. A book titled *When Grass Was King*, by Maurice Frink, W. Turrentine Jackson, and Agnes Wright Spring, offers an academic analysis of the foreign investment. The book is dense with stockholder accounts, balance sheets, and reports for various branches of Her Majesty's government. It's not an easy book to read, nearly impenetrable for a simple cowboy, but it details a bullish period of investment:

> During the 1860s, continental [European] herds were ravaged by anthrax, and to protect her own cattle, Britain enacted quarantine regulations. In spite of precautions, the disease came into Britain from Ireland, and because of its highly contagious character, spread rapidly throughout its herds. Progress in its eradication was slow even though thousands of animals were slaughtered. As the demand for beef increased, production steadily declined in Britain and prices soared. The hungry British had the money to buy meat in the world market, and they were particularly interested in the United States.[1]

Over the following decade, the longhorn cattle that had run wild in Texas during the Civil War were rounded up and driven north to the empty ranges of Colorado, Wyoming, and Montana. The northern cold-weather grasses were highly nutritious. Cattle could be free-ranged during the winter and emerge in spring in better condition than they had been in the fall. This was a new system of agriculture that was made possible partly by a period of mild winters. Large ranches, many of which are considered historic ranches today, grew to supply the foreign demand. At the same time, refrigeration methods used in railcars were incorporated into transoceanic ships, and exports of fresh beef to the U.K. increased dramatically.[2] Frink, Jackson, and Spring provide the numbers:

> The total annual import of fresh beef into Britain during 1876 was 1,732 tons; for the years 1878–1880 the average annual import was more than 30,000 tons. The United States was responsible for eighty to ninety percent of this foreign supply. A multi-million-dollar business had emerged in short order.[3]

Thus were the northern prairies stocked with cattle. Large herds roamed the open range. Western romanticists refer to this as the unfenced days or the days of the open range or the days before barbed wire. The American cowboy, a mounted stockman who had hybridized his methods for handling cattle mostly from techniques learned from the Spanish, became a fixture of the plains. He developed a unique style of clothing and gear. He assumed the character of someone who mostly stayed out of town and was apt to shoot out the lights whenever he came in off the trail. In the early 1880s, the cowboy had his wild heyday, and the British funded it. Their fascination with the West, an interest that extended beyond the beef on their tables, peaked in 1882. According to Nebraska writer Mari Sandoz:

> Around Cheyenne and in Boston and in Edinburgh it was said that a man could buy a calf in the forenoon and sell it in the afternoon for enough profit to pay for his dinner, with a hearty nip or two thrown in for sauce. Indeed, the only way to avoid making money in beef was not to go near the business at all or to punch cows for the other fellow at $25 a month.... Truly 1882 was the year the cow jumped over the moon.[4]

The bubble burst shortly thereafter. The summer of 1886 was dry. The cattle went into the fall in poor condition. The wildlife began acting strangely. The pronghorn left the country. Arctic owls appeared in Montana for the first time in memory. The ranchers had little time to consider the omens before the blue northers arrived. Winter came hard, and the cattle drifted south before the wind, piling up in canyons and coulees, anywhere they found shelter, and that's where they were for the spring thaw: frozen in heaps, piled in the arroyos, clogging streams and creeks:

> The spring roundup of 1887 was darkest, grimmest ever known to all the cattle country. It was the first time that white men ever saw turkey buzzards soar the Wyoming sky in great dark flocks, circling slowly down.[5]

The winter of 1886–1887 has been called the "big die-up," and it marked the beginning of the end of the open range days. One cowboy who was there to see it, and later write about it, was E. C. "Teddy Blue" Abbott. His book, *We Pointed Them North: Recollections of a Cowpuncher,* is an entertaining account of cowboying in the West. Compared to the majority of other sources from the period, his accounts of Indigenous people are refreshingly non-discriminatory. He writes about his friendship with the artist Charles M. Russell, about working for British and New England bosses, and about the process of tallying cattle on the open range, one of the biggest hurdles to bookkeepers in the East or overseas. He also talks about the big die-up that killed the business. He was working in Montana at the time. Cattle that had spent a previous winter or two winters in the area fared better than those who had recently been driven from the south. The newly arrived cattle, he wrote, suffered:

> Double-wintered Texas steers in the Big Dry country got through in the best shape of any cattle in the state. But the loss on trail cattle that had just come into the country was 90 per cent. Fully 60 per cent of all the cattle in Montana were dead by March 15, 1887; that is why everything on the range dates from that winter.[6]

After that winter, Abbott spent another year cowboying and then gave it up (along with whiskey and tobacco) for a woman whom he married in 1889. The heyday of the cowboy was finished. Barbed wire fenced the ranges. What we see today is an evolution of what began in the nineteenth century, and the first ranch I camped at west of Casper, a large operation that had diversified its portfolio beyond just cattle, was a good indication of how much the West has changed.

———

I rode in the front gate of Pathfinder Ranches on the afternoon of July 8. Matt Hoobler, director of operations for the ranch, had told me to meet him at the big ranch house under the cottonwood trees and to throw my horses in the pole corral beside the house. The house was two stories and made of brick. The ranch brand, the letter *J* with short bars on either side, appeared on two chimneys. Off the back of the house, a wooden deck looked over Pathfinder Reservoir a mile to the south. Between treeless ranges of burled granite, the reservoir appeared as a thin reflective sheet under a pale sky streaked with mare's-tail cirrus clouds. The ranch remuda of a dozen or so horses meandered along the serrated margin of grass and water.

About sundown, Matt drove up in a gray Ford pickup with Wyoming specialty license plates that said "wildlife conservation." The truck was loaded with new wooden fence posts and new plastic toolboxes and a new DeWalt cordless drill still in the box, as though Matt had just spun the ranch credit card through Home Depot. He told me that the materials were for a volunteer day later in the week. The volunteers were going to replace an old woven wire fence that snagged wildlife nearly as easily as it confined livestock. The new fence would have horizontal toprails so that elk and deer could jump over it with less risk of entanglement. The volunteer day was at the end of the week. At the beginning of the following week, he would be hosting a range-management workshop for livestock producers, conservationists, and hunting outfitters.

"This is an extremely busy time for us right now," Matt said.

The week before I was there, Pathfinder had hosted beef buyers from Singapore. One afternoon, as Matt and one of the Singaporean buyers returned to the house, they found a skunk in the yard.

"I like skunks, don't get me wrong, but we can't have them living under the house," he said. "So I said to this guy, 'Look, I'm going to get out of this truck and shoot that skunk with a handgun. But if that bothers you, I won't do it.' I didn't want to offend him or anything like that, but, turns out, he thought that was some real cowboy action. It was all he talked about for the rest of the week."

Matt was telling me this as he unloaded the cab of the pickup. He handed me two sacks of groceries and asked me if I'd eat an elk steak for dinner, and I told him that I'd eat an elk steak any hour of the day. He said that he had a room for me in the house, but I told him that I'd just sleep with my horses, and he gave me the same look I'd seen from everyone else whose invitation to sleep inside I had declined. "All right, suit yourself," he said.

The inside of the big house felt like I expected, like a nice Rocky Mountain country house. The kitchen was clean and free of clutter. The appliances were modern. Most of the floorplan was open, and a large bar area with a stone fireplace on one wall dominated the space. Above the fireplace mantle hung the mounted head of a large horned bull. Its hide was speckled brown and white like the mostly wild, Texas-bred longhorns that first walked up the trails in the 1800s. Old Wyoming license plates and Western art decorated the walls, and half a dozen small bronze sculptures of cowboys and Native Americans and frontiersmen sat on various surfaces. The bar was wooden, chest high, and square so that a bartender could stand in the center and dole out drinks in four directions to beef buyers from Singapore or a tired crew of volunteer fencers.

Matt poured us each a glass of whiskey and began to tell me the story of the current ranching operation. Pathfinder Ranches is a conglomerate of around a dozen contiguous ranches, and it oversees about 630,000 acres of rangeland, nearly 1,000 square miles. In 2009, a Dallas-based equity firm, Sammons Enterprises, began buying the ranches along with several other investors under the name Sweetwater River Conservancy, with plans to develop a windfarm. Sammons's idea was to maintain the existing ranching operations while also selling wind energy.

At the same time, the greater sage grouse, a sensitive, chicken-like bird indigenous to western North America, was proposed for protection under the Endangered Species Act.[7] The sage grouse is a ground-nesting bird that is easily disturbed, and when it's disturbed—anything taller than a fence post will upset the bird—it will not reproduce. Conservationists wanting federal protections for the bird and energy companies wanting to maintain the ability to work in sage grouse country lobbied hard for and against Endangered Species Act protections. An alliance of federal and state governments, private ranchers, and energy companies, called the Sage Grouse Task Force, began a management plan to keep the bird from being listed under the Endangered Species Act. The efforts were successful, and in 2015, it was determined that the grouse didn't require listing. That ruling, however, imposed restrictions on oil and gas development to further protect sage grouse habitat, prompting lawsuits from energy companies. One report from the energy industry claimed those restrictions cost the U.S. $5.6 billion in annual economic output.[8]

In several places in the West, sage grouse habitat lies over carbon-rich sedimentary rock. On one hand, it's an unfortunate coincidence for the bird. On the other hand, it's generated conversation and discourse on the future of range management in the West that might not have occurred with less financial implication. In that way, the sage grouse has become a fulcrum upon which stakeholders in the landscape are learning to balance their interests. Eleven Western states have developed various forms of cooperative sage grouse conservation and management plans, and each involves wildlife advocacy groups, representatives of natural resource development industries, livestock producer associations, state wildlife commissions, and the Fish and Wildlife Service.[9]

As the conversation over protecting sage grouse was unfolding, Sammons realized that its plans for a windfarm would disrupt a core area of sage grouse habitat. Sage grouse don't like wind turbines any more than they do oil rigs or phone towers.[10] So the firm scrapped the idea of a windfarm, changed its name to Pathfinder Ranches, and drafted plans for what would become the nation's first sage grouse habitat bank. A habitat bank is an area of permanently protected land with natural resources that benefit endangered, threatened, or otherwise at-risk species of wildlife. The owners of a habitat bank sell credits to developers or other project proponents looking to offset their impacts on a species elsewhere. Pathfinder Ranches, through selling habitat credits, was looking to augment its bottom line.

"Because, let's face it, everyone knows you can't pay for a ranch with cattle anymore," Matt said.

The elk steaks came off the grill, we poured another glass of whiskey, and Matt told me that he had set up an intern program with the University of Wyoming to survey Pathfinder land for grouse. The value of grouse habitat as real stock needs to be supported by the habitat verifiably holding and supporting a sage grouse population. Which meant that data must be collected, and that's what the interns did: inventory the rangeland. I asked him who was buying the grouse credits, and he told me that any entity that disturbs grouse habitat is required to offset that disturbance and that, initially, Pathfinder expected large energy producers to line up for the chance to demonstrate a commitment to environmental stewardship.

"That turned out not to be the case," he said. "Do the big energy companies really care about the sage grouse? No. They want their permits, and that's it. But other companies do care. We sold a hundred credits to PepsiCo, and they used it in their ad campaign."

Matt saw the program at Pathfinder as benefitting the sage grouse, the companies looking to offset their environmental impacts, and the land under Pathfinder's stewardship. In a larger way, Matt also saw the program benefitting Wyoming by protecting and preserving sage grouse, an endemic part of the Rocky Mountain ecosystem in Wyoming. And that's why the university was involved.

"Why shouldn't this whole ranch be a classroom for the University of Wyoming?" he asked. "It should be, and it is. What I can't believe is that the two interns I got right now, one is from Colorado and the other's from Texas of all places."

The next morning, Ella, the intern from Texas, showed up to take us out to the grouse range. Ella was going to be a senior at the university in the fall, and Matt told me that when she wasn't looking for grouse, she was fly-fishing. "If you want to see some big trout, look at Ella's Instagram," he said.

The three of us climbed into Matt's truck and drove a few miles west of the house through low sage prairie. The range looked healthy. The stands of sagebrush were spaced five or six feet apart. Grass, mostly western wheatgrass, the state grass of Wyoming, filled the matrix between the sage. We drove over an old pipeline route and though the grass had filled in the scar, the sage had not.

"Sagebrush doesn't regenerate quickly or easily," Matt said. "It's not easy to get it to germinate."

At an unremarkable spot between granite mountains, Matt stopped the truck, and we walked out into the sage. Ella set down her backpack and pulled out a notebook and a large GPS unit. She walked in circles to establish eco-points for data collection. At each point she observed certain environmental criteria within a square meter, like height of plants, evidence of wildlife, and grade of slope. Matt asked her what she was looking at, and she said, "A rill."

"Will, do you know what a rill is?" Matt asked me. I shook my head.

"A shallow channel where water once flowed."

Ella walked to a new point some feet away and did the same data collection, putting together what Matt called a stratified random sample. We leaned against his truck and talked about grouse. The data that the interns collected validated the value of the habitat, and where grouse habitat had been damaged, the data reflected the restoration efforts. Restoring grouse habitat mostly consists of removing invasive species, repairing damaged riparian areas, and rotationally grazing the range in a way that benefits the grasses and the sagebrush.

"We use livestock grazing as a tool for improving grouse habitat," Matt says. "We're trying to better define the value of the land."

By then, Ella had wandered off two hundred yards from us. Her backpack sat in the sage somewhere between her and us. I told Matt that Badger had nearly stepped on a rattlesnake outside the front gate of the ranch, and I asked if he ever worried about his interns out here alone.

"No, no, there's always two of them," he said. "That's the rule. That there has to be two of them in the field."

———

After a morning with Matt and Ella, I rode out of Pathfinder on the trace of the Oregon Trail. I never saw or talked to any of the ranchers whose ranches had been absorbed by Sammons, but I know that not everyone in the West would be excited about a Texas-based equity firm buying up acreage in Wyoming. Pathfinder has been dedicated to keeping the original ranching families on the land, and it's hard to argue against what appeared to be a sustainable plan for an area of land nearly the size of Rhode Island, but I figured there'd be a few naysayers to the changing landscape lurking somewhere on the range. Foreign investment, though, whether from Texas or the U.K., is nothing new to the West. And while dramatic changes to the Pathfinder range may be happening on paper, most of the valley, from Pathfinder toward the Continental Divide, has changed relatively little compared to nearly every mile of country I'd seen between there and Missouri.

The Sweetwater Valley was a wide valley of gently undulating hills, about thirteen miles between the Rattlesnake Hills to the north and the Ferris Mountains to south. Other than a few scattered pockets of cottonwoods, the only trees visible in that huge expanse of country were the dark forests on the slopes of the faraway Ferris Mountains. In the afternoon, I passed Independence Rock State Historic Site, a large granite monolith that looks like the topside of an elephant half submerged in the prairie. I passed alkali flats as white as snow, red-stemmed bunch grasses, and small pink flowers about an inch tall. Small horned toads, which are actually lizards, scurried before the horses. Yucca blossoms hummed with bees, and I passed so many anthills—one every thirty feet or so—that I thought ants must have been the predominant animate lifeform of the ecosystem. A U.S. Geological Survey benchmark out in the middle of the sage recorded the elevation as 6,129 feet above sea level. After Pathfinder, I camped at the Mormon historic site of Martin's Cove, and then, twenty miles later, at the old Split Rock Ranch, and after two and a half day's quiet riding, entered the small town of Jeffrey City on U.S. Highway 287.

Jeffrey City is pretty much a ghost town. What's left of it is a holdover from a uranium mining boom that began in the 1950s and ended about the time the Three Mile Island incident in 1979 killed the uranium industry. In 1980, four thousand people lived in Jeffrey City. Nearly everyone had left by 1982. Today, twenty-three people live there, and when I rode in from the east, the town looked like the setting for a post-apocalyptic Cormac McCarthy novel. The miners' dormitories sat vacant, with "no trespassing" signs posted on them. One of many shuttered gas stations had as its only signage the word *Jesus* painted on it. Most buildings were abandoned, their windows boarded over and the paint faded and peeling, and those buildings that weren't abandoned looked like they soon might be. The elementary school and the St. Brendan Mission Church were closed for good. A street sign warned drivers to slow down for children playing, but there are no children playing in Jeffrey City these days. The only functioning cash register in town was at the Split Rock Bar and Cafe, and that's where I met Laurie Redland, who I had first met two years prior and who agreed to put up my horses for the night.

Laurie Redland was the last cowgirl of the Sweetwater Valley. There may have been others like her in the area, but I would have had to meet them to believe it. She and her husband, Tom, moved to Jeffrey City in 1976. Tom had taken a variety of jobs since then, but over the past forty-six years, Laurie had mostly cowboyed.

The definition of *cowboy* varies, but essentially it means someone who handles cattle on horseback. Day-hire cowboy work, which is what Laurie mostly did, involves helping ranchers when they need it but not having a place on the permanent payroll. Day-hire cowboys usually help with seasonal jobs like gathering cattle in the fall or branding calves in the spring or monitoring first-time mothers during the calving process. A lot of people call themselves cowboys, but anyone who's done day work is probably a legitimate cowboy because the only way they find work is through their word-of-mouth reputation—and if they're not good at it or don't ride good horses or aren't handy with a rope, they won't have work. It's a good way to make money if you like to be horseback, but it generally doesn't pay well. I once heard a Montana rancher say that you couldn't make enough money cowboying to raise a pantleg. Which means that providing for a family or educating children on a cowboy's wages is difficult. But it's all Laurie ever wanted to do, and when I asked if she ever worked with other cowgirls like herself, she shook her head.

"Over the years, I had a lot of wives and girlfriends ask me to teach them to rope and ride because, you know, they'd see me out there with their husbands and they'd get jealous. I tried, but none of 'em ever amounted to much on a horse."

Laurie lived at the cul-de-sac end of a blacktop road that had been paved with ambitions for a neighborhood that never materialized. Driveways and street curbs had been installed, but no houses were ever built and none probably ever will be. The neighborhood idea played out with the uranium market, and Laurie's house was one of only a handful on the west end of town. But no matter where you live in Jeffrey City, there is no escape from its hard environment. Just below the Continental Divide and hardly a tree between it and town, the winters are so cold and windy that they can bury a Conex shipping container in drifting snow. The summers, though, are arguably worse because of one condition: the mosquitoes. Jeffrey City, which sits a few miles south of the Sweetwater River, is famous for its mosquitoes. The place rivals Alaska for the severity and density of its mosquitoes. They can be infuriating and demoralizing, and the only relief comes from a stiff wind or insect repellent.

"Sometimes I think they're getting noticeably worse," Laurie said, "but really, they've always been bad. When I moved here, they sprayed [from the air] for two years, and then quit."

I asked why they quit.

"Because everybody left town."

On the front porch of her house, Laurie kept a citronella coil smoldering on a sheet of tin. An electric bug zapper with blue lights and heavy screens hung from an eave above the porch, and a small mound of charred insect hulls lay beneath it. Inside the front door, several cans of insect repellent and a tube of insect-repellent lotion sat on a small table. I set up my small tent in Laurie's yard, and the mosquitoes immediately began to pile up on the screens.

That evening, Laurie and I drove an hour into Lander to pick up a six-pack of beer and a pizza from Pizza Hut. As we flew past more country than I could ride in three days, she pointed out corrals where she'd worked cattle, roping arenas where she'd spent evenings chasing steers under the lights, and just west of Jeffrey City she pointed to the east end of the Granite Mountains. The treeless mountains stand on the north side of the Sweetwater River. At its western end, the rounded white spine of the range had weathered differentially into clefts and pockets and spires. The crenulated slopes hung like drapery folds over the mountains in vertically walled gorges that ran deep and shadowy.

"When we first moved here, word was, there was the bones of a cavalry man up in the rocks there. He crawled up there to die, I guess, get away from the Indians. That's what the story was anyway. There was also a stack of teepee poles around the other side of the mountain—and I saw those—but I think someone took them, is what I heard. Both of those were on private land, and no one was supposed to say anything about where they were, fear of people looking around too much."

Laurie talked a lot about the good old days. Her husband, Tom, worked the daylight hours of every day, mostly as a welder. He left the house before daylight and returned home after dark with hardly enough energy to get through a conversation. Laurie woke early every morning to see him off. She tended her hummingbird feeders, watered her patio plants, laid out a shallow water trough for a resident mule deer and her fawn. Every day she drove across town to feed her two horses that she kept in a leased corral. She still rode, helped local ranchers gather cattle or brand calves, but she was getting older, and the community wasn't what it once was. The good old days were the summer nights at the local roping arena, where the horse sweat and beer ran thick. The good old days were back when they sprayed insecticide over the town and people could actually tolerate being outdoors, back before the Three Mile Island meltdown ramped up federal mining regulations to save both people's health and the environment, with the collateral damage being the death of Jeffrey City. All that was past, and the brightest light in town when I saw it was Laurie Redland.

We ate most of the pizza and drank a few beers, and she wrapped up two leftover pieces in tinfoil for my lunch the next day. We talked about my road ahead and about looking after my horses. I stood up to leave and she looked at me and said,

"Be careful. I'll be glad when you finally get to California, and make sure you let me know just as soon as you do."

———

Jeffrey City evoked demise. Decay has been too slow there, as though some benevolent god should have scuttled the town long ago. In stark contrast to it was the pristine, if austere, landscape of the upper Sweetwater Valley. From where the Pony Express Trail leaves U.S. Highway 287 and runs up and over the Continental Divide, the path is about fifty miles of travel through BLM land. My buddy Scott Zimmerman, who lived in Jackson, Wyoming, agreed to join me with a horse for a few nights to make the trip. Scott's horse—a big red mare named Spooks—had experience with an electric fence and a camping routine, which made his joining me easy and unlikely to upset Chicken Fry or Badger. In Central Asia, Scott and I had played a horseback game together that's as close as you can get today to horseback warfare, and I figured he wasn't apt to complain about a hard day or bad camp.

A few days before he met me, I sent Scott a list of provisions that included summer sausage, cheddar cheese, tortillas, hot sauce, oatmeal, and other comparatively luxurious foods. On the evening of July 12, he pulled up to my camp at an abandoned gas station on the side of the highway. He rolled down the window, and the first thing he said was, "I forgot our groceries on my kitchen counter. Lander's forty minutes from here. I can drop my horse and be back in two hours.

I began my journey on May 5, 2019, from the Pony Express National Museum in St. Joseph, Missouri. Horses for the Pony Express were kept in the building behind me, though at the time of the mail service it was made of wood and called the Pike's Peak Stable. *(Photo by Claire Antoszewski)*

Mammatus clouds over an abandoned barn portend heavy weather in northeastern Kansas. The electric fence, though only a single strand of rope, held the horses through the storm. Not once during the entire journey did the fence fail to confine the horses. *(Photo by the author)*

Fifth-grade students from Valley Heights Junior High School greeted Chicken Fry and Badger at the Pony Express Barn & Museum in Marysville, Kansas. Whether as a break from walking or just eager for the alternative company I couldn't tell, but the horses always seemed to appreciate passerby attention. *(Photo by Claire Antoszewski)*

My load-out of gear lies in the center of this farm shop in Nebraska.
Stormy weather on the Great Plains forced me to camp in many shops
and barns for the first month of my journey. *(Photo by the author)*

The Phelps County Canal in Nebraska provided a reprieve from riding along the shoulders of highways and county roads. The high amount of precipitation through the spring meant that finding grass for my horses was easy as far west as the Continental Divide. *(Photo by Nate Bressler)*

Joe and Dianne Jeffrey live on the Pony Express Trail near Lexington, Nebraska. People's willingness to welcome me into their homes—shown here for morning coffee—was an encouraging consistency at nearly every place I stopped. *(Photo by Nate Bressler)*

The staff at the McDonald's in Torrington, Wyoming, was eager to give me baggies of apple slices for Chicken Fry and Badger. Chicken Fry navigated the drive-thru on autopilot as though he had previously picked up fast food. *(Photo by Bill Frakes)*

Ruins of a stagecoach stop near South Pass, Wyoming, have been fenced off to prevent cattle from damaging the structures. Though not a Pony Express station, these buildings are likely similar to what the mail service used. *(Photo by Scott Zimmerman)*

The roan stallion in the background, who appears in the preface of the book, stands off after I threw rocks at him to prevent him harassing Chicken Fry and Badger. Chicken Fry, unfazed by the encounter moments before, has lowered his head to graze. *(Photo by the author)*

To avoid wild horses stampeding Chicken Fry and Badger in the middle of the night, I corralled my horses in this five-foot fence near Simpson Springs, Utah. This was the afternoon of August 5, and the temperature was about 100° F. *(Photo by the author)*

Each pannier weighed between 35 and 40 pounds depending on how much food and water I carried. One was marked port, the other starboard. I used a Decker-style packsaddle and a basket-hitch rigging to lash the panniers to the packsaddle. The morning routine—from my first cup of coffee to when I stepped in the saddle—took about 45 minutes. *(Photo by Tom Fowlks)*

Central Nevada was hot, dry, and sparsely populated. After 106 days on the trail, the horses and my gear were showing the miles. Badger, who I rode almost exclusively at this point, never lagged from the heart-attack pace of 3.8 miles per hour, which is quite a feat for a horse to maintain over so long a period. *(Photo by Tom Fowlks)*

Javier Colonio and Omar Cajachagua, both from Peru, were working at the Robert's Creek Ranch in Central Nevada on three-year visas. Here, we're looking at the National Park Service map of the Pony Express Trail before dinner. *(Photo by Tom Fowlks)*

Calculating distances between campsites and coordinating permission to camp on private land were unending chores. Paper maps — as pages cut out of an atlas — were essential because charging my phone was not always possible. *(Photo by Tom Fowlks)*

On an alkali flat in western Nevada, Badger looks east from where we'd come. Having traveled some 1,500 miles, the horses were unlikely to run away and leave me afoot. *(Photo by the author)*

A bronze statue in Old Sacramento marks the western terminus of the Pony Express Trail. I finished my journey on September 21, 2019. *(Photo by Claire Antoszewski)*

The thing is, I have a bunch of dehydrated backpacker meals under the back seat of the truck."

That'll work, I told him.

"The good news is I remembered the whiskey."

We started up the Sweetwater the next morning, and for most of the day we talked about the horse game in the Central Asian country of Kyrgyzstan. It's called kok boru, which means "blue wolf" in Kyrgyz, and the object is to throw a headless goat carcass into a goal that's about the size and shape of a hot tub. Here's what that means: A goat is killed immediately before the game, and even without its head, it must weigh at least seventy pounds. Players reach down from their horses to pick up the carcass by one of its legs or a handful of hair. Having hauled the goat into the saddle, the horse then runs like hell for the goal while the other team attempts to steal the goat, knock the opposing players off their horses, interfere in such a way as to prevent the goat from entering the goal. It's a dangerous, difficult, very fast game that's been played in Central Asia for the past 3,000 years, or so we'd been told by the Kyrgyz.

Scott and I had been part of the U.S. Kok Boru Team that competed at the World Nomad Games in Kyrgyzstan in 2018. That experience fostered a bond between us. It was a rich and exhilarating experience. On the Pony Express Trail, with nothing but time and space on our hands, Scott and I were free to relive our kok boru days and dream about the future without upsetting loved ones or ruining dinner with talk of headless goats.

We camped the first night west of Rocky Ridge, one of the highest points on the Oregon and Mormon trails, at 7,300 feet above sea level. Because eating the dehydrated packages of food required boiling water, we had no food we could eat in the saddle. The dinner was not good, nor was breakfast. By the afternoon of the second day, I felt as though I wasn't getting enough calories when we rode up to the Mormon historic site of Rock Creek Hollow. A family or two of missionaries are usually camped in a motorhome at Mormon historic sites, and Scott and I were hoping for a ham sandwich or something similar as we dismounted our horses at the front gate.

A large travel trailer motorhome was parked near a block of bathrooms, and as we approached the RV, a woman stepped out. She was probably in her late sixties. A white cotton hat was held snugly on her head by a chinstrap pulled tight, and she held a water bottle clasped between both hands at her chest. A woman with a diminutive stature, something like a field mouse, she seemed kind.

"You boys look like you've had a busy day," she said.

We nodded.

"Where are you coming from?" she asked.

I told her that we'd camped the previous night near Rocky Ridge. She looked past me to Badger and then at Chicken Fry carrying the packs and at Scott's horse with loaded saddlebags. "How long have you been traveling like this?" she asked.

"I've been with him two days," Scott said.

She looked at me, and I told that her that I'd left Missouri on May 5.

"Oh, my," she said.

She looked around me again at the horses, who had half-closed their eyes and were dozing, and silence hung between the three of us. I dangled my bridle reins in the dirt between my boots and waited for her to invite us in for lunch. After a few seconds, she said, "I wish I could offer you guys something to eat, but my husband and I are leaving tomorrow, and I'm afraid we gave all of our food to some other missionaries. I could give you some cold milk if you'd like."

I looked at Scott, and he said, "I would love some milk, thank you."

I almost never drink milk. The last time I'd had it—without coffee—was in the parking lot of the coliseum where we played kok boru in Kyrgyzstan, a year prior. That was fermented mare's milk drawn from a bag made out of the stomach of an animal, maybe a sheep or goat, and it was an extenuating circumstance. I don't really like to drink milk, never did as a kid, but standing in the yard at Rock Creek Hollow, I figured what the hell and said I'd love some milk and thanked her. She returned to the trailer and reemerged with two Styrofoam cups and six small chocolate cookies the size of coins. Scott and I each took a cup and three cookies, and she pointed to a kiosk of water jugs, what she called the water buffalo, where we could fill our water bottles. We drank and ate and thanked her again. Using a tablet, she took photos of us as we climbed on our horses and rode out the gate.

We camped that night at a historic spot, Burnt Ranch, that was also the site of a Pony Express station. We leaned against our saddles and talked about how a Pony Express rider might avoid freezing to death or becoming lost while crossing South Pass on a January night. I had a few questions about the riders that I didn't think anyone could answer—like if a rider carried a toothbrush in his boot, as I'd seen Mongolians do, so that he could brush his teeth that night. Another question I had was what kind of socks the riders wore to keep their feet warm. Anyone who's spent time on horseback in the winter knows that your feet can get cold in a hurry, and I wondered how hard a pair of wool socks would be to come by out there in 1860. We finished the whiskey around dark, and the mosquitoes clouded around us. A small tornado of them, hardly visible in the low light, gyrated over Scott's head.

"I hear this constant whine," he said, futilely swinging his hand through the air as though to clear the insects. "A normal person would not be okay with this."

The next morning, we left the Sweetwater River and rode ten miles over low-sage prairie to the Continental Divide at South Pass. We made the pass at one o'clock. The pass is a low-slung, wind-swept saddle between treeless hills. Every interpretive site in the area relates that the divide itself was so gentle that emigrants hardly knew they had passed from the Atlantic watershed to the Pacific. That low grade is what allowed passage for wagons. It was the only place between the Canadian border and Guadalupe Pass near Mexico where a wagon could cross the Continental Divide. Historian Will Bagley's book *South Pass: Gateway to a Continent* gives a thorough explanation of the pass's role in the development of the West:

Geography made South Pass the gateway to a continent and one of the most significant historic landmarks in the United States....Without this natural road, wagons could not have left the Missouri River and reached the Pacific in a single season, and the European conquest and settlement of the American West might have taken several more generations.[11]

At the summit of South Pass, Scott and I dismounted our horses. The air was thin and clean. Fair-weather cumulus clouds ran to the western horizon, and the horizon looked dry. The country was beige, yellow, and red, and it looked rough, as though a thousand folds of scrubland separated the watershed summit where we stood and whatever far-off country lay to the west. We were tired and hungry and dirty. The horses dozed standing right where we'd slid from our saddles. The landscape was quiet. The gentle wind, the breathing of the horses, and the creak of saddle leather as the horses shifted position were the only sounds. More so than any subdued feeling of ceremony at having crossed the continental watershed, I felt an authenticity. I'd been horseback for seventy-one days. I'd come a thousand miles from Missouri. I had a thousand miles ahead of me. At that moment, what sense I made from the elements was: This is the West.

Chapter 7
"The Mormon 500"

When I was a kid, I had a book titled *Don't Squat with Yer Spurs On! A Cowboy's Guide to Life*. It was a small, thin book, filled with Western aphorisms that I took seriously, like "Nobody ever drowned in his own sweat" and "Never go to your room in the daytime." One was "The only way to drive cattle fast is slowly." It means that if you try to move a herd of cattle too quickly, they will scatter, and you'll be delayed trying to regather them. In the end, the more efficient execution is slow and deliberate. An older reference to a similar principle is *festina lente*, Latin for "hasten slowly." It was a widely used motto for Roman emperors, often represented with a porpoise wrapped around a ship's anchor.[1] What I realized halfway across Wyoming was that the slower I traveled, the faster I'd get to California.

Crossing South Pass changed my sense of time. I'd been riding for two months and ten days. My routine was established. Chicken Fry and Badger had reached a flow state with the work, and the system was functioning as planned. I was neither at the beginning nor the end of my journey; I was in the middle. And so the calendar days were lost to the rhythm of the horses. I stopped worrying about crossing the Sierra Nevada before the snow flew or about riding late into the fall. There were no shortcuts or quick fixes to my situation. My existence could be distilled into one of two conditions: I either had the ability to travel or I did not. That logic led me to believe that any opportunity to rest my horses was an opportunity to bolster my chance of actually making it to California, and was therefore to be passed up at the risk of decreasing the probability that I could cover the remaining 1,000 or so miles ahead of me, most of which was desert. Which meant that when a local rancher on the west side of South Pass suggested I lay over a couple of days at the ranch, I took her up on it.

Melissa Misner met Scott and me at a pull-off on Highway 28. I'd first met Melissa and her husband, Andy, in 2017. They run a ranch outside the small town of Farson, population 211. Melissa shuttled Scott and his horse back to Sweetwater Station, where he'd first joined me. What took us three days to cover on horseback took us an hour in a truck. Once we'd dropped Scott and were headed back toward Farson, Melissa told me that they had some new faces at the ranch. When I visited her and Andy in 2018, they had a ranch hand working for them who'd come from Oregon. He chewed apple-flavored

Skoal snuff and drank Crown Royal a little earlier in the day than most employers would be comfortable with. So he was gone. Now they had a new hand, Tim, a young man from Texas.

Finding good ranch help, Melissa told me, had been difficult. It's a unique job that often involves working alone, so the hand has to be trustworthy. And it can be dangerous work, so you don't want to hire someone prone to recklessness. Attention to safety is critical when operating tools and equipment like chainsaws and tractors. And, of course, a good ranch hand has to be quiet and capable with the livestock. It helps if he or she can recognize a cow that's mere hours from giving birth. There are no set hours to a ranch hand job, but you can be sure the days will be long. Hot in the summer, cold in the winter. As much fresh air as you can stand, and no two days are the same, but if you don't love it, you probably won't last long. So far, Tim had been working out, but, Melissa said, "Time will tell."

They also had a young man staying with them who was at the ranch to clean up. Jason, who was in high school, had been running with a bad crowd. Drugs and alcohol had become a problem. Jason's parents sent him to Andy and Melissa so that he could stack hay bales and stretch barbed wire, wake up early, go to bed early, and hopefully realign some of his priorities with plenty of time to think about them in the middle of nowhere Wyoming.

Andy and Melissa's ranch is at the other end of the agricultural spectrum from Pathfinder Ranches. It is a family-run ranch. They and Tim and Jason did all the work. Tim and Jason lived in a bunkhouse behind the main house and ate their meals with Andy and Melissa. After we turned out my horses in a large green pasture that was half-flooded with irrigation water, Melissa told me I could sleep in their guest room. I told her that I didn't want to soften up by sleeping inside so I'd just unroll my bedroll beside the barn.

"No way. Trust me, you need a shower," she said.

I'll take the shower, I said, but I'm sleeping outside.

"You really think a few nights inside is gonna make you soft?" Andy asked.

Nah, I told him, just not doing that on this trip.

When I walked into the house for dinner, Melissa opened the refrigerator and handed me a Bud Light. That was an unexpected gesture of hospitality because Andy and Melissa are members of the Church of Jesus Christ of Latter-day Saints. They do not consume alcohol. Probably the most common notion about Mormons is that they abstain from alcohol. Runners-up would be that they show a preference for helping church members more so than non-church members, that they're hardworking, family-oriented, and perhaps lastly, shrewd in their business. Stereotypical notions may be rooted in truth or partial truths, but such generalizations often lead to trouble, and one thing I can tell you about the Misner Ranch is that Melissa was an integral part of running a tight operation.

As we sat down to a dinner of cheeseburgers, Melissa told Tim to remember to put any receipts from the day on the desk. Melissa kept the ranch books. All receipts needed to be put on the desk at the end of the day. Fuel, fencing supplies, hardware, horse feed—any expense incurred needed to pass through her, and when Tim said, "I know, I know," she gave him a look that conveyed she wasn't so sure.

I've had a few dinners at Andy and Melissa's house, and I recall most of them being cheeseburgers. I mentioned this to Melissa as she was serving the plates, and she said, "Andy loves a good burger."

"To me, eating is a chore," Andy said. "If I didn't have to eat, I wouldn't. If there was a pill I could take instead of eating dinner, I'd take the pill."

While we were eating, he asked me what the craziest experience with wildlife I'd had so far on my trip had been. Nothing crazy, I told him. Melissa told him that Scott and I had played some kind of dead-goat game in Asia the prior summer, and that it sounded pretty crazy.

"I'd love to be able to do stuff like that, travel, whatnot, but we can't hardly leave the ranch," he said and leaned forward, resting his elbows on the table and kneading his hands. "This is what I've always wanted—to run a ranch of my own. Now that I have it, it's important for me to make it work in the best way I can."

With that, Andy rose from the table to go check on the hay meadow. Andy and Melissa leased a field, a few miles from their house, where they grew hay that would feed their cattle through the winter. They were irrigating the hay at that time, the third week of July, with a center-pivot system. Center-pivot irrigation systems, often called just pivots, water a crop with a long arm that rotates around a center pivot where the water is pumped into the arm. Andy and Melissa's pivot was a half mile long, and it ran twenty-four hours a day, constantly watering the hay. Because of the high value of water and that so much of it is held in the pipe of the pivot, the system needed to be checked regularly—every two hours—for any leaks or malfunction. I asked Andy if he woke in the middle of the night to check it. He nodded as he pulled on a coat, and said, "One thing that I've found as I get older is that I don't need as much sleep. That helps, makes it easier."

I rested for two days at their place. Hay season was in full swing, and everyone put in long hours in the fields. On the afternoon of my second day there, Melissa and Tim walked in the house while I was lying on the couch enjoying the air conditioning. I heard the shuffling of boots in the mudroom. They walked into the kitchen in their socks, and Tim said he was starving. The smell of freshly cut hay wafted in with them. The knees and thighs of Tim's jeans were stained green, and his hair was damp with sweat and matted into a shape resembling the inside of his cowboy hat. He laid four slices of white bread on the countertop and covered two with thick slices of ham. Melissa had one hand on her hip and held a pair of leather gloves in the other. I heard her say something about Jason as I sat at the kitchen counter.

"Has he ever asked you to buy him vaping stuff?" she asked Tim.

"Yes, and I told him I couldn't do that because I'd lose my job if I did."

She watched him squeeze mustard out of a bottle onto the slices of ham.

"What else has he asked you?"

"Lotsa things."

"Like what?"

"He asked me if I'd ever smoked pot and if I'd ever done mushrooms." He finished making the sandwiches and immediately began to eat one. "He asked me if I'd ever vaped while on mushrooms," he said with his mouth full.

Melissa looked at him while he ate. "And what did you tell him?"

"That anyone who thinks vaping is cool is an idiot!"

She watched Tim finish one sandwich and begin on the other. They stood across the kitchen from each other, and Tim looked like he was ready to answer another question. His forehead was white to a line just above his eyebrows, and his face glowed red. Melissa finally sighed heavily, shook her head while looking at the floor and then turned to me with a resigned expression. "What am I going to do with these boys?" she said, frustrated but not totally upset.

———

Staying with Andy and Melissa gave me a respite. Dry country lay beyond their ranch. Eighty-five miles of sagebrush from there to Mountain View, Wyoming, and most of it was BLM land. A country empty of people. The landscape was still and quiet. The only recent tracks in the fine dust of the road were left by coyotes, birds, rodents. The solitude was a comforting buffer between Chicken Fry, Badger, and I and the rest of the world. In the late morning I found a rifle magazine beside the road. It was curved and looked like it would fit an AK-47. The outside was heavily rusted. Sand had filled in around the cartridges. I slid two of them into my palm. They were 7.62 x 39 AK rounds. I left the magazine in the middle of the road where someone might find it, and put the two rifle shells in my pocket.

The sage hills gave way to badlands—drab, bald hills of weathered sedimentary rock that supported only scant vegetation. I passed a soda ash mine to the south. About 2,500 miles of underground tunnels had been bored under the prairie.[2] The facility on the surface looked like an international airport, and I skirted a few miles north of it with no desire to be any closer. The miles passed with hours and days. I camped on the banks of the Hams Fork river, where the water ran the color of oak tannins. I crossed the Church Buttes Gas Field, where derricks steepled the horizon and far-off scarves of rising dust betrayed energy trucks on their errands. Chicken Fry nearly sank in quicksand on the banks of Blacks Fork river, and I spent that evening beside a nightjar, a large nocturnal bird, that sat atop a fence post until dusk settled and it left without a noise.

On the afternoon of June 20, I crossed under Interstate 80 and left the desert behind. Pastor Joe Reynolds had given me permission to camp at the Heart of the Valley Baptist Church in the town of Mountain View. As I neared the town,

I meandered along county roads that ran between irrigated meadows. The landscape had changed from gray and dry to green and humid, and with the change came blue herons and songbirds and tall cottonwood trees and all the biting insects that Western water sources support. I was skirting a hay meadow on the shoulder of a paved county road, when a pickup truck stopped on the opposite shoulder. I recognized the truck, which had passed me an hour prior, because of its tool boxes and a welder strapped to the flat deck, and when it stopped, I noticed that a bundle of lumber was now tied to the truck as though the man who climbed out had been to the hardware store.

I pulled up Badger while the man walked across the road to me. He wore a mesh feed-store hat, aviator sunglasses, a pearl-snap shirt with a wallet in one breast pocket and folded papers and a pen in the other, and wide suspenders. "Where ya headed?" he asked.

Heart of the Valley Baptist Church, I said.

He looked at Chicken Fry. "Much gear as you're packing, I'd say you're headed farther than that."

The plan is to ride to California, I said.

"I got a mule that I think you need. She just might work for what you got going on here."

At that, I slid off Badger. Whenever someone offered the possibility of a remount, a fresh horse if one of mine could not travel, I made a point of taking down his or her information in the small spiral notebook I kept in the pocket of my vest. I asked the man, what's the story with the mule?

"Well, she is the prettiest mule you've ever seen in your life—I mean this is one gorgeous mule—but last week she tried to kill me."

Giving the man the benefit of the doubt that sometimes dangerous situations arise by no fault of the animal or handler, I asked, how so?

"Well, I was riding her in an indoor arena, and she took off running on me, and for the life of me, I couldn't stop her. Just tearing around that arena with me leanin' into the reins, and I could not get her shut down." He looked at me with a blank expression and stuck out his hands with his palms up as though he were empty-handed as to any other option than sit out the windy ride and hope for the best. He shook his head and half-laughed like he was glad the situation was behind him.

"She finally balled up in a corner, and I got the hell off her and thought, no more of that shit. I'm too old for that business, you know? I'm thinking that if she were part of your outfit, it would do her good."

A suicide mule was the last thing I needed. A horse or mule in stampede mode can out-muscle a rider. The man standing in front of me was no small man, and the thought of him holding on for his life as that mule whipped around the arena made me think that he was lucky to escape without injury and that on a half-busy road with traffic flying by at fifty miles per hour, like the one that we then stood beside, his jenny mule would be a serious liability to herself, me, and anyone who happened to be driving down the road.

The man began petting Badger on the neck. "This bay horse is a nice horse," he said. He seemed happy to be in our presence. I'd seen it before: people liked what I was doing. It inspired them. All along the way, I'd had people tell me they would ride with me if they were younger or had more time on their hands, and I reckoned that was part of the reason people had been so generous to me. I didn't want to insult this man's time and offer by flat-out rejecting it, so I wrote down his name and phone number and "xtra pack mule." He offered to come retrieve me at my camp that evening and drive me to see the mule. I told him we'd be in touch. He tipped his hat, looked both ways down the road, and walked over to his truck and drove off.

I didn't have to ask Chicken Fry and Badger what they thought of the idea. Of course, 1,000 miles to California would benefit the mule. Assuming she made it in one piece. The first fifty miles, though, could be a little dicey. I wasn't certain if the man was offering to give me the mule or if he was wanting me to train her for him, but either way, I saw his original intention as trying to support a passerby horseman, and that was a hospitable gesture.

I camped behind the Baptist church, and I never went to see the mule. She sounded too fractious. I spent the next night at Pastor Joe's, nine miles up the road. From the fertile bottomland of the Blacks Fork Valley, I rode straight west, and on a long, flat bench of sagebrush I approached a sheepherder's camp. I couldn't see any sheep, but a tin-sided sheep wagon was parked a hundred feet from the dirt road. Beyond the wagon, four horses were picketed along a shallow ditch. The horses were spaced fifty or so feet apart, and they were tied by a front foot to stakes in the ground. They raised their heads from grazing as I approached.

The doorway at the front of the wagon was open and dark. The wagon had no windows on the side facing me. One solar panel was mounted to two boards on the roof, and another solar panel hung from ropes slung over the top of the wagon. A blackened smokestack emerged from the cylindrical roof, and three orange five-gallon water jugs sat on the ground beside it.

When I came abreast of the wagon, a dark-faced man wearing a red t-shirt filled the empty space of the open door. He seemed to be squinting in the light. He leaned against the door jamb with one arm above his head and the other on his hip. I sensed he may have been sleeping. He watched me for a second and I thought he might wave, but he faded into the darkness and left the doorway empty. As I rode past, I saw that the wagon had a single small rectangular window in the center of the rear wall. It was a windy, unforgiving camp. The horses had returned to grazing. In the distance, a long row of wind turbines turned on the cusp of the horizon, lower than the stomachs of the horses, lower than the silhouette of the sheep wagon, and for all appearances, the product of a wholly different world than the shadeless camp of a herder and his horses.

I spent that night at the ghost town of Piedmont. I unrolled my gear in the lee of a collapsed cabin that had been mostly dismantled by cattle. I penned the horses in grass to their bellies, and we shared water from a narrow seep that smelled so strongly of rotting organic matter that I couldn't drink it without adding lemonade powder. That night I lay on my bedroll thinking about the sheep wagon. Not since passing isolated nomad camps on the Mongolian steppe had I seen such an austere way to spend the summer grazing season. The herder was either with his sheep or in the wagon for the whole summer. Something about the camp was distant. What it represented seemed faint and shrouded. I saw it as an undertone of the West, as though the job of herding sheep had fallen through the cracks of progress, and I appreciated that the man and his job and his camp were partly beyond my scope of the West, that I might never understand the life of a sheepherder on the range.

———

Two days later, I rode into Utah. No signage on the unpaved county road marked the state line, but a small steel sign on a barbed wire fence told me that I had entered Mormon country. The sign said "Ensign Ranches" and gave a phone number for the ranch office. The word *ensign* is part of the Mormon vocabulary, and like a lot of other towns, rivers, or anything else in Utah that needs a name, it comes from the Old Testament. The sign told me that the ranch was a Mormon business, and any ranch that provides an office number is likely a significant operation. Ensign certainly qualifies as a significant cattle operation. The ranch is one of several owned by an investment firm, the Ensign Group, and is neighbors with Deseret Land and Livestock Ranch, which is owned by the Church of Latter-day Saints. And the church, reportedly the largest landowner in Florida and Illinois and the fifth-largest landowner in the nation, has extensive agricultural holdings.[34] An oft-cited testament of what farms and ranches mean to the church comes from a State-of-the-Church address given by Church President Gordon B. Hinckley in 1991:

> We have felt that good farms, over a long period, represent a safe investment where the assets of the Church may be preserved and enhanced, while at the same time they are available as an agricultural resource to feed people should there come a time of need.[5]

The church's largest ranch is in Florida. Deseret Ranches owns more than a quarter million acres around Orlando, and though the land is mostly orange groves and cattle pasture, it's also the freshwater source for the greater Orlando area, home to 2.6 million people.[6] *Deseret* is also part of the Mormon vocabulary, and it means "honey bee."[7] The honey bee is a Mormon icon for cooperative industriousness. The image of a yellow, layer-cake-type hive appears on the state flag, on state highway signs, and on the doors of Utah Highway Patrol vehicles. Images of beehives are on Salt Lake City manhole covers. Two large sculptures of beehives sit in front of the state capitol. The Salt Lake City minor-league baseball team is known as the Bees. And nearly as prevalent as the image of a beehive is the word *Deseret*.

Brigham Young, leader of the church and of the Mormons' westward hegira, wanted to call the land that would become Utah the State of Deseret, but the federal government rejected it.[8] When the vanguard of Mormon pioneers arrived in the Salt Lake area in 1847, they carried with them five of the layer-cake-type hives made of coiled straw, called skep hives, because just as the seeds they'd carried from Illinois were necessary for cultivation of food crops in their frontier Zion, so too were pollinators necessary for the propagation of those crops. Brigham Young chose the beehive as a symbol for the new settlement because the beehive suggested that hard work produces sweet results when all bodies are working toward a collective goal.[9] That worker-bee mentality survives today, and it's appreciated by some of the highest profile institutions and corporations in the country.

Harvard Business School has had a significant Mormon contingent for years on end. Typically, ten percent of a class at the school is Mormons. A former Mormon dean of the school, Kim Clark, led the program until he was recalled by the head of the church to lead Brigham Young University-Idaho in 2005. When asked if it was a difficult decision to leave Cambridge for Idaho, Clark replied that a phone call from the head of the church was as good as a phone call from a prophet.[10] Clayton Christensen, a church leader who developed the theory of disrupted innovation and authored the book *The Innovator's Dilemma: The Revolutionary Book That*

Will Change the Way You Do Business, is a star business school professor for the Mormons. Another star is Mitt Romney, who graduated from Brigham Young University in 1971 and then attended Harvard Business School. A common track for entrepreneurial Mormons is to attend Brigham Young University, which costs church members half of what it does everyone else, the BYU Marriott School of Business, and then Harvard Business School.[11] From there, Goldman Sachs will be ready to talk. It happens enough to warrant a reputation.

One Harvard Business School graduate told me that certain qualities of Mormons make them desirable partners or employees. Every church member is strongly encouraged to do a two-year or eighteen-month mission, which means he or she is likely bilingual and has some international travel experience. Church policy prohibits alcohol or drugs among its members. Most have families and children, which is thought to incline them toward long-term stability. And, at least by reputation, they are instilled with the kind of hardworking cohesion implied by the iconography of a beehive.

In eastern Utah, from the Wyoming line to Salt Lake City, that cohesion runs strong. Ensign Ranches runs between five and six thousand mother cows. Its neighbor, Deseret Land and Livestock Company, is about the same size. They operate on the same scale as Pathfinder Ranches in the Sweetwater Valley, and like Pathfinder, the ranches have implemented partnerships and policies with researchers, the state wildlife commission, and others to benefit the land. The ranches are large operations that collectively have a larger footprint than if they weren't all working together. They're the kind of ranches that post a phone number for the office on the fence, and if you call the number, you're more likely to get an administrator than a cowboy who just walked off the range.

Jeff Young, general manager of Ensign Ranches, told me a few days prior to my arrival that I could camp at an "old shearing shed that blew down" a few miles inside the state line. The shed was right beside the road, Jeff said, I couldn't miss it. He told me to call him when I arrived.

The shearing shed was a long, tin-sided barn that lay in a twisted heap of rafters and sheet metal. Two walls remained standing, and the insides of the walls were covered in signatures and dates. Many of the names were Hispanic. Some were written in elaborate, hardly decipherable cursive. They were a variety of colors—black, blue, orange, red, green—dated to the 1950s, farther back to the '30s, and yet farther back to just after the turn of the century, and they were the names of men and women who'd been part of the shearing operations.

I penned my horses beside the wrecked shed in grass taller than their backs and walked across the road to look over the abandoned ranch headquarters. The house had been vandalized. All the windows were broken out and illegible graffiti decorated the stucco walls. Broken glass was everywhere around the house. Two barns and a couple outbuildings stood empty but for trash. The barn doors hung badly askew on failing hinges. The corrals of the ranch were in good shape, though, and had clearly been used to work cattle in the recent past.

Jeff drove up in a clean white pickup as I was sorting my gear. He wore clean clothes and a clean straw cowboy hat. He wanted to show me which gates to go through, which locks to unlock, and which roads to follow so that I didn't get lost as I rode through the ranch, which we thought would take me slightly more than a full day.

"It can be confusing," he said with a smile. "Jump in, and we'll go have a look."

We drove under Interstate 80, and we went through a ranch gate that had a chain of padlocks on it. Each padlock represented a different access to the land, and by opening any one lock you can open the gate. We drove a mile over a two-track road to a bottleneck of three gates. He said to go through the middle gate, and he told me that he'd secured permission for me to use the Ensign easement across land owned by Deseret Land and Livestock, the neighbors. He drove through the gate and rattled up the rough road, and he pointed to several roads that I should not take. At the last gate, he pointed out the windshield to a green, rolling landscape that climbed slightly uphill for miles, and he said that all the country before us was either Deseret or Ensign.

That evening I cooked dinner on the ruins of the shearing shed. The light played angular shadows over the wall of signatures. Sage grouse warbled nearby, and a family of nighthawks cut circles through the pink sky, diving with their mouths open so that the passing air made a humming sound like blowing over the top of a beer bottle. Chicken Fry and Badger had more grass available than they could eat in a week. With the last light, I unrolled my bedroll in the tall grass and heard both of the horses lie down somewhere beside me.

I woke a half hour past midnight to the sound of a car stopping in the gravel drive of the abandoned ranch. The motor shut off, and all four doors opened and then slammed shut. There were four young men, and they sounded drunk, speaking loudly. I heard them climb over the same iron gate I'd climbed over a few hours prior. A bottle bounced off the wall of the abandoned house, and the men laughed. I heard it bounce off a second time. The bottle shattered on the third attempt, and the men cheered. Another bottle smashed with a sound like falling water. The voices lowered, and then I heard nothing, not even my horses breathing. Finally, an eruption of laughter came from significantly closer, and the gate rattled a second time.

"I drink basically every night," one of the men said. It was the only intelligible sentence I could make out. The car doors opened and closed, and the motor started. The car sat idling until I heard the sound of the tires turning on the gravel. The headlights panned south of me and then swung around and lit up the seed heads and stems of the grass over me. The wrecked shearing shed glowed for a moment like artwork lit up in a city park. The car left slowly and finally sped away, and I heard one of my horses clear his lungs with a quiet sigh.

The next morning, an Ensign cowboy, Trever Carpenter, showed up at the corrals. He was nineteen and had been working for the ranch since the previous fall. He kept a string of six horses at a pasture behind the abandoned ranch and

was about ready to distribute salt blocks to the cattle. I told
him about the bottle breakers from the night before.

"Yep, I'm not surprised," he said. "Always something going
on up here at night."

As I was planning my approach to Salt Lake City, I'd
learned that livestock were prohibited from the valleys east of
the city. It was the municipal watershed, and the city didn't
want dogs or horses or cattle polluting the water. Obtaining a
special permit to ride through the watershed was possible, but
the bureaucratic wheels were turning so slowly that I figured
I'd arrive at Big Mountain Pass, the easiest route for me,
before the permit was issued. Trever didn't know about the
livestock ban.

"News to me," he said. "I know Big Mountain Pass, but
I've never been over there on horseback. Quite a lot of traffic
through there."

He told me to call him if I needed any help, and I rode
away from the shearing shed on the morning of July 26. I
camped another night on Ensign land. The following morning, I called Trever to ask him if he could shuttle my horses
and me around the city to a ranch on the outskirts of town.
He agreed to meet me on Big Mountain Pass the following
afternoon.

I planned to camp at East Canyon State Park east of the
pass, but by the time I rode into the valley above East Canyon
Reservoir late in the afternoon, I had a bad feeling about the
place. All day I'd seen trucks pulling boats and loaded with
kayaks and rafts. It was Saturday, and before I saw the scene

on the water, I could hear the music. The lake was small, but full of activity and sound. Stereos blared. Boats sat idle, with people strewn about the decks like drying laundry. Other boats pulled people on water skis and rubber innertubes. Two people pedaled a square paddleboat with an ice chest dragging in the water behind. I saw a dog wearing a neon personal flotation device. It looked to be the size of a bulldog, and it stood on the front of a stand-up paddleboard. Its owner stood over it. The scene reminded me of the smell of coconut sunscreen. It was the first clear sign that I was approaching a large urban center, and it was no place to camp with horses.

Across the highway, though, a green hillside of wheat grass looked more suitable. I couldn't find any landowner information on my phone, but I saw that it was an 85-acre tract. There was no fence between the grassy slope and the highway. A small, wooded-over creek ran at the base of the hill. So I bivouacked where I had no permission to do so, and I put a $50 bill in the breast pocket of my shirt to give the landowner if he showed up wanting to know why I was sleeping on his land.

I broke camp early the next morning. I rode past lakeside campers cooking breakfast and drinking coffee. The reservoir was glassy and quiet. Five hours later I crested the Wasatch Range at Big Mountain Pass. It was also a trailhead, and a dozen cars were parked in the parking lot. People in tight-fitting, brightly colored clothes were gearing up for a hike. Two people with mountain bikes were making adjustments to one of their bikes, which stood upside down on the gravel lot. To the west, the Salt Lake Valley sat under a thick haze. The urban sprawl stretched out like a ragged, multicolored canvas spread over the valley floor. I unloaded Chicken Fry and unsaddled Badger in the shade of an aspen grove and took a nap leaning against my saddle and holding their lead ropes. A few hours later, Trever Carpenter rolled into the parking lot with his horse trailer and drove me around the city.

————

Trever delivered me and my horses to a feedlot outside Eagle Mountain, a suburb of Salt Lake City. A man named Zane Dansie owned the feedlot and raised a breed of cattle called corrientes that are specifically bred for roping competitions. Zane was friends with a member of my dead-goat team in Asia, Ladd Howell. Ladd had arranged for me to stay at Zane's for a week or so to rest Chicken Fry and Badger before riding into the West Desert beyond the city.

A feedlot is not an ideal place to rest for a week. Two hundred or so roping steers were kept in large corrals, and on the afternoon of July 28, when I unloaded Chicken Fry and Badger in Zane's feedlot, the temperature was 103° Fahrenheit. The cattle stood lowing quietly in the heat, flicking their tails at the flies and chewing their cud. Zane was there to meet me. We put Chicken Fry and Badger in a corral at the far end, past eight other roping horses in corrals—Zane's, and his sons'. Zane had a bunkhouse he said I could stay in. It was a small log cabin type of building that might have come in a kit, and the inside was about like what you'd expect of a feedlot bunkhouse. A pair of dirty jeans lay on the couch. A half-open pizza box sat on the kitchen table with a few pieces of crust inside it. He showed me to the shower, which looked like cowboys had been using it, and turned it on, and a stream as wide as a pencil trickled from the head.

"There's no water pressure on these hot days because the cattle are all standing around the drinkers," he said. "The system can't keep up. It's better in the mornings."

No one lived at the feedlot—only the cattle, the horses, a dog with a litter of puppies, and a lot of rats. The two hundred or so cattle on the place consumed a lot of hay and grain, and the rats were a nuisance.

"I got a heck of a deal for ya in the morning," Zane said. "Got a guy coming with minks."

Minks? I asked.

"Traps, poison, nothing's worked as well as the minks. You'll see."

The next morning the young man showed up with his minks and promptly filled one five-gallon bucket after another with dead rats, using his minks in a sort of quasi-falconry way: the minks just acted on instinct and the young man, who had a history of falconry, used a squeaking sound to recall the minks after freeing them of the rat they had just ferreted out of a burrow. He'd pull the dead rat from the mink's mouth, and then give the mink a morsel of meat from his pocket. After half an hour of this business, the minks were tired, the man's hands were red with blood, and there must have been 100 dead rats in several buckets.

Between the rats and the cattle, I wasn't so sure I wanted to camp at the feedlot for a week. So I called a friend of Claire's who had worked in a hospital emergency room with her in Santa Fe and then moved to Salt Lake City. I asked him about camping in his yard for a few days while I reprovisioned and rested my horses at Zane's. He said no problem and told me that his wife was out of town and that I could borrow her car for the next five days. His name was Nate Unkefer, and his generosity allowed me to prepare for crossing the desert.

Late summer is the worst time of year to cross the West Desert of Utah. The scant water sources are at their scantest, and the heat is at its peak.[12] Because of the lack of feed and water, I hired Trever Carpenter's younger brother, Nathan, to drop hay and water at six locations along the 133 miles between Salt Lake and the Nevada state line. I shared waypoints with him through the app onX, and he agreed to drop ninety pounds of hay—a high-protein mix of grass and alfalfa—and seventy gallons of water in large tubs at each location. I paid him $400 to do it, and it took him two days of driving to drop the hay and water. The three risks involved were, one, that wild horses would find and eat the hay, two, that something would drink the water or upset the coverless tubs, and, three, that one of us would have the location wrong.

To get a better idea of what traveling through the country might entail, I called a friend of Zane's who is a hunter. His name is Dylan Rydlach. I told him that I was considering ditching my tent to lighten the load and instead just sleeping under a tarp if it unexpectedly rained. I asked him if he thought rattlesnakes would be a problem if I slept under a tarp.

"I'd be more worried about bugs. Spiders, ants, fleas. Everyone always talks about the snakes, but the bugs can be pretty bad out there."

I asked him about water sources in the desert, and he said that the BLM had installed low-evaporation water cisterns, called guzzlers, for the wild horses and other wildlife. He said I could probably find a little water in one of those guzzlers.

"You'll be on about a hundred game cameras at any one of them," he said. "But there's nothing you can do about that."

I asked him if he had cameras out there, and he said he did, and I asked what they turned up.

"Coyotes, bobcats, mountain lions. Wild horses, of course. Weird people."

Weird people?

"Yeah, whatever the heck people are doing out there, I don't know."

More concerning than strange people or rattlesnakes or bugs were the wild horses. The Onaqui herd lives in a dry valley about sixty miles west of the city center. The herd is advertised as a popular day-drive destination for city and suburban people. Pictures of the Onaqui horses turn up easily in a Google search. At the south end of the wild horses' range is the site of the Simpson Springs Pony Express Station, a place I planned to camp. For information on the herd, I called Tami Howell, a wild horse specialist with the BLM in Salt Lake, and asked her if she thought the horses might be in the area.

"Probably. I was out there earlier this week, and they were there."

I asked her how far from the springs they were.

"A quarter mile or so."

A quarter mile is nothing for a horse. So they're at the springs? I asked.

"Oh yeah, it's a water source for the herd."

I asked her how many horses she saw.

"Two hundred fifty. Something like that."

Two hundred fifty horses were loitering at the water source I wanted to camp at. That was only about half of the herd, which was reported to contain more than five hundred, and that would amount to the most horses I'd seen since Mongolia. I asked her if she thought they would give me any trouble.

"I talked to a woman who'd been riding out there last month with some friends, and she said that a pair of studs followed them for a while. But I think one of them was riding a mare."

I hung up from Tami unsure about how to prevent Chicken Fry and Badger from stampeding off with two hundred fifty wild horses. Back in Wyoming, Roy Dougherty had suggested I keep my revolver handy. I wasn't sure that was the best option, but probably a good idea. By the time I get there, I figured, the herd will probably have moved on to another part of its range.

In Salt Lake City, I paid $12 for a haircut at Supercuts. I bought two new pairs of underwear, six new pairs of heavy-weight merino wool socks, a new pearl-snap shirt, and a personal locator beacon. Claire had encouraged me to get the beacon since I'd be crossing more than a hundred miles of desert without much civilization or cellular phone service and little passerby traffic. I laded eight days of food in the paniers and bought a liter of Canadian whiskey from the state-run liquor store. I visited the church-owned bookstore and bought a copy of *Butch Cassidy and Other Mormon Outlaws of the Old West.*

The night before I left Zane's, I rolled out my bedroll on the deck of a flatbed pickup because I thought it would be harder for the rats to find me on an elevated surface. City lights glowed to the east, and coyotes barked in the desert to the west. I viewed the next week of traveling as a test. Until then, I had so far not undergone any acute test. No miles had come easy, but I'd been able to find plenty of feed for my horses, plenty of water for the three of us, and had been nowhere near as remote as I was about to be. The West Desert is not a hospitable place, especially not in the first week of August. The road ahead was not ideal, but it was the path of the Pony Express, and therefore my future.

CHAPTER 8
A Hundred Miles of Mirage

SALT LAKE CITY marks the western edge of the Rocky Mountains. From there to the Sierra Nevada is the Great Basin, which can be described in three ways. As a hydrologic basin, it covers most of Nevada, as well as parts of Utah, Idaho, Oregon, and California, and it has no outlet to the ocean. All the precipitation and snowmelt drains internally. As a landscape, or physiographic province, it's known as the Basin and Range, and it runs south into Arizona, southern California, and Mexico. The surface topography is consecutive mountain ranges oriented north-south that are the result of extensional tectonic stress on the continent. These consecutive ridges, which have been described on geologic maps as looking like "an army of caterpillars marching toward

Mexico," make Nevada the most mountainous state in the nation.[1] And thirdly, it can be described as the Great Basin Desert, one of the four major deserts in the U.S. (the others are the Mojave, Sonoran, and Chihuahuan). In the Great Basin Desert, the juxtaposition of the dry, sagebrush-steppe communities of the valleys with the montane communities of the ranges creates a highly biodiverse region. The mountain ranges are sometimes referred to as island communities because the deserts between confine the higher-existing species of plants and animals to geographically small areas.[2]

Most people are familiar with the Great Basin as flyover country. You can see it outside Las Vegas and south and west of Phoenix. Interstate 80 crosses it from Salt Lake City to Reno, Nevada. The stretch of the interstate across western Utah runs over the Bonneville Salt Flats, where the white plains are as level as a billiard table. That area is the Great Salt Lake Desert, known locally as the West Desert, and it includes the Great Salt Lake. The lake is saline because all the fresh water running into it contains naturally occurring salt, and as the water has evaporated, the salinity has increased. It used to be something much grander, with significantly more water, known as Lake Bonneville.

At its peak depth, Lake Bonneville held nearly as much water as Lake Michigan, was nearly 1,000 feet deep, and had no river draining it. It covered most of the West Desert of present-day Utah and was the largest of many lakes to form in western North America starting about 30,000 years ago, in an era known as the late Pleistocene. Lake Bonneville eventually breached a natural dam along its northern shore, and a third of its water drained into the Snake River Basin in what's called a megaflood event. The lake level ebbed over the next 4,000 years, due mostly to evaporation, and by 13,000 years ago, the water level stood at the current elevation of the Great Salt Lake. The old water levels, called paleo-shorelines, are visible throughout western Utah today as sedimentary benches high above the valley floor.[3] Much of the old lakebed is paved with minerals left over from the evaporation, and it's an inhospitable environment that famously taxed and delayed the Donner Party so that they became trapped in the Sierra Nevada and resorted to cannibalism.[4]

The Pony Express skirted the Great Salt Desert along its southern margin, where the dry scrubland hills rise from the white plain. It was and is an austere stretch of the mail route. When I entered the West Desert at Five Mile Pass, I left civilization behind. The landscape was mostly a dry sagebrush steppe surrounded by far-off mountains. From the top of the pass, Rush Valley stretched out before me, running north to south for forty miles. It was twenty-five miles wide, ringed by mountains on three sides, and for all the country that lay before me I could hardly see a tree other than the scrubby junipers that barely cast shade enough for a dog. The mountains appeared raw and empty. I camped that night on the bank of Faust Creek at the bottom of the valley. It was the last live-water source I'd camp at for the planned future, until somewhere in or near Nevada. The slow water smelled like swamp water, like rotting vegetation, and mosquitoes swarmed over its surface. That night, clouds blacked out the stars and dry thunderstorms boomed on the ranges above me.

From Faust Creek, I crossed the last paved road I would see for one hundred miles. A BLM sign warned, "Travel ahead is through extensive desert regions. Extra fuel, water, and equipment is recommended." I carried one half gallon of water and had shed whatever superfluous equipment I could. To the north, a small fire burned atop a spine of mountains. A helicopter carrying a large bucket was making trips between a somewhere water source and the thin plume of smoke. A convoy of three wildland firetrucks drove past me on the road, and the firefighters waved their yellow-shirted arms out the windows as they passed.

Dry as the country was, it became drier. Each mountain range was like a demarcation of increased aridity. I camped that night on the top of Lookout Pass, and the spine of mountains was thin enough for me to see the desert fall away on either side. To the east, Faust Creek ran a thin band of green down the center of the wide valley. To the west lay nothing but treeless rock, successive ridges that hued to blue and purple in the evening light. The desert felt foreign and strange, and it looked like Afghanistan.

The window of comfortable travel time opened with light enough to avoid stepping on a rattlesnake or anything else, and closed by early afternoon. My plan was to find my hay and water cache between two and three, before the heat of the day. First light came just after six o'clock, and I dropped out of the mountains onto a plain surprisingly thick with wheat grass. The grass stems were green at their bases and yellowed to thick, dry seed heads so that the golden plain bowed and rippled between the dark basalt ridges. And for the first time in my life, I was sorry to see horse tracks in the dirt. Many of them. Manure heaps showed where stallions marked the same territory. I had entered the Onaqui range.

The Onaqui herd of wild horses was about 500 head. (When you talk about numbers of livestock you use the collective singular noun "head" because each animal has only one head, it's usually held where you can see it, and it's easier than counting the legs and then dividing by four.) The BLM manages wild horses in the West according to the Wild Free-Roaming Horses and Burros Act of 1971, and in the Onaqui Mountain Herd Management Area, the agency has determined that the carrying capacity of the land is 121 to 210 horses. The BLM has two ways of controlling the population: contraceptives and removal. To implement either of these methods, the wild horses are gathered into corrals with helicopters, cowboys, and ATVs, and it can be a messy business. Once corralled, eligible mares are given contraceptives. In 2019, eighty-six mares of the Onaqui herd were given a drug called PZP. Also that year, 241 horses were removed.[5] Which means they were either trucked to a pasture where they would be effectively warehoused on the taxpayer dollar at $2 per day or sent to a gentling facility where they will eventually be put up for adoption.[6] Or just put up for adoption without the gentling process, and usually offered at auction or advertised on the BLM website. That's an oversimplification of how the BLM reduces wild horse populations, and if you hang around Utah or Nevada or Wyoming and ask how the wild horse management program is going, you'll get a lot of different answers, but more than few will be that the system is a classic example of the federal government's inability to manage Western rangelands.

Wild horses in the West are a problem because they're not native. They're feral. The majority of wild horses in the West live in the Great Basin, and the sensitive desert ecosystem that we see today did not evolve with horses. Horses went extinct in North America at the end of the last ice age, about ten thousand years ago.[7] The forage and the water and the wildlife evolved toward an ecological equilibrium in which opposing pressures become equal, and those pressures did not include an ungulate that weighs as much as 1,000 pounds and has the mountain lion as its only natural enemy in the area. While total eradication of the feral horses for the sake of a uniquely North American landscape might seem like an option, it's not. Wild horses of the West have assumed cultural value. They have advocates, some with a lot of money, like Madeleine Pickens, ex-wife of tycoon T. Boone Pickens. She bought a 600,000-acre ranch in eastern Nevada so she could adopt and warehouse her own herd of about a thousand horses.[8] Organizations all over the country—Pickens's is called Saving America's Mustangs—support the horses as free-roaming symbols of the West, and many of them bemoan the BLM's handling of the horses.

Opposing the advocates are those who see the horses as detrimental to the landscape or their livelihood. Livestock producers say the horses degrade the range to a higher degree than cattle because the horses aren't managed in the same way, namely rotated to different areas.[9] Researchers have shown that the horses have negative effects on the greater sagebrush community, using exclusion-type test plots where the range responded positively without horses.[10] There's also a contingent that say the horses aren't feral, that they should be considered native wildlife. That argument suggests that because the mustangs are genetically similar to the native horses that roamed here before the ice age, they should be regarded as a reintroduced native subspecies.[11] There are a lot of different sides to the conversation over wild horses, and it's one of several issues facing the West that has eluded an easy solution.

For me the wild horses were a problem because I didn't want to lose Chicken Fry and Badger to a herd of them. Which happens. Matt Hoobler of Pathfinder Ranches told me that in one pasture on the ranch where wild horses graze—and where they don't gather cattle on horseback because of them—he saw a horse in a wild herd wearing a halter, indicating that the horse had escaped from its owner. Any good horseman will criticize a horse owner who pastures his horse in a halter because of the risk to the animal. It can strangle itself in the halter or get injured in any number of ways while scratching its head on a fence post, a tree limb, or with its back foot, and I wondered how long the newly wild horse on Pathfinder would have to wear the halter. If Chicken Fry and Badger got away from me, they'd be wearing saddles and headgear, and the thought of them running wild with a herd of mustangs made me cringe.

At 10:30 in the morning, I rode up to a water trough that the BLM built to provide water for the wild horses as a way to relieve the scarcity of natural water sources. The trough was thirty feet long, about knee high and eight inches wide, and it was filled with cool, clear water that seemed an anomaly amid all that rock and wind and sky. The soil around the trough was fully covered in horse tracks, and sitting on the ground beside it was an apple. The apple had been in the place where I found it for not more than a day or so, but long enough to have swelled and slightly changed color so that it looked like a plastic apple fading in the sun. It was untouched by horses or anything else, and I saw it more as a choking hazard to the wild horses than as a treat.

I first saw a wild horse when I rounded a toe of low hills east of Simpson Springs. My hay and water cache was in a corral beside a BLM tank—a small, muddy pond for the horses—and when I came into view of the tank, I saw a roan stallion rolling in the mud. You may remember him from the preface of this book. I was one mile from the tank and the roan stallion, and I decided to take a nap in the shade of elm trees that grew around the springs. I thought that in an hour's time, the stallion might wander off, but when I woke from dozing, two horses—one white, one black—had joined the roan. By throwing rocks at the stallion to keep him at bay, I was able to get Chicken Fry and Badger safely inside the corral.

When I reached the corral, the afternoon heat was at its peak. The corral was built of heavy lumber, and I tied the gate closed such that the wild horses would have to tear down the whole corral before the gate would open. I strung a shade-fly tarp off the east side of the corral, facing the water hole and the roan stallion. I lay on my saddle blankets with my boots and socks off. The white and the black horses that I had seen earlier stood dozing in the sun. Both horses looked like old stallions, their backs swayed and their hips jutting out like rafters. Eight small black birds sat atop the white horse, picking insects from its back and trading places with each other in hops and short flights. The horse stood hipshot, motionless, asleep. Beyond the white horse, the miraged image of the black waved like a flame a quarter mile away, and I about half expected the horse to melt into some Dalí-esque equine puddle under the desert sun.

A white pickup truck pulled up to my camp. A man with pale skin, wearing a golf shirt and a ball cap, sat in the driver's seat. A similarly complexioned woman sat beside him. Three children sat in the back seat. The man said that he had brought his family out from Salt Lake City for the day to see the Onaqui horses and that they came out there often. I asked him where the herd was now.

"Just the other side of that hill," he said pointing behind him. I asked him how many were in the herd, and he said, "All of them. Looks like all of them to me."

The man asked if I needed anything, and I said no, that I was fine.

"How about a soda and a bottle of water?" he asked. I nodded and thanked him. When he stepped out of the truck, I saw that he had a pistol on his hip. He wore white shorts, white socks, and white sneakers. The gun was a black automatic pistol, and it hung on his thin leather belt in a plastic Kydex holster. He walked to the bed of the truck and opened a cooler, and when he reached into the cooler, I saw the Glock logo on the butt of the gun. He handed me a Dr Pepper and two bottles of water, and all three were wet and had little slivers of ice clinging to them. I pressed the water bottles to my forehead and to my neck and thanked him. He asked again if I needed anything and told me to be safe. When he left me, he drove to the sleeping white horse beside the water tank. The black birds lit from the horse, and the woman, who had been sitting next to the man, and a young girl, both wearing long dresses, stood in front of the white horse while the man with the pistol took photos with his phone, and I thought that seeing wild horses without two domestic ones was a lot more enjoyable experience.

As the sun lowered in the west, the water tank drew traffic. A western kingbird landed with a large yellow grasshopper in its bill. It looked in either direction, banged the grasshopper on a small flat rock, and then swallowed it. It flew to the water's edge for a drink, lifting its head several times to let the water run through its craw. A dozen pronghorn does with fawns walked up in silence and delicately drank at the water's edge, hardly creating a ripple. A pair of golden eagles came and drank, and went through the same tipping-back-of-head routine that nearly all birds, save pigeons and doves, must do, and then the eagles left with big, audible heaving motions of their wings. A small falcon-type raptor landed without a sound and stood looking at me before it drank. Its head-on, rectangular profile reminded of a Christmas-time nutcracker. Droves of small, drab birds the color of the desert circled and landed and drank in tight clusters. The roan stallion, who had been loitering within a half mile, came to the tank. He walked into the water, took a long drink, and then raised his head and looked at me and Chicken Fry and Badger. A thin stream of water trickled from his mouth and made a sound like a leaky faucet. The stallion took another long drink and then turned and left. He walked in a straight northeasterly line, and in ten minutes, he had disappeared, somehow ghosted into a landscape that looked completely visible, as though I could see every square foot of treeless desert between myself and Davis Mountain, some seven miles away.

I woke the next morning at 3:30. I rode the sun up, and by six o'clock I was between a herd of about eighty horses two miles north of me and a much larger herd of about two hundred horses three miles south of me where the desert plain ramped into the Simpson Mountains. The horses quartered along the strike of a flatiron hill that appeared yellow with wheat and cheatgrass, and the herd stretched out for nearly a mile in small groups surrounding a single large group that moved as a long oval. Over a low rise, I raised a herd of thirty or so horses that galloped a wide arc around me and then stampeded north toward the main herd. They looked like young horses, and they left a long ribbon of dust trailing into the pastel sky.

The road ahead of me, the original trace of the Pony Express route, was twenty-two miles, straight as a rifle shot, from Simpson Springs to Dugway Pass. I might as well have been riding over the surface of Mars. The desert changed colors with lithology and soil—from sienna to yellow to white, brown, orange, red, pink. Nine miles from Simpson Springs the map showed Government Well No. 36. I found it to be an iron cistern thirty feet tall and covered in graffiti. A small concrete pumphouse stood beside the cistern, and a pipe ran from the cistern into an empty, fifty-foot-long water trough, built by the BLM for wild horses.

On the other side of the gentle valley, I climbed through red and gray strata to my hay and water cache at the top of Dugway Pass. The Dugway Pony Express Station was near the pass, and in 1860, Sir Richard Burton's party stopped for a meal there. He describes the station as a primitive habitation:

> It was a mere "dug-out"—a hole four feet deep, roofed over with split cedar trunks, and provided with a rude adobe chimney. The tenants were two rough young fellows—station master and express rider—with their friend, an English bulldog.[12]

One other point that Burton makes about Dugway Station is that "Water is brought to the station in casks."[13] The year prior, Horace Greeley had said the same thing: the water "which was given our mules had been carted in a barrel from Simpson's Spring."[14] This is one of the conundrums of the Pony Express: the waterless stations. According to Pony Express expert Joe Nardone, fifteen stations needed water hauled in. Nothing I've read about the mail service has ever confronted the job of hauling water for the livestock.

Hauling water is not easy. At each cache, I had sixty to seventy gallons of water for my horses, usually in three large, uncovered plastic tubs, each weighing about one hundred sixty pounds. Upon arriving at camp, my horses would drink twenty gallons. Over the next three hours, they would drink nearly another twenty gallons, and by first light the next morning, only a few inches of water would remain in the third tub. Most veterinarians and a quick internet search will tell you that an average horse will drink ten gallons of water per day. Chicken Fry and Badger were working harder than an average horse, and we were crossing one of the driest, least hospitable environments in the U.S., but they drank far more than ten gallons.

The Pony Express horses were working hard in the same country. We don't know how many horses were kept at Dugway Station, but Burton reported ten horses at the Fish Springs Station, the next station farther west.[15] At least six horses at each would probably have been needed to accommodate the twice-weekly service running both east and west.

If each horse could survive on thirty gallons of water per day, the station would need 180 gallons of water daily, or 1,260 gallons weekly. There are two ways water could have been hauled. One is in casks or barrels; the other is in a 500-gallon water wagon, which was a long, cylindrical tank made of wooden staves sealed with pitch and mounted on the chassis of a mule-drawn wagon.

I ran the calculations, and whether in casks or a water tank, supplying water to Dugway Station would have required three to four weekly trips. The water would be hauled from either Simpson Springs or Fish Springs, and each round trip would require a full day of driving the team. This would have been a critical supply line for outposted stations like Dugway where water is life and there is no water. A horse starved for water is a sorry sight, and when you're burning through 180 gallons daily, any disruption in the service would levy an ugly toll in a matter of hours. Each dry station would have needed a dedicated worker to supply it with water.

What this means is that the cost of shortening the relay between two stations—Simpson Springs and Fish Springs—by building Dugway Station between them, is part of the reason the mail service was prohibitively expensive to operate. Supplying water to Dugway Station would have been a full-time job. So, too, would hauling hay have been a full-time, year-round job for many stations, not only at places in the desert where there hasn't been grass enough to graze a horse for the past 9,000 years, but also in places where the horses were kept in corrals to avoid losing them to theft. Provisioning the men at the stations and supplying the gear and horseflesh for the mail runs would also have required freighting. More men on the payroll, more livestock to look after, and more equipage in the way of harness and wagons that needed maintaining.

When credit is lauded on the mail service for its brief but bold stroke in history, the riders are first to receive the acclaim. They carried the mail. They braved the road. They executed the most famous courier service in the world at that time. But they could hardly have done what they did without the station keepers and stock tenders who receive less credit than the riders but more than the men hauling water or shoeing the horses or distributing the hay. Compounding the difficulty of all of this on both the animals and the people was the remote and severe nature of the environment. Living at Dugway Station, though busy enough with the coming and going of the express riders and the water wagons and the hay haulers, would have been a hard existence.

I camped on Dugway Pass in a stand of cheatgrass so dry it hissed like a starving fire in the gentle breeze. The night was warm and quiet. I could hear the insects moving in the grass around me. On the west side of the pass the next morning, I passed a Great Basin rattlesnake. The snake was more yellow than any rattlesnake I'd previously seen, and it coiled and buzzed and lifted its front third off the ground. Behind it, a salt-white expanse of desert dwindled to the blue horizon. I was at the edge of the salt flats, and for all its aridity, at the south end of that nearly lifeless expanse lies a large oasis called Fish Springs.

Fish Springs, which is now Fish Springs National Wildlife Refuge and so named because of the native Utah chub found in its waters, contains 10,000 acres of marshland. Several artesian springs—points where water flows to the surface through hydrostatic pressure within the aquifer—discharge roughly 25,000 acre-feet of water, or about eight billion gallons, each year.[16] The water at the surface fell as rain 9,000 years ago, and since then it's been percolating toward the springs at the rate of a half inch per year where it pools into marshlands that support flocks of Pacific Flyway migrators crossing the driest part of North America.[17] Today the wildlife refuge diverts and impounds the water into several large ponds that are visible on a satellite image, looking like turquoise stones set in snow.

Fish Springs Flat surrounds the wildlife refuge as a level plain, bounded on the east and west by volcanic mountains and on the north by only the white horizon. As I approached the springs, the vegetation slowly thickened until the scrubby greasewood gave way to meadows of salt grass, as thick and green as a tidal flat. From the back of my horse, I had a higher perspective than anything for miles around me but still could not see any water, only the salt grass prairie that stretched out like a green carpet. Livestock is prohibited from entering the wildlife refuge so I saw nothing of the springs other than a few pelicans circling a mile or so away and a small colony of avocets that flew over as I rode past the refuge headquarters.

I camped at a gravel pit that had been quarried into the side of the mountain above the refuge. Under gray carbonate cliffs, I penned the horses on pure rock, without soil, that was ungracious but cool in its north-facing aspect. As the sun lowered in the west, the grassy plain around the refuge hued from green to citrus. The blue sky went pink in the east, and before night had fallen, the moon hung squarely over the ridges beyond and nearly full. Two hours later, a veil of clouds hid the moon.

I woke to a starless morning. The air was damp. First light revealed the rarity of a foggy summer day in the West Desert. I rolled my gear and led the horses out of the gravel pit, and as I was closing a barbed-wire gate, Badger quickly lifted his head. The leather reins jerked my hand across the wire. One of the barbs hooked the base of my thumb and laid open a cut across the meaty part of my hand. It immediately began to bleed. The same thing has happened to cowboys wherever they close wire gates, which is all over the West. Unfortunately, my med kit was safely packed away at the bottom of the starboard pannier on Chicken Fry, so I dug out a small package of tissues that had been in my saddlebag since Nebraska and began blotting the cut. It wasn't painful, but it was bloody. Once the bleeding stopped, I climbed onto Badger and held my left hand away from the horse, as far from any source of infection as I could keep it while I held both the reins and the lead rope in my right hand. I rode like that for nine hours, with my left hand held away from my horse and my dirty jeans. My arm cramped and the muscles ached from the unnatural carriage of my hand, but I genuinely feared infection.

I hadn't seen a cottonwood tree in eight days when I rode into the cool shade of Callao on the afternoon of August 8. Callao, pronounced KAL-ee-oh, sits at the base of the Deep Creek Range, whose summits reach to 12,000 feet and hold snow all year. The snowpack of the Deep Creeks supplies the water that grows the massive cottonwood trees, and though the community is too small to be included on the census, it has good water. Callao smelled like water. It was more of an expression of the color green than I'd seen since the city parks of Salt Lake City, and with the verdancy came a feeling of relief.

At the edge of town, a sign made of unfinished boards had been painted with a map of who lives where. About a dozen names were located on it. Beside the name Anderson appeared "Willow Springs Sta." At the entrance to the Anderson place, a stone obelisk with a bronze Pony Express medallion marks the site, though the station sat one hundred yards from the road. I rode into the drive under the shade of the cottonwoods, with the wind running through the leaves like creek water tumbling over rocks. An oscillating sprinkler ran beside the house. I felt as though I could hydrate myself simply by absorbing atmospheric water in such a place. I slid off Badger at the edge of the front yard and the horses pulled at me to graze, but I dragged them to the front door and knocked on the wooden frame of the screen door.

Don Anderson opened the door. He was wearing a blue t-shirt and a feed-store ball cap, and he had gray hair. We shook hands and he said he'd get his wife, who would show me where to put the horses. He let the screen door close and walked back into the house, and I heard him holler, "Beth, there's a cowboy on our front step here to see you."

Beth opened the door with a smile. She had a warm face, reddened by the sun, and she spoke softly. She looked at my horses and at me and then down at my left hand and moaned disapprovingly. The cut had glazed over to a dark crimson and the dried blood showed the creases in my palm because I'd spared my water in case I became delayed: I thought it might be more important for drinking than rinsing the cut.

"Have you got something to clean that up with?" she asked.

I told her that I did in my packs.

"Let's get your horses situated." We walked around the back of the house and put Chicken Fry and Badger in a corral with a rivulet of irrigation water running through it, and they dropped their heads to green grass for the first time in a week. I put my saddles in the tack room, and Beth said that a small tin-sided building attached to the tack room was a cold house for storing butchered animals.

"It's a long way to a grocery store out here," she said.

I asked her how far, and she said, "Eighty miles to Wendover, half of it on dirt roads."

Yep, I said, that's a long way.

"We didn't get electricity until 1972. In 1986 we got a

telephone, and Daddy was against it. He thought we didn't need one."

I sat against the base of one of the cottonwood trees and unpacked the pannier with the med kit. I ran my hand under a hydrant in the yard, and Beth asked if I need a bandage or anything. I told her, no, that it was the first time since leaving Missouri that I'd had to mop up my own blood. For nine hours, I'd managed to avoid touching my hand to anything. Handling both horses with only my right hand made the day one of the most difficult of the journey. The cut didn't hurt—the only pain was in my arm muscles—but it had been a significant inconvenience. After all that, the cold water soothed the discomfort, and I smeared the cut with antibiotic ointment and wrapped it with gauze and cling wrap.

Once I'd patched up my hand, Beth pointed to an old house and told me that she was raised in that house but that it was empty now and that I could put my gear in it. The house was small and painted white. Two sprawling willow trees covered it and the driveway before it. The willows were originally set as green-log posts for the clothesline, and in the same way that a coppice fence takes on a life of its own, the trees had since become massive entanglements of long thin branches and slender leaves that gently swung in the breeze. Beside the house stood an old clapboard building that was the Willow Springs Pony Express Station. It's the only intact, in situ Pony Express station in the country, Beth said.

"My family, Bagley—Bagley is my maiden name—bought the ranch in 1886, and I'm the fifth generation to live here."

Two large cottonwood trees stood in front of the station on either side of the door, and Beth told me that the tree on the right was the largest-diameter Fremont cottonwood tree in the state of Utah and the second largest in the nation, behind a larger one in California. "The oldest photograph of the tree we have is from 1900," she said.

The station had a pitched roof and a screened porch running off the front. Both the exterior and the interior had been remade several times over the years. The original log frame had been walled with adobe bricks, and where the top coat of paint had crumbled off or broken, the inner-wall bricks appeared very old and white as ash. One hundred sixty years of settling had left not a joint or corner square in the place, but the integrity of the small building remained. The front door led to an anteroom that led to the kitchen.

The wood paneling of the kitchen had been painted lime green some time ago. Dusty articles, pots and pans and tools and more cookery, cluttered the countertops and shelves. The room smelled old. An enameled tin chamber pot sat on the floor with a small piece of paper on it, and on the paper was written "1st indoor plumbing." A pair of rusted antique ice skates hung from a plastered wall, and a treble hook for curing meat hung from a ceiling beam. Old photographs of family and horses decorated the walls, and on a long table sat a framed certificate complimenting the Bagley family for its preservation of the historic site.

The Bagleys, and now the Andersons, have been stewards of both the building and the history. They maintain a connection to their past through the modest building set between the two large cottonwood trees, and to me the connection seemed free from the veil I've encountered at historic sites preserved by federal or state governments. I found intimacy in the dust-covered shelves, the sagging ceiling joists, the layers of paint distinguishing one rustic renovation from another.

As Beth showed me through the old building, I felt like we were at an intersection of history and its people. Our shared Western heritage somehow made us whisper in the cool bed-room where the express riders and station keepers had slept. It was like being in a church, and standing there in the Willow Springs Station, having come more than a thousand miles on the old mail route, having considered every day what workaday constitution the riders must have needed, having weathered storms of similar circumstance, I was moved to a hallowed place. No one, I thought, knows the ride of a Pony Express rider, but I'd come pretty close. My time in the desert, free from the distractions of population or vegetation or paved roads, had revealed what no book had conveyed, what I could not fully articulate, but what I knew was a past informant to our current psyche.

Beth told me she needed to move sprinklers, and she left me to sort my gear. Don walked out of the house and asked to look over my horses. We leaned on the fence while Beth dragged hoses over the green grass. I told Don that I felt like I'd arrived at an oasis.

"Well, there's not the water there once was," he said. Don and Beth moved to the ranch from Southern California in

1994 to take over the operation. In the nearly thirty years that he'd been there, he said, he's seen the water table drop.

"As people have expanded their operations and are irrigating more acreage, they're using more water. Used to be, you'd dig a post hole and come back half an hour later and it'd be full of water. Not the case these days."

I told him that I'd had a hot and dry pull from Salt Lake, and I asked if it might be all right if I laid over a day to rest my horses. He nodded and told me I could stay as long as I pleased.

"Supper's at six. Come on up to the house."

At six, Beth hollered for supper. She served chicken and dumplings and green beans and passed slices of warm bread. Don asked me if I wanted to shower after supper, and I told him that I'd be fine, that I was going to lay over a few days at the Bateman Ranch two days' ride from Callao and would wash up there. He asked if I needed to use the phone to call Claire to tell her that I was all right, and I told him, no, that she was expecting me to call the day after tomorrow. He asked if I needed any food or gear or bandages for my hand, and I told him that Claire had mailed a resupply package to the Batemans, so I was all set with food and still had enough bandaging material. He asked if I needed anything at all, and I told him no and thanked him.

"Now look," he said and set his knife and fork on the table and looked at me, "we don't want to be responsible for the cowboy someone found lying beside the road with his two horses, or maybe just one horse—I don't know if your horses would stick with you or leave you or what—but we don't want to get a call from the neighbors about you."

I rested a day at the Andersons', and on the following morning I woke at four o'clock and rode north out of Callao with first light. The road angled along the slope of the Deep Creek Range until it climbed to Overland Canyon. From the mouth of the canyon, some 1,000 feet over the valley floor, the Great Salt Lake Desert ran from Callao to the northern horizon as an unbroken white sheet between successive ridges of basalt and granite that shone hazy and ethereal in the afternoon sun. That was my last look at the West Desert of Utah.

I rode up through the dry, serpentine arroyo of Overland Canyon while the sun robbed all shade from the dry slopes. In the windless air of the loose-sand thalweg, the dust of my horses hung behind me. I made camp that afternoon on Clifton Flat above the head of the canyon. Nathan's final cache was hidden under a juniper tree beside a long water trough for sheep that took water from Skinner Spring, one hundred yards uphill of it. The narrow trough was filled mostly with moss and algae, but a few inches of clear water ran down the center. I penned the horses around one end and went to fill my water bottle from the other when a rattlesnake hissed and so surprised me that I almost fell over backward. It recoiled up against the base of the trough, and it worked its tongue in and out of its raised head. It held the rattles of its tail upright but ceased to buzz as it inched backward away from me in a coiled heap, looking for crevice or cover.

I considered killing the snake or chasing it away. I didn't want it to crawl in my bedroll with me later that night, and I didn't want Chicken Fry or Badger to step on it. But I didn't kill it or otherwise harass it. I left it because the water trough was probably its home, and I was only a visitor. I'd be gone in a matter of hours. The snake knew the horses had arrived, and I figured it would stay clear of them. I also figured that it didn't want trouble any more than I did and probably wouldn't try to share my bedroll. I was the passerby, he the resident, and because the karmic stakes seemed too high amid all that empty desert, I avoided that end of the trough. I did not see the snake again.

By half past eight that evening the country finally started to cool off. Flights of mourning doves whistled overhead in fast passes and then settled in twos and threes beside the horses where the trough overflowed at its bottom end. A waxing gibbous moon hung over the top of Overland Canyon, and the eastern sky turned a deep, abyssal blue. Leaving the desert behind me to the east was like returning to Earth.

———◆———

I was four hours coming off Clifton Flat to the first paved road I'd seen in a week's time and one hundred miles of travel. I followed the cracked highway straight south, and when I met a cattle guard on the north side of Ibapah, three cars pulled up to me at the same time. It was more traffic than I'd seen since Salt Lake City. A pickup stopped on the road in front of me, and a skinny man with a gray moustache and thin gray hair got out of the truck and walked at me, and I slid off Badger.

"Kyle Bateman. I'm Luke's father."

We shook hands. Kyle was wearing beige Western-style slacks, heeled boots that were clean and polished, and a clean white shirt. Church had just finished, he said, and dinner would be served in two hours. I'd forgotten it was Sunday. Claire had mailed a resupply package to Luke, and I asked about it.

"Yep, your box came. Luke's got it." He pointed to the ranch house a half mile distant under sprawling cottonwood trees and told me he'd meet me there for dinner.

Luke Bateman and his family, a wife and four children, live in an old log house that's been refurbished and added onto over the years. Kyle and his wife live in a similar house opposite the drive from Luke's house, and the collection of attendant ranch buildings and the church and the school and the community center are all that stands for Ibapah. There is no town. It is and has been a Mormon community on the edge of Goshute Indian land, first established in 1859 as a church farm on the banks of Deep Creek. The place became a Pony Express station the following year, but its original purpose was to graft agriculture onto Goshute life, which worked about as well as similar efforts all over the West, in which cultures and people who were not already farming at the time of contact with European Americans could hardly take up the plow in a season's time after generations of nomadic ambulation over a desert that required the acute, sporadic procurement of its widely spaced resources.[18]

The Goshutes were hunter-gatherers. Depictions of their lifestyle when the European Americans arrived are consistently bleak. They were often derogatorily called Digger Indians. The Ibapah interpretive kiosk, a concrete wall opposite the school, says:

> The term "Gosiute" means "Kusiutta," describing their original dusty, well-traveled look. . . . Living in small family groups, they ate berries, pine nuts, pickleweed, insects and small game, and lived in roofless, brush wind-breaks or cedar bow wikiups. Clothing was scarce.

Goshute lore says that the people have always inhabited the deserts of the Great Basin. Scientists suggest they migrated into the area from the Death Valley region about 1,000 years ago.[19] Either way, they made a life where comparatively little lived and little grew, and the settlers who found them clad in rabbit-skin capes and carrying all that they owned in baskets reckoned the Goshutes would do well to cultivate more than so meager a diet. But the harsh desert soil was not so hospitable to the sowings of white ambition, and the church farm at Ibapah was abandoned the year after it broke ground.

Goshutes suffered under the influx of whites. The population diminished. In 1912 the Skull Valley Reservation, which houses the Skull Valley Band of the Goshutes, was formed. The Confederated Tribes of the Goshute Reservation at Deep

Creek followed two years later.[20] The Deep Creek tribal head-quarters is three miles south of Ibapah. It's a low, concrete building with a bunker-like profile. A few thirsty trees shade the entrance, and it's from this building that the Goshutes are trying to preserve their identity, their language, their tenuous hold on their culture amid alcoholism, drug use, and hardly a job to be had. Preserving their existence means making money, and one way they make some money is through selling trophy elk hunts in the nearby Deep Creek Range.

Historically, elk did not live in the Deep Creeks, but the Goshutes introduced a herd in 1987, and sales of hunting permits benefit the tribe financially. In another venture, from 1975 to the late 1990s, the tribe leased land to a rocket-test company, though later the company moved its operations elsewhere.[21] Then in 2000 the Goshutes offered space for the nation's largest open-air nuclear storage facility for spent power plant fuel rods, but that never played out because everyone other than the Goshutes—as well as many tribal members—opposed it.[22] In 2007, the tribe proposed damming Deep Creek to create a reservoir and generate hydroelectric power, but nothing ever became of the water-impoundment project.[23]

That was the last big effort by the Goshutes to bring devel-opment to the reservation, as far as Kyle had heard. He told me this as we were driving south past the tribal headquarters the day after I had arrived. We were going to look at an injured horse owned by his cousin who lived on the far side of the reservation. We found Marilyn Linares sitting on her front porch while hummingbirds swarmed around her, darting between the half dozen feeders filled with red nectar. Downhill from her house, a bay mare stood motionless in a corral. She was a nice-looking mare, dappled through her barrel, with a thick neck, dark legs, a dark face, and the heavy deep jowls of the old foundation breeding preferred by some cowboys. A cloud of flies orbited her face. Flies crawled over her lip and in the corners of her eye, but her problem was at the base of her right front leg.

A few months prior, the mare had become tangled in wire and in her effort to free herself had nearly sawed off her foot between the long and short pastern bones of her ankle. The cut was on the backside of her leg, just above her hoof. The entire foot was swollen and, like her face, supported an orbit of flies. From the cut, puss the color of lemon meringue pie ran down the shiny black heel and had made the dirt wet. Tight concentric circles in the dust around the hoof betrayed that the mare had for some time been standing as we then saw her. She didn't look like a horse that wanted to move. She hardly acknowledged our approach. We leaned on the fence, and she stood without regard for us, as though she were in some traction of pain, denied what horses most need: the ability to move, walk, run. As the mare stood glaring at us, Marilyn was clearly upset by the situation.

"I can come put her down if that's what needs to happen," Kyle said.

"She's been such a good mare for us," Marilyn said. "She's raised us some really good colts over the years."

The injury was severe enough that the mare might never be the same, probably never fully recover soundness from a cut so deep. She'd been on and off antibiotics for weeks, Marilyn said, and she wasn't healing. A horse without a foot is no horse at all, and Kyle shook his head, and Marilyn sighed.

"Well, let me know if I can help in any way," Kyle said.

We left Marilyn with her mare, and we walked out the shadeless drive to the truck, and Kyle said that he didn't like the look of the foot. "Not pretty," he said and clicked his teeth. As we approached the Goshute tribal headquarters on our way home, we raised a woman and a child walking north along the side of the road. Kyle slowed the truck, lowered his window, and said to me, "I know this woman."

She was a dark-skinned woman with jet-black hair that was wild and windblown. She wore a red t-shirt and black sweatpants that were pulled to her knees so that her calves were exposed, and she had thin sandals on her feet. She led the child by the hand, and the child, a young girl maybe four or five years old, was dressed similarly to the woman. When Kyle pulled up beside her, she turned and looked at him once and then looked forward and continued walking. He rolled beside her and asked after her health. I couldn't hear a reply. He asked after her mother's health. I could hear Kyle but not anything the woman said or even if she had said anything at all, but she seemed disinclined to talk. Her face was grave, mostly without expression, and that was enough expression for me to know that she was either not fond of Kyle, not in the mood for chatting, or maybe not too happy about walking down the side of a desert highway on a hot, cloudless August afternoon. Kyle offered her a ride, but she must have declined the offer because nothing happened. We rolled beside her for another second and Kyle acted like he wasn't sure whether to drive on, but he said, "Okay, well, take care," and we left her, hatless, leading the child under an unforgiving sun down a straight and unchanging road.

It was hard for me to find optimism on the Goshute land. I felt that the land had long ago brought about a seminomadic equilibrium in the Goshute people, that they had evolved a lifeway as a result of the land's demands and constraints, and that the current situation was less organic and less sustainable. They are an isolated people, far more isolated than any of the federally recognized twenty-three peoples in New Mexico, where I live. Two hundred people live on the reservation south of Ibapah. The emptiness of the land all around dwarfed the Goshute reservation in the same way that it did the thin line of Pony Express stations. As Kyle and I drove back to Ibapah, we were two miles past the woman and child before we saw a house that could be her destination. I mentioned to him that I reckoned the house to be where she was headed, and he looked out his open window at the house as we flew past it and then looked at me and shook his head, but he didn't say anything.

I camped three nights at the Bateman ranch. I slept in the vacant mobile-home bunkhouse. The cut on my hand closed and became less painful to the touch. After a week of healing, I no longer feared infection. I mapped my way across Nevada.

Two weeks of riding would get me halfway across the state. Nevada sounded too big and too dry. I figured it was all rattle-snakes and mustangs, country so big a man could ride all day without seeing a fence. There were mountains ahead of me. Fourteen consecutive ranges trending north-south between Utah and California, and I'd cross each one straight abeam. Up and over fourteen passes, across as many valleys between. I had good maps and a list of phone numbers, and my horses had the flesh for the trip—or what I expected of the trip—so there was nothing to do but cross the state line in the name of progress toward California.

For the first time the thought of making California emerged from the abstract. With the next full moon, I should be at the foot of the Sierra Nevada. I was 101 nights out from St. Joseph, Missouri. I had originally planned to arrive in Sacramento after 100 days, but I still had all of Nevada ahead of me. It didn't matter. The horses were setting the rhythm. I needed to rest at every opportunity that I could, but if we could keep up our pace and routine, the only things that could stop us were the same things that could have stopped us any day before: a nail in the road, an unseen rattlesnake, a piece of gear failing into catastrophe and injury. Just as it could all end in the space of a heartbeat, so was it also new every day, reborn for what the day before had made of it. With every night and every mile the logbook thickened. The concentric layers of my experience—an experience that was indivisibly of and within the American West—were added by blind turns on a road so straight I could see two weeks ahead, halfway across Nevada, some 200 miles from the bunkhouse where I sat. The idea that the pioneer spirit of the West runs close to the surface of the modern landscape is what inspired me to compass the country horseback. I made up to pull out for Nevada under moonlight the next morning, and I lay in my bedroll on the floor of the bunkhouse thinking there was no way that Nevada could be drier than the West Desert of Utah.

CHAPTER 9

"*They weren't all bad—
some were just wild*"

I'D BEEN THINKING about Nevada ever since I first considered riding the Pony Express Trail. Nevada is the American outback, the sagebrush steppe, a lonely corner of the West. It was mostly unknown to me, but I knew that it was big country. The trail enters Nevada's White Pine County, which is larger than New Jersey but averages about one person per square mile.[1] That's a population density less than Alaska. Nevada is the driest state.[2] It sits almost entirely within the rain shadow of the Sierra Nevada. A rain shadow is a dry area behind, or downwind, of a mountain range. The mountain range creates the desert rain shadow because as moisture-laden air moves up and over the mountains, the air cools, the moisture condenses and falls as precipitation, and the downwind area is left dry. The Sierra Nevada mountains, which run north-south along the eastern edge of California, take the moisture from winds coming off the Pacific Ocean and create the desert of the Great Basin.

Nevada is also the most mountainous state: nearly all of the topography is alternating north-south-trending valleys and ridges, basins and ranges. That was my perception of what lay in store when I crossed the state line—and entered the Pacific Time Zone—before dawn on August 14. I was 102 days from St. Joseph, Missouri, having traveled a distance that the Pony Express mail would have covered in seven days. But crossing into Nevada was a milestone because it represented the last big stretch of open desert before California.

I rode the sun up on a wide, flat playa vegetated by low, yellow-topped shrubs that grew no taller than a boot. Drab badland hills rose on either side of the playa, and the road ran over the level valley floor where there should have been a thalweg or arroyo or some marker of a drainage, but there was no indicator that enough precipitation had occurred in the region in the past millennia to produce surface flow. The valley was dry and quiet and felt very old.

I followed a southwesterly bearing all day toward a line of mountains that I'd been looking at for three days while at the Bateman Ranch. The Antelope Range stood like a wall over the valley. Folds and fissures of naked rock came into focus with the hours and the miles. I camped that night near the site of the Antelope Springs Pony Express Station, which shows up on maps today as Tippett. It's a ranch, not a community or a town or anything more than the most remote single-family residence I'd seen since leaving Missouri. When Richard Burton stopped here in 1861, the Pony Express station had been burned down and the only permanent fixture of the mail service amounted to a pole corral for the horses.[3]

The next day, I skirted the Antelope Range along its southern slopes, and as I angled along the strike of the hills, gradually gaining elevation, the dry valley gave way to a more verdant landscape. Sagebrush and piñon pines and juniper trees replaced the stunted vegetation. The country did not look like Utah, though it was hard for me to define exactly why. I could see mountains to the north and south, faint ridges that appeared blue and hazy in the distance, but I could see no effects of the hand of man other than the road that I followed. As I turned to the northwest to enter Spring Valley, I flushed a trio of mustangs—two reds and a black. They saw me when I came into view at a hundred yards, craning their necks upward, and then they turned tail-to and disappeared into the mountain scrub.

At the bottom of Spring Valley, I turned north for a ranch called the Need More Sheep Company, owned by Hank Vogler, who had said I could camp at his corrals for the night. Hank's ranch was the first sheep-raising operation I would camp at, and one thing I'd heard about sheep ranching in Nevada is that South American herders do most of the work (this was true of other states in the West as well). The herders arrive as temporary laborers. A program through the U.S. Citizenship and Immigration Services issues H-2A visas that authorize foreign labor, on a short-term basis, that's used all over the country.[4] In the West, South Americans, usually Peruvians and Chileans, herd sheep and goats (cattle are less prone to predation and death and therefore don't need a herder living with them on the range). Operations like Hank's are required, per federal regulations, to advertise herding jobs locally, but in fifty years of hiring herders, Hank told me, only three of them have been "white guys" and the one who lasted the longest worked for nine days before quitting.[5]

At the ranch headquarters, I found two men at a hydrant, washing a red truck in front of a red steel-sided shop. I said howdy and they didn't respond. I said hola, and they both said hola and nodded. The older man looked to be about sixty years old, and he wore a black mesh ball cap, black heeled boots, and blue jeans that were too large in the waist and had been pulled into tight folds with a leather belt. The younger man wore silver tracksuit pants and a featureless gray t-shirt and had olive skin, black, short-cropped hair, blue eyes, and the chiseled muscling of a worker.

In Spanish I told them that I had talked to Hank on the phone three days prior, and that he'd told me I could pen the horses here for the night. The younger man stepped to the side to get a better look at Chicken Fry and the packsaddle. I told them that I'd ridden from Missouri and was headed for California. The older man nodded and said something to the younger one, and then they both smiled. "Okay, venga," the younger one said, and turned and gestured with his hand for me to follow him.

As I rode behind the young man with blue eyes, he told

me that he was Chilean and that the older man was also Chilean. I asked how many men worked at the ranch, and he said, "Diez y siete." Seventeen ranch hands are a considerable workforce and made me wonder how many sheep the ranch raised. The young man nodded toward the old man, who had by then turned off the water hydrant and was walking into the shop, and said, "Manager."

Where's Hank, I asked. The young man jerked his chin at a house uphill from the barns. "Allí."

I put Chicken Fry and Badger in a large corral, forked them some hay, and then walked up the hill to see Hank. He was a tall man with square shoulders that spread out like an inverted triangle from his narrow hips. He wore wide black suspenders over a flannel shirt, and his gray hair was combed over to one side in a neat fold. I entered what turned out to be his office, and there I saw the first computer I'd seen in weeks.

Hank is a vocal man. He regularly writes columns for Nevada newspapers and trade publications like *Range* magazine, and these days most of his energy is directed at stopping the city of Las Vegas from buying up all the water in northern Nevada. The Southern Nevada Water Authority, the state agency charged with keeping the swimming pools full and the taps running for the city's two million residents and forty-one million annual visitors, started buying up ranches for the water rights in 2006. The plan was to one day pipe the water south to Las Vegas. The water authority has since accumulated more than twenty-three thousand acres of deeded ranch land, grazing rights to nearly a million acres, and water rights to twenty-two billion gallons of water a year, all of it under the name Great Basin Ranches.[6]

The agency's northern acreage borders Hank's south pasture, and their permitted grazing regions interfinger in the mountains on either side of the valley. Hank doesn't think it's legal for a tax-free state agency to enter into private enterprise by competing with private livestock producers, and he is completely certain that state and federal officials have abused their powers. To Hank, giving more water to Las Vegas, the biggest city in the state, is like buying a liquor store for a drunk. A pig is still a pig even if you put lipstick on it, he says. He rolls out his tongue like a mule skinner's lash, and he'll tell you that his politics are unclear, that he's been known to throw a skunk on the table at a garden party. He says that the list of people trying to put him out of business is longer than a polygamist's clothesline. He thinks that no one in America buys lamb anymore because no one in America cooks anymore and that if you want to hide something from a woman where she won't find it, hide it in the oven. He survived pancreatic cancer and says that he's been read his last rites so many times that he'll be able to read them for himself when the time comes. The country around his ranch, he told me, is hard on women and horses, and his main hired man, the older man I met when I arrived, had outlasted at least one wife.

But when I met Hank, he was short on time. I felt as though I had interrupted him.

"You're like a badger digging a hole in a gravel road," he

said. "You're in the middle of a hard job that most people wouldn't take on, and I don't want to interfere with you."

With that he stuck out his hand and wished me luck. I was thinking that a cold beer and a hot dinner wouldn't interfere with me, but instead I told him that I had put my horses in a corral and that one of his men showed me to the hay.

"Yes, for chrissake feed your horses. But if you build a fire, don't do it in the corrals."

I told him I wouldn't need a fire, and he reminded me that I was at 7,000-feet elevation. As I turned to leave, he said, "And if you want my opinion, the Pony Express was a government ploy to scout for mineral resources in Nevada. The Silver Rush was in '59. The Pony Express came along in '60." He paused and looked at me as though what he just told me was common knowledge.

"I mean, come on. They wanted to know what else was out here."

I hadn't heard that theory, I told him, and he said that it was only his opinion. We nodded at each other, and I walked down the hill to the corrals. I laid my saddle blankets over the thin grass beside the tack room and boiled water for ramen noodles. Two border collie pups about two months old appeared out of nowhere and crawled on my saddles and over the panniers. Then, as I was eating the noodles, a man I hadn't seen before walked by holding a yellow and brown bull snake. It was about four feet long. He gripped the snake behind its head with his left hand, and its mouth gaped into a small pink pocket. The rest of the snake was wrapped around his arm. "En el baño," he said, smiling, and lifted the snake slightly in my direction.

You found the snake in the bathroom? I asked.

"Sí, sí," he said with a big smile. Through gesturing, he made it clear that he had discovered the snake while sitting on the toilet. I watched as he walked over to the hay meadow and released it. At the far edge of the same meadow sat a massive pile of split firewood, and two men were throwing the wood, two pieces of it at a time, into a high-sided truck. When they finished, half an hour later, they drove by where I was sitting. The driver nodded at Chicken Fry and Badger and whistled between his teeth. "Se venden tus caballos?" he asked.

I smiled and thanked the man but said they were not for sale.

Around nightfall, the manager came over and asked me, "Quieres cafecito?"

I nodded and stood and said thank you and asked him where, and he said, "En la casa," and pointed to a small pink house across the ranch yard. I followed him into the house and set my hat on the washing machine in the entryway mudroom. In the kitchen, the man set out coffee cups and began preparing his dinner.

I asked him his name, and he said, "Leonet Rivas Reyes."

He told me that he had been coming to the ranch to work for Hank for thirty years and that he was now the oldest and oversaw the others. He split his time between his home in Chile and Hank's ranch, what he called "mi otro país." *My other country.* Then the man I saw with the snake walked through the front door, washed his hands in the mudroom, and sat at the table with us with a cup of coffee.

"Mi sobrino," the old man said, nodding at his nephew.

"Mi tío, mi tío, mi tío," said the younger while stirring sugar into his coffee. He rose and said something to his uncle that I couldn't understand and laid out a few lamb chops beside a hot-plate grilland nodded at them assuringly. "Borrego del rancho. Muy bien."

I asked where all the sheep were at that moment.

"En las montañas," the older man said.

Which mountains? I asked

He made a circle with his hand over his head, pointing his index finger outward as he rounded the compass and said, "Todos las montañas."

I asked if most of the ranch's seventeen herders were in the hills with the sheep at that moment, and the old man nodded. He said that each herder looked after about five hundred "borregos." The man said that all of the ranch's herders were from Chile and Peru, only Chile and Peru, not any other country. Their visas usually lasted a few years. It was hard work, he said, and it was not for every man. "Una vida muy básica," he said. "Un hombre con caballo, uno or dos perros. Los borregos. No hay mucho mas." *A very basic life. A man with a horse, one or two dogs. The sheep. There is not much more.*

Time and space to think, I responded.

He smiled and agreed. "Sí, mucho tiempo para pensar todo. Mucha soledad."

The young man cooked the lamb and some chicken, and

the kitchen flooded with the smell of meat. I had anticipated a meal with Hank, but his hired men had made me the most comfortable I'd been in a long time. It was different than having a meal with Don and Beth Anderson in Callao or the Batemans in Ibapah because this felt like the bunkhouse. I was among workers. With these men, I didn't worry about smelling like a horse or having dirt under my fingernails. We had common ground and a mutual respect. It was like talking to cowboys about their work except that it was sheepmen about sheep, and that fascinated me, maybe because I didn't know much about the animals or the business of raising them.

I fell asleep that night thinking of the herders and their sheep. They moved when the sheep needed fresh pasturage, once every week or ten days. They spent the summer in the mountains and the winter in valleys. Their dogs were notoriously faithful. Like Leonet had said, it was a basic existence: the sheep, the mountains, the solitude.

The job and life of a sheepherder is easy to romanticize until you think about it enough. You get plenty of fresh air. There's very little oversight while working, which is always— you're on the job all day every day for ten months of the year. The ranch provides you with all the mutton you can eat, a horse to ride, and a dog to keep you warm at night. Once every week or ten days a resupply man brings food, water, news. Pretty soon, you learn the ways of the land, pick up slight cues in the atmosphere as to changes in weather, be able to read the behavior of your sheep, and know the best forage for them. You'll likely never get a shower or see anyone other than your resupply man, and you might spend about half the year out of phone service, but you will have participated in a form of animal husbandry that's practiced all over the world but assumes a unique nature in the American West.

———

Peruvian and Chilean herders started coming to the Western U.S. in 1952 through a Department of Labor program that granted three-year visas. At that time, sheep ranchers in Nevada, Idaho, and Wyoming were suffering from a lack of workforce, due partly to the disruptions of World War II and partly to the vacancy left by the discontinuation of a similar program that had brought Basque herders to the West since the late nineteenth century. The Basque herders were the first immigrant herders of any significant number to follow sheep over the ranges of the Great Basin.[7]

The Basque ethnic group originated in the westernmost regions of the Spain-France border in the Pyrenees mountains, in the vicinity of the Bay of Biscay. Ethnically, they are one of the oldest people in Europe. Their language is a language isolate, meaning that it is unrelated to any other language. The Basques came from the mountains and were accustomed to tending livestock, but they did not have the experience in herding sheep that would come to define the Basque experience in the Great Basin until later.[8]

The first Basques immigrated to the U.S. during the Gold Rush, which began in 1849. They eventually dispersed eastward over the Sierra Nevada, found jobs tending livestock, and by the turn of the century they had both established themselves as able sheepmen and become part of an agricultural system unique to its time and place. They also established cultural enclaves, and those can still be seen today at Basque hotels and restaurants in the intermountain West. In the 1950s, South Americans replaced the Basques, and they do most of the herding today.

I left Hank Vogler's Need More Sheep Company and climbed the Schell Creek Range west of the ranch. Over the next few days, I crossed the Steptoe Valley and the Cherry Creek Mountains and then the Butte Valley and the Butte Mountains. The country was quiet and dry and mostly inhabited by rattlesnakes, badgers, and mustangs. The days were hot and the mornings cool. This was a remote part of the Great Basin. It's between highways, between towns, and it's almost all government-owned land. Dirt roads cross the ranges and run up the valleys, but the roads see little traffic.

For much of the time, the old trace of the Pony Express Trail was visible beside the modern dirt road, and somehow over the past 150 years, evidence of the nineteenth-century travelers remained. I found old rusted horseshoes and mule shoes and shoes made for the cloven hooves of oxen. The shoes were left by not only those associated with the Pony Express, but also the ox- and mule-team freighters that traveled the same route until the Transcontinental Railroad was completed in 1869, some one hundred miles north of the Pony Express Trail. The road gets so little traffic today that the shoes were lying on top of the sand as though no one had been through there in a century and a half. The ox shoes were shaped like commas. Each foot had two shoes on it so that each ox wore eight shoes. A twelve-yoke team of oxen would need 192 shoes, and that is a significant amount of blacksmithing. I passed the sites of several stations, and at the site of the Mountain Springs Pony Express Station, I looked down into a hand-rocked well that had been covered by a sheet of plywood. The well was dank and mossy but held no water. The old station site was marked by debris—charred wood, bits of masonry, scraps of rusted metal, shards of dishware—and among the remains I found a white porcelain button that looked like it would fit a jacket of some kind or maybe the shirt of a Pony Express rider.

I crossed Long Valley and the Maverick Springs Range, and then Newark Valley, the Diamond Mountains, and the Diamond Valley. After six hot, dusty days, I called a man named Martín Etcheverry about camping at his ranch. Martin was of Basque descent; his surname means "new house" in Basque. He and his brother, Mark, owned the Roberts Creek Ranch, site of the Roberts Creek Pony Express Station, and when I told him over the phone that I'd ridden from Missouri, he said, "I got two questions for you. One, how crazy does a guy have to be to ride a horse from Missouri to California? And two, how sore is your ass right about now?"

I told him that my ass was fine but that I'd had a hard pull for the past week and wondered if I might be able to rest a few days at his ranch. He said that I could stay as long as I liked but that he wouldn't be at the ranch because he was harvesting almonds in Bakersfield, California. He had two hired men at the ranch who would take care of me. He said they were Peruvian and didn't speak English. "How's your Spanish?" he asked.

———

The Roberts Creek Ranch sits at the southern base of the Roberts Mountains, and both were named for Bolivar Roberts, superintendent for the Pony Express line from Carson City to Roberts Creek. Halfway up the mountain, slightly west of the ranch, the Gold Bar Mine sprawls in a jagged scar where the forest has been replaced by open pits, roads, leach heaps, and the workings to produce more than 30,000 ounces of gold annually.[9] The mine remains the biggest change to a landscape that otherwise looks mostly like it did in 1860.

I met Martín's hired men, Javier Colonio and Omar Cajachagua, in the cool shade of two massive cottonwood trees sprawling over the small ranch house. A large, two-story building beside the trees was apparently the site of the old timber-and-adobe Pony Express station. Omar and Javier were both young men, thirty-five or so years old, and both were dressed in long-sleeve shirts and dark pants and wore large straw hats with wide, turned-down brims. They were also wearing rubber boots because they'd been repairing a waterline. We shook hands. Javier said, "Bienvenidos a Roberts Creek Ranch," and after no more than a minute of conversation, Omar asked me what years the Pony Express ran. When I told him, he asked if

Lincoln was president, and I told him that Lincoln was elected while the Pony Express was running but that James Buchanan was in office when it began. He nodded.

"Quíen era el presidente antes de Buchanan?" he asked.

Franklin Pierce was in office before Buchanan, I told him. I worried he was about to ask me who preceded Pierce when Javier interrupted and told me they needed to finish the afternoon chores. Dinner would be at six thirty. As they turned to unload their truck full of tools, Javier asked, "Te gusta comida Peruana?"

I nodded and said that a Peruvian dinner sounded like just what I needed. "Bueno," he said.

Javier and Omar's house was clean and cool. The ranch is off the electrical grid, and an extension cable ran from a generator on the porch and through a window to a large television in the main room of the house. A soccer game was playing on the television when I walked in. On the table was a heaping skillet of chicken with tomatoes, onions, and potatoes, and a pot of rice. After the flatware and cups for water were laid out, Omar brought over a bottle of Sriracha and said, "Y el chile," as though the table was now ready for us to sit down to.

Omar and Javier are from the same village in the Andes. They were at the Roberts Creek Ranch on three-year visas, and they worked every day. There was not much else to do. At night they spoke to their wives and children on the phone and watched soccer. When I asked them if they ate full Peruvian dinners every night, they nodded. They didn't mind the solitude, and they said that the quietest nights come in the winter and that on a cold and moonless night in January, the stars will shine like a million diamonds in the sky. Omar arced his arm through the air and looked up through the kitchen ceiling. "El cielo es toda luz." *The sky is all light.*

We talked about my journey and about traveling by horseback, and they said that horses are still used by mountain people in the Andes. I asked them if they saw wild horses near the ranch. Javier said, "A veces," and pointed over his right shoulder and said the wild horses came from the south, "del sur." Were they ever a problem? I asked. They looked as if the answer was more complicated than a simple yes or no. One morning, Omar said, they walked out to the corrals and found a wild stallion in with two of their mares. "El caballo se saltó la cerca," he said—*the stallion jumped the fence.* They left the horse in the corral because they didn't want to open the gate and risk losing their mares. They didn't want to rope the stallion, either, because catching a wild horse around the neck isn't easy, and removing the rope from the stallion, to turn it loose once outside the corral, would have been even more difficult than getting the rope on it. Unsure of what to do, they fed all three horses and went about their work. The stallion stayed for three days, and then one morning they came out to see that it had disappeared.

After we ate dinner, we walked outside and looked at the unadulterated sky above. The moon had yet to rise, and the Milky Way glowed over us. After a while Omar broke the silence and said, "Nos vemos por la mañana," *See you in the morning.*

I rested three days at the Roberts Creek Ranch. They lent me a pickup to reprovision my groceries in the small town of Eureka, but otherwise I slept in the shade, looked over maps, and planned my next steps. Omar and Javier, like Hank Vogler's hired men, were as warm and hospitable as anyone else I'd met since leaving Missouri, and I thought that they treated me as they themselves wanted to be treated, with respect and generosity. My grasp of Spanish is serviceable but still our conversations were sparse. But that didn't bother me. Drinking coffee in near silence is one of the most enjoyable ways to get to know someone, and with a lot of barren desert ahead of me, I wasn't anxious to leave the Roberts Creek Ranch.

While I was at the ranch, a man delivering hay told me that his cousin, Tom Damele, owned a ranch that was the site of the Dry Creek Pony Express Station and that he would probably let me camp there for a night. The man said that it would be a good place for me to see because Tom had "kept everything in the old way." The Dry Creek Ranch was thirty miles southwest of Roberts Creek. I decided to split the distance into two days because the hard days of travel had begun to take their toll on Chicken Fry and Badger. They were both sound and strong, but I could feel a general ebbing of their energy. Safer to ride two days of fifteen miles than one day of thirty, I reasoned. I left Roberts Creek on the morning of August 25 without being able to reach Tom Damele but confident that if I couldn't camp at his ranch, I'd be able to someplace nearby.

———

I had been calling Tom's phone without luck for three days when I rode up to the ranch gate at three o'clock on the afternoon of August 26. The gate was closed, and the fine soil around it showed boot tracks. I could see horse tracks on the inside. I knew that once I dismounted, and walked through the gate, I would have announced my presence by leaving my own tracks.

I entered the ranch as an unknown, uninvited, unexpected visitor. At the ranch buildings a quarter mile from the gate, I hobbled my horses in the front yard and knocked at the door to the old stone house. The place was quiet. I hollered at the open door of a Quonset shop but received no answer anywhere.

The barn was below the house and built into the hillside. It was more of a roofed dugout than what most people would think of as a barn, and it looked as old as any barn I'd ever seen in my life, not because it had been standing longer than any other, but because it was constructed in a rudimentary, primitive way. The roof was slightly pitched and covered in soil. The framing was all hand-cut logs that showed the adze and axe marks of someone who was handy at hewing out framing timbers. The walls were made of uncut rocks, white and gray and yellow, loosely mortared with a cement made from the same material, and some of the mortar looked more like adobe chinking. The inside of the barn was cool and dark and smelled like earth, and it looked almost exactly like the

replica barn at the Pony Express Barn & Museum in Marysville, Kansas, except that this was the real deal. I wondered
what kind of person saddled a horse in a barn like this.

Two hours later, a blue pickup appeared on the ranch
road a quarter mile or so from me. It came slowly, and I
told the horses that we were about to find out if we could
camp there or would have to repack and move to public
land. The truck was old, and the engine loped along with
the growling, reassuring heaviness of a work truck. A man
had one arm cocked on the door when he drove up to us.
I told him my name, that I'd been trying to reach him for
a few days, that I'd been horseback for nearly four months,
and that if I might be able to camp in his hay meadow for
the night, I'd be no trouble. He looked me over and then
squinted at my horses, and then said, "Get in the truck.
Everything's cool."

We drove past the house and Quonset shop and up a broken
road parallel to the creek. At the top end of the ranch, thirty
or so horses stood swishing their tails in the shade of another
pole barn. Tom climbed out of the truck and shut a gate to
prevent "a mixup" of my horses and his. He'd hardly said a
word since I climbed in the truck.

"When I saw your tracks at the gate," he said finally, "I
thought maybe a beautiful woman with two horses had come
to visit me."

Tom is a skinny man of medium height and medium build,
about the right size to sit a horse. When I met him, he was
wearing a beaten gray felt hat that looked like it had been on

his head for the past fifty years. He wore a light blue shirt with a hole at one elbow. He was using a three-quarter-inch leather bridle rein for a belt, and he wore heeled leather boots like a logger might wear. The instep of the right boot had been once repaired with a patch, but the stitching had come undone and looked as though it might spill out a socked foot any day now. As I followed him into his house, he smelled like grass and diesel fuel.

The house, like the barn, was partially built into the hillside. The entryway was a cool, concrete-floored room with several gambrels for processing slaughtered animals hanging from ropes run through blocks at the ceiling and cleated off along one wall. A meat saw hung on a nail. On a sunny shelf at the front of the room, a longhaired gray cat slept on a saddle blanket, and when we entered, the cat stretched and yawned. "You like wine?" Tom asked as he pulled two glasses from a cabinet in the kitchen.

He filled our glasses from a gallon jug of Carlo Rossi Paisano wine and told me that he had bills to pay and then we could visit. We sat at a long wooden table, and he used the spine of a kitchen knife to open two envelopes. He moaned and ran his hand through his short, strawberry hair. He seemed tired. He set down the bill and looked at me.

"Two horses. All the way from Missouri," he said, shaking his head. He took a sip from his wine. "Same two horses?"

I nodded, same two horses. He looked down at the bill, which was from AT&T. He squinted at it and then held it at arm's length and moaned again. "Only two bills for this place. Telephone and propane. But the bastards want more every year."

He asked me to read the amount he was being billed and then wrote out a check.

"We're not supposed to care if we don't make any money, right? That's the deal. We get to live in a beautiful place, but we'll never get rich, and that's okay, but goddamn these guys, they're making it harder on us every year."

Tom's house was comfortable. The kitchen joined a large living room that ran the length of the house. Bookshelves in the big main room were lined with photos of men and horses and men on horses, a set of World Book encyclopedias, a dozen or so volumes of Reader's Digest condensed books, a copy of *Lonesome Dove*, and other books mostly about horses and the early West. An open-faced gun cabinet at one end of the room held a dozen or so rifles and shotguns and half as many pistols, and a dried rattlesnake skin was pinned below one of the rifles. Bridles, hackamores, rawhide quirts and reatas, horsehair mecates, and various pieces of tack and saddlery hung from a standing coat rack and from long rusty spikes driven into the walls. In one corner sat the largest freestanding wood stove I may have ever seen—a large iron barrel that was the size of a washing machine. I nodded at it.

"Well, it's an old house, and it gets a little drafty in the winter," Tom said.

The cat met us on the stone porch of Tom's house, where we sat in two chairs facing east toward a solitary landform some nine or ten miles away that rose from the level plains around it like a golden cone of Mexican piloncillo sugar set upon the desert tableland. We sat in silence for most of the first glass of wine.

Tom refilled the glasses. We began to talk about the Pony Express. I told Tom I'd seen quite a few old horse- and mule shoes on the trail.

"My dad found a gun ten feet off the trail under some sagebrush," he said. "A .32-caliber side-hammer Colt. All rusted solid, and the hammer was broken off. We figured that broken hammer was why he threw it into the brush."

That's a light-caliber pistol with a short barrel. It wouldn't be very effective for self-defense, especially not from the back of a moving horse. "It's a peashooter," Tom said.

I told him that at the Pony Express National Museum in St. Joseph, Missouri, I'd seen a life-size diorama of a rider, atop a plastic horse, carrying a large, Navy-style holster on his hip.

"Who the hell knows," he said.

No one knows, I said.

"Nobody really knows," he said. He refilled our glasses, holding the jug by its glass ring and using his other hand to lift the bottom.

Tom said that the Dry Creek Ranch went by a different name during the Pony Express and that the ranch was responsible for supplying horses for it. Up at the top of the ranch, he'd seen remnants of two long wing fences that had been used to catch wild horses. Each fence was a mile long on either side of a canyon and led to a large round corral at the bottom of the valley. Wild horses could be driven between the wing fences and then funneled down into the corral. From there, it'd take a couple of salty cowboys to get them ready to carry the mail, and that would be no small job. We agreed that making a good saddle horse generally takes about two years of consistent work, "if you want one that you're not risking your life every time you ride it," Tom said. Supplying horses for the Pony Express meant working on a much tighter timeframe.

"If those guys were breaking horses for the Pony Express, and the whole thing only lasted eighteen months, they weren't riding no gentle kids' horses," Tom said.

But if you could get one half-broke to where he'd let you saddle him and climb aboard, then all the horse would have to do would be run to the next station. Most people today want their horses to stop when they say whoa, turn left when they pull the left rein, walk quietly for an afternoon trail ride. But the Pony Express needed only one job out of its horses: run to the next station. If the horse understood that, maybe in a month's time you could get a wild one broke enough to ride. It wouldn't be no gentle kid's horse, but it might be able handle the work. And once the horse knew the job, we agreed, he'd be your best bet to get the mail through. Because those Nevada mustangs have hooves as hard as anvils. They know how to run through the sagebrush and avoid the badger holes. They're tough, not the sort to feel sorry for themselves or balk at a headwind. The Great Basin is not a mild climate or mild landscape. It makes strong horses, and if you had to run the twenty-five-mile mail relay through a nighttime blizzard in January, the horse most likely to get you there would be the mustang.

Tom refilled our glasses. We were uncovering the mysteries of the Pony Express while the gray cat turned figure eights through our legs and the sun set behind us. The Dry Creek Ranch comes up often in the history of the Pony Express because Paiutes attacked it on the morning of May 21, 1860. The station keeper, Ralph Rosier, was fetching water when he was shot dead in the front yard. Another man, John Applegate, ran to the door and was shot through the hips. The two remaining men piled sandbags in the windows and prepared to defend the station. As the story goes, a suffering Applegate borrowed a pistol with the premise that he would help defend the station, but instead shot himself through the head. The two others escaped on foot and arrived at Grubb's Well, twenty miles to the east, with bloody feet, having fled without boots. Emigrants later found the two dead men at the station scalped and mutilated.[10]

That incident was part of a conflict with the Paiute nation that became known as the Pyramid Lake War, and it shut down the mail service for three months. I asked Tom about the shooting scrape at Dry Creek, and he said, "I always heard it was over a woman. That's why they came and shot up the place."

I told him that the books I'd read hadn't mentioned a woman.

"I don't know if she was here on her own accord or whether they were keeping her here, but they raped her and all hell broke loose," he said. "The guys working for the Pony Express and everyone else out here, they weren't all bad—some were just wild—but some of them were bad men."

Finding good men to run the Pony Express may have been just as difficult as finding good horses for it. The only way for a line superintendent—there were five of them responsible for different sections of the mail route—to know if a station keeper had the horses in good working order, the corrals in good shape, firewood stacked, and food for the passing riders, was to ride the line and stop at each station. Those superintendents must have been constantly on the move, we agreed. If they found a man who wasn't working out, I asked Tom, how would they replace him?

"Might not have been a lot of other guys around to pick from," he said. "Hell, it can take a year to settle into a job."

We sat in silence for a while as Venus became a pinhead of light over the eastern horizon. The cat had gone to sleep in the house. One inch of wine remained in the jug, and small dots of purple showed on the flagstones where it had splattered while being poured. The country before us was shadowed and wide, and the landscape appeared very peaceful.

"I've been looking at this view my whole life," Tom said, "and I never get tired of it."

Below us in the valley, the failing light had accentuated two irrigated hay circles that showed like dark coins amid the sand-colored desert. They looked out of place, as though farming had no role in the desert. I asked Tom about the meadows.

"God damn sodbusters!" he roared and stood. He tilted his

head back, drained his wine, slung the dregs into the grass of the yard, and said, "Okay, I've had enough. See you in the morning."

———

The Dry Creek Ranch was the climax of my journey. Nothing had brought into focus the reality of the Pony Express like Tom Damele and a gallon of Paisano wine. The mail service lasted only eighteen months because the schedule was too tight and the land too hard. That's what I concluded. That the desert gave no quarter, and the cost of running horses over that desert was too high to maintain. I was walking Chicken Fry and Badger, covering about three miles to the hour. To make an average of eleven miles per hour, which is what the ten-day delivery schedule required, a rider would need a lot of fresh horses. Each one of those horses would need care and housing. And if there was another rider following, coming along three days behind, who would need the same, as well as two riders on the same schedule but traveling the other direction, then the support needed to carry that eleven-mile-an-hour average would not only be difficult to install and maintain, but also expensive to operate.

The history of the Pony Express is filled with gaps in the record, contradictory reports, and missing information, but the biggest unknown for me has always been the reality of it. No one knows what it looked like from a rider's perspective. But I got close. I'd seen the country, and I'd read the books, but Tom Damele brought the details to light. To me, he was a timeless man, as though he had survived the Old West and was here to tell me about it. I could just about see him breaking wild horses in an old log corral so that the young couriers of the Pony Express could fly their mailbags over the driest, most mountainous state in the nation. Tom was like a relic of that time, but he did not suggest an end. Rather, he was a living connection between the past and present. You could see it in the crow's-foot folds of his eyes and in that old weathered felt hat and in his house and his barn and the thirty horses milling in the corral. That's what I was looking for when I left St. Joseph, Missouri: the last man standing from the Pony Express.

From the Dry Creek Ranch, I rode up and over the Simpson Park Mountains, up and over the Toiyabe Range, and across the valleys between. I camped on Railroad Pass, at Cold Springs, at Middlegate, at Sand Springs. I slept on a salt pan, on a mudflat, and beside a 600-foot-tall sand dune. When I rolled up my bedroll on the morning of September 9, I found a black widow spider beneath it. That night, a woman from Fallon, Nevada, named Starr Schwoerer, brought hay and water for my horses to our desert camp. She also surprised me with dinner: half a dozen soft tacos wrapped in tinfoil. I told her about the black widow.

"They're bad this year," she said. "So are the scorpions. Do me a favor and sleep in your tent. You're almost to California."

Chicken Fry and Badger were tired. I could feel it in Badger when I stepped into the saddle. He would immediately start walking as I climbed on him, and I interpreted this as a way to balance my weight, similar to how balancing a bicycle is easier in motion than idle. When I loaded the panniers on Chicken Fry, I could see him give slightly to the weight. Both horses' faces looked tired. Their eyes looked tired. They were ready to be done with the twenty-five-mile days.

My last night in the desert was September 10. I camped at a place called Hooten Wells. To the northeast, the Dead Camel Mountains turned the color of bourbon. An ATV whined in the distance. From somewhere came the sound of an owl calling, but there were no trees within miles of me. The air was still and warm. The next day I would ride ten miles to a camp on the Carson River where Claire would meet me. She was driving up from New Mexico to see me through California. The desert was behind me. The Great Basin and the Rocky Mountains and the Great Plains were behind me. The mystery had been solved. I knew what could be learned from the months of solitary travel, and I owed it all to my horses. We could see California, and it looked like the end of a dream that I didn't want to wake from.

CHAPTER 10

The Final Miles of the Pony Express

MY EMERGENCE FROM the desert brought relief. On the afternoon of September 11, I rode into the shade of tall cottonwood trees along the Carson River. That was the end of the dry miles. Two days later, Claire arrived from New Mexico to see me through California and then haul the horses home once I rode up to the bronze Pony Express statue in Old Sacramento, which would mark the end of my journey. She was just as eager for the trip to end as I was. I rested the horses another three days in preparation for crossing the Sierra Nevada. On September 16, we drove the horses to a vet north of Carson City for current health papers because if there was any state that I expected to check my horses at the border, it was California. We camped just outside town, and that night a cold front dusted snow to a hundred feet above us.

The cold weather was a significant environmental change. The Sierra Nevada stand over Carson City like a wall demarcating a wholly different ecosystem. The other change was the sudden increase of population. Whereas not many people live out in the sagebrush and greasewood of the inner Great Basin, a lot of people live around Carson City, home to about 55,000 residents. The greater Reno-Sparks area, just thirty miles north, is home to nearly half a million. Just west of Carson City, Lake Tahoe is a major tourist and recreation destination. Between Lake Tahoe and Sacramento is the heavily trafficked thoroughfare U.S. Highway 50. In 1860, it was the route of the Pony Express.

The Carson City area was so densely populated that I handled it like Casper and Salt Lake City: hauled the horses around it. Claire and I camped just inside the Sierras at a place called Hope Valley, where one branch of the Pony Express route ran south of the main route through Tahoe. Hope Valley was a wide, boggy park that looked like the kind of place where you could find a moose, but there are no moose in California. That night we built the first campfire of my journey. I hadn't needed a fire before then because the nights had been mostly warm, but mid-September in the Sierra Nevada felt more like fall than summer.

From Hope Valley, I followed an old road grade from the valley and climbed into a forest that was unmistakably Californian. The trees were taller than any I'd seen since leaving

Missouri. They were old, venerable conifers with bases about the size of a hot tub, and many of the tallest ones had been decrowned by wind or lightning or heavy snow. The boughed tiers of the canopy brought a constant array of birdsong, so different from the silence of the desert. The understory was lush with aspen and red-branched madrones and fruit-bearing shrubs, and I saw the diversity of life as a sign of all that water coming off the Pacific Ocean. The biggest difference from the desert of the Great Basin, though, was that out there I could see three days' ride into the future, up and down valleys that could take a week to cover by horseback. In that California forest, I had fifty feet of visibility.

I topped out on the 7,740-foot summit of Luther Pass just after noon. At a pullout on Luther Pass Road, a black-and-yellow pole was graduated in six-inch increments to measure snow depth. The pole ran up to ten feet, tall enough so that I would have had to stand on my saddle to reach the top of it, and it suggested hard passage for a horseman in the winter. The coldest place on the trail for the Pony Express riders was probably where it crossed the Continental Divide at South Pass, Wyoming, but the snowiest miles were undoubtably through the Sierra Nevada. Not surprisingly, the snow caused delays. During December and January and into February of that first winter, delivery times were slower than the advertised ten-day schedule—one relay took twenty-two days, several took fifteen or sixteen days, and at least one did not go at all.[1] The only way the riders could get through was on a beaten track. Ten feet of snow isn't navigable on a horse, so the only way for them to ride up the valley and across the passes in the winter would have been on a packed trail over the snow.

The Pony Express followed the main wagon road connecting Sacramento with the silver mines in present-day Nevada. In 1860, like today, it was a busy throughfare, and it was notoriously steep. The trail plunged down out of the mountains and clung to the slopes above the American River. The stagecoach and wagon drivers who drove their teams up and down the Sierra became well known for their skill at handling a team of horses or mules along such precipitous roads, and one of the most famous of those drivers was a man named Hank Monk, who held the reins to Horace Greeley's wagon along this stretch of trail in 1859. Greely's ride became a well-worn yarn in the far West, though Greeley apparently never cared much for the story.

In short, it was a wild ride. In his book *An Overland Journey, From New York to San Francisco, in the Summer of 1859*, Greeley wrote that the road was the width of a wagon, with a sheer drop on one side. The driver "was of course skillful" but he drove the team "just as fast as four wild California horses, whom two men could scarcely harness, could draw it."[2] He comments that speed of the wagon and the narrowness of the road could have resulted in a collision or that the wagon could have plunged off the road, but he makes comparatively quick work of what Mark Twain, and several others, could not resist. Twain told the story four times in his book *Roughing It*. Each time, someone he met on the road told him the story of Greeley's ride and that "the coach bounced up and down in such a terrific way that it jolted the buttons all off of Horace's coat, and finally shot his head clean through the roof of the stage." Once Greeley arrived at Placerville, "what was left of him" crawled out of the stage as a bruised and battered man.[3]

William Banning, co-author of the book *Six Horses*, writes that Greeley took personal offense to the incident and that he misjudged Monk and overstated the danger. Banning notes that Monk, whom he calls a "Sierra whip," may have been giving Greeley a demonstration of how to make good time on a California road and that Greeley was simply unfamiliar with traveling in that part of California. He also writes that Greeley later resented Monk for personally humiliating him that day, that Greeley felt he had been "misused."

One look at the old wagon road today was enough to know why Greeley was concerned. It's just as steep a century and a half later. The same road gave me concerns, but for different reasons. California was full of people. The traffic on the highways was fast, and there was hardly a shoulder to ride on. The night after I climbed Luther Pass, Claire and I camped on the bank of the Silver Fork of the American River. It was a clear-running freestone river that plunged between granite boulders into calm pools where trout might have lived, and it was clearly a popular campsite: abandoned piles of toilet paper littered the ground in every direction. The human impact on the landscape was depressing. There was no quiet way to descend from the Sierra Nevada. The mountains were full of people, the traffic was too fast, and I had little stomach for it. There was a part of me that felt that Chicken Fry and Badger deserved better.

This was the final stretch of the Pony Express Trail, the last leg of a long journey that had taken me all summer. Since May 5, I'd been riding toward California, and when I arrived here, I found it demoralizing. In the desert, the solitude and space were comforting. I could handle rattlesnakes and dry miles and swarms of biting insects, but I could not handle the cars and people of California. Human manure was never far away, and the highway hummed with traffic all night. I thought of the West Desert of Utah, where I could hear the footsteps of beetles and the world was so quiet that dawn broke like a pistol shot across the open plains.

Hell with it, I told the horses, it's enough. All throughout my journey, I never held myself to completing a certain number of miles per day. I never set out to do anything more than follow the Pony Express Trail from one end to the other, and now that I was within sight of the end, I didn't want to risk riding along the highways. I'd managed to cover nearly 2,000 miles with zero bloodshed to the horses. As far as I was concerned, there was only one job left to do: ride up to the Pony Express statue in Old Sacramento. But I wasn't going to ride the seventy-five miles to get there. Any vestiges of the Old West were now behind me, and I wanted only to finish. Claire agreed to help me by hauling me and the horses into town so I could put a lid on this journey with one final push.

———

The Pony Express station in Old Sacramento was the end of the fast-horse mail relay. From there, the mail was shipped down the American River to San Francisco. Pony Express historian Joe Nardone identified an overland route to San Francisco that used a horse relay, but the majority of the mail was put on a steamer in the part of town known today as Old Sacramento, where a larger-than-life bronze statue commemorates the mail service. That was my destination. I'd seen it on Google maps, I'd seen photos of it, and I planned to ride to it on a thirteen-mile greenbelt trail system that led from the outskirts of the city right to Old Sacramento.

On the morning of Saturday, September 21, I unloaded Chicken Fry and Badger on the shoulder of the greenbelt and assured them that they were nearly done. We took off at a high trot. The trail was a wide gravel road that ran between neighborhood housing on one side and the American River on the other. It was a warm, humid morning, and the horses must have sensed something was different because they showed a renewed energy and freshness. For the first time since somewhere in Nebraska, I was moving faster than a walk. We'd been traveling at three miles per hour for nearly the entire journey, and now at last we were making good time toward the finish line.

Unfortunately, as we were trotting past fields where children's soccer games were going on, I looked back to see Chicken Fry limping. My guess was that he stepped on a rock in such a way that it bruised his foot. It was disappointing. Getting into Sacramento was proving difficult and frustrating, but I was determined to finish at the bronze Pony Express statue. So I called Claire, who had driven ahead, and told her that we needed yet another ride. Two hours later, we parked the horse trailer a few blocks from the statue.

Old Sacramento had a frontier feel. The buildings looked old. A candy store with Victorian architecture advertised salt-water taffy for sale and "over 400 fine candies." The Wells, Fargo & Co. sign was painted in an old font. On the small city streets, the traffic moved slowly. There were pedestrians on the sidewalks, crossing the roads, peering into storefront windows. From where I unloaded the horses, I trotted down 2nd Street past the California State Railroad Museum to the Old Sacramento State Historic Park, which is about a half block in area. An old woman in a gaudy nineteenth-century dress was talking to tourists. A baseball team wearing old-style uniforms, like something out of the movie *Field of Dreams*, loafed in the shade at one end of the park. The horses felt good, as though they knew that I had one thing on my mind, and they obliged me. Chicken Fry, who was always the horse to ride in challenging situations, no longer limped, and as we clicked over the concrete, Badger clung to his hip for security amid all the sound and commotion of the city.

I trotted across the park and turned the horses down J Street, and we fell into traffic. The road was narrow, so I trotted right down the center yellow line to part traffic. A silver Toyota SUV stopped as I approached, and I could see a child in the passenger seat craning to see the horses. I wove between a line of cars stopped at a stoplight, managed to avoid clipping any side mirrors with my stirrups, and rode out into more traffic. The cars coming from both directions stopped as I did so. I tipped my hat to them, crossed the intersection on a diagonal, and pulled up Chicken Fry and Badger beneath the bronze statue of a Pony Express rider.

That was the end of my trail. That was the goal that I had been working toward for 142 days. That was the reason for all the early mornings and the long hauls and the constant progression westward. That was the location where the Pony Express horse would be freed of its burden, where the saddle would be pulled off and the horse turned out to pasture. It was the end of the line, and for me, it was like the twilight of a day that had been five months long. We had accomplished our objective, and it was a deeply satisfying feeling.

———

Claire and I spent three days driving home to Santa Fe. I tried to make sense of all that had transpired. I began on May 5, and I finished on September 22. I'm not sure how many miles I traveled because I never tallied mileage. The Pony Express Trail is 1,966 miles, but my route had been convoluted, and I might have covered more than that. I'd been on the road for fourteen weeks. My boots had holes in the soles. I'd completely worn out one pair of jeans and one shirt and had gone through about a dozen pairs of wool socks. But I didn't lose any weight, never adjusted my belt from the day I started, and I was no worse for the journey.

Images of all those days on horseback flashed through my head. I saw a dead steer, bloated and stiff-legged under a high sun, with thirty or so of its brethren standing around it. I saw minks trained to kill rats and a pet Canada goose. I saw the blood of a lamb and a horse with a broken neck. I saw a pronghorn fawn so small it could hide under a cowboy hat, and I saw a pygmy rabbit, the world's smallest member of the rabbit family and no bigger than a tennis ball. I rode through valleys of grass carpeted with wildflowers, and I found water in the desert where no water should have been. I met a rattle-snake crossing the road on a cool morning. Most of all, I saw the details of the American West, its unique landscape and its people.

I tried to think through what this all meant and what I had learned. I learned that groundwater in parts of Nebraska is unfit for drinking because of nitrogen-heavy runoff from farming operations, a problem that will remain in our lifetime. Cheatgrass is arguably the biggest environmental threat to the West. Hay producers in Nevada pack shipping containers with bales of alfalfa and send them to South Korea to be fed to racehorses. People drown in corn every year in the Midwest. Fire is the biggest ecological component missing from the Great Plains. But all that was just information. The lessons were more abstract.

I learned that we have mostly lost our palate for water. Municipal water, bottled water, well water—none of it tastes markedly different. In Utah, I filled a bottle with water that smelled like a swamp and was green with algae. I tried to filter out the algae with a sock, but the sock water was worse than the moss water. I drank water from an irrigation ditch downstream of a herd of mother cows, and the water tasted like cow manure. Springwater from a mudhole in Kansas tasted like mud. At the other end of the spectrum, water from the Sweetwater River in Wyoming tasted the way its name suggests. Springwater at the Dry Creek Ranch was the same, like liquid saccharine. When you drink surface water, you realize that not all of it tastes good.

I learned that optimism is fundamental to maintaining morale while traveling. A rough night's camp was bearable because the following night would almost certainly be better. Two consecutive hard nights further increased the chance that things were about to improve. Moving was the remedy for a bad situation, and the most important aspect of moving was to be organized and efficient.

I learned that the only way to cope with unavoidable risk was to have faith in my ability to deal with the situation. As I saw it, there was always some kind of wreck waiting for me down the road. The only way to square moving forward with the well-being of the horses was to assume that I had the means and wherewithal to minimize the damage—and a plan. If my horse stepped on a nail, I'd immediately jump from the saddle and remove the nail with my pliers. If my horses got loose on the side of the highway, I'd call 9-1-1. If my horse bucked me off out in the sagebrush and left me with a broken pelvis, I'd use the BIC lighter in my vest pocket to light the sage, start a grass fire, send up a smoke signal. None of that ever came to pass, but I tried to avoid over-worrying myself by telling myself that I'd know what to do when the time came.

But the most significant thing I learned between St. Joseph and Sacramento was that the Pony Express was more impressive than anyone knows. I couldn't wrap my head around hauling water to the waterless Dugway station. I couldn't understand how you could keep half a dozen working horses at a desert corral that had no water source. I could hardly believe that the Pony Express riders crossed South Pass at night in the winter without getting lost or freezing to death. Fundamentally, I couldn't quite see how a bundle of letters in a saddlebag could be relayed by horseback from Missouri to California in ten days in 1860. It didn't seem possible. Figures and distances and statistics attempt to approach the truth, but there's a lot missing. I calculated the number of horse exchanges, points where a rider would get a fresh horse or hand off the mail to another rider, during one week when the service was running twice weekly in both directions. It was 532 exchanges per week. No one fully understands that number because connecting the dots could take 142 days, but it represents a massive coordination of manhours, a lot of running horses, and slightly more than 5,500 miles of horseback travel in one week.

Postal experts estimate that the Pony Express carried a total of 39,500 pieces of mail. Some estimates say that between 400 and 500 horses were used, but I'll bet the Pony Express burned up at least that many with hard riding. If you assume there were six horses at each of the 190 stations—though we know that many stations had more—the service would require 1,140 horses. My guess is that the Pony Express used between 1,500 and 2,000 horses and mules and that it was rigorous work. The number of riders has been given as 180, but that's just a rough guess because we know that some station keepers and livestock tenders substituted for regular riders. And we know that not all claims of riding for the express are accurate. In places like the Pony Express National Museum, as well as in most books about the Pony Express, Buffalo Bill is listed as a rider. He claimed to have ridden in Wyoming, to have covered 350 miles in one epic relay. But a leading expert on the Pony Express, historian Joe Nardone told me that he was certain that Buffalo Bill did not ride for the Pony Express because William Frederick Cody is listed on the Census of 1860 as being at school in Kansas.

Everyone knows that the historical record suffers from a lack of verifiable information. You can shoot holes in any book for its inaccuracies, but the biggest piece of missing information, what no one could tell me after all that I'd been through, is what a corral full of Pony Express horses looked like. That's what I wanted to see: twenty-five of those hardy mail horses circling in a log corral like a school of sharks. They probably wouldn't look dissimilar from horses today, but to me they were different. They were part of the Pony Express. That was the luster: that horses for the Pony Express were no ordinary horses; they were part of a fast-horse mail service whose legacy informed the national identity. And after compassing the full length of that transcontinental beat, I saw Chicken

Fry and Badger right among those Pony Express horses, milling in the same log corral, having earned their places in a rareified cavvy.

Claire and I arrived in Santa Fe on the evening of September 25. When I turned loose Chicken Fry and Badger in the pasture that they'd last seen five months prior, they threw their heads up, flagged their tails, and ran a wide circle around me. I could hardly breathe. They were so happy to be home. They moved a little stiffly, as though three days in a horse trailer wasn't exactly the best therapy after some 2,000 miles of walking, but they were sound, and they were in good flesh. There was nothing more I could have asked for.

EPILOGUE

A WEEK AFTER I finished riding, Claire and I bought a house outside Santa Fe. It had a barn with six box stalls, corrals for horses, and space for plenty of hay. We moved in with five horses. For Chicken Fry and Badger it was a comfortable place to enjoy sedentary life—they'd earned it, having traveled farther in a summer than most horses will their whole lives. As the days cooled and shortened, their coats grew long and their bellies round. The hard muscling of the Pony Express Trail faded from their shoulders and their hindquarters. Winter rolled into northern New Mexico, and hardly a day passed that I didn't look up at the snowy mountains around town and be glad I wasn't camped there. Spring brought strong westerlies that blew juniper pollen in yellow clouds, and along with the wind came the coronavirus pandemic and global lockdown.

Claire pulled hard shifts in the hospital emergency room while

I sat at my desk all day. I hardly left the house or the corrals. In the evenings, I'd go to the horses. I seldom rode either Chicken Fry or Badger, though whenever coyotes needed chasing out of the barnyard, Badger was the horse for the job—still the best at fast work and tight handling. We had few visitors, but we taught a friend's daughter—who had never formally learned—to ride. She was eight years old. I put her on Chicken Fry. She began slowly, walking circles around me in the corral, riding out to get the mail, sitting atop Chicken Fry while he grazed dry grama grass in the pale evening light. For the young girl, Chicken Fry may have been the best horse in the world to learn on.

Three years went into writing this book. I kept in touch with many people whom I met and stayed with during my summer on the Pony Express Trail. Not all the news was good. In February 2020, the old mountain man Roy Dougherty, who I had met on the plains of Wyoming, passed away. Two years later, his pal Bill Sinnard also passed. Ray Robinson, the trucker from Sidney Nebraska, died in the summer of 2022. Joe Nardone, a Pony Express expert from Southern California, died in July 2021, one week after I met him at his house. In the fall of 2021, my friend and mentor, Jack Brainard, died. He had lived to the age of one hundred years, three months, twelve days. Also among those who have passed since I rode across the West is my mother, to whom this book is dedicated. She is the reason that I write.

Will Grant
Santa Fe, New Mexico
January 2023

Acknowledgments

Claire is the person most responsible for me being able to write this book. She helped me and supported me more than anyone, and she put up with it for longer than anyone. I could not have done this without her. My agent, Ethan Bassoff, was also a consistent supporter of the original idea, and he remained committed to the book's success throughout the process. I owe the final form of the book to my editor at Little, Brown, Pronoy Sarkar. Pronoy helped me develop a logic to the narrative, to refine my perceptions of the West, and to contextualize what I experienced on my journey. Pronoy's input was critical to executing the book that I envisioned.

Jonah Ogles deserves credit sowing the seed of a book about the Pony Express. I'm grateful for his editorial direction, criticism, and encouragement from the beginning. Elizabeth Hightower Allen was a helpful editorial backboard for me while writing this book, and her pointed criticism of it in the late stages made the story better. Kaelyn Lynch proved to be an indefatigable fact checker, and I appreciate her dogged efforts to retrace my steps.

ACKNOWLEDGMENTS

Throughout my life, my father has encouraged my pursuit of the character of the West, and I am thankful every day for his support, guidance, and insight. Likewise, support from Claire's parents, Stephanie and Jurek Antoszewski, enabled me to complete this project.

I also have to thank everyone along the Pony Express Trail who made it possible for me to ride from Missouri to California:

The Buchanan County Sheriff's Office for escorting me over the Missouri River. Lyle Ladner for helping me cross northeast Kansas. Norman Meng for showing me his dairy farm. Betty Bunck of Bunck Seed Farms for letting me camp at the old barn. Jack and Linette McKee for putting me up and sending me on my way with a bag of peanut-butter energy balls. Roy Winkler for his insight and a night's pasturage. Sarah Pralle for letting Claire and I camp in her yard. Darrell Mosier for letting me ride in his tractor. John and Lynn Greer for letting me wait out storms and telling me how someone could drown in corn. Larry Overy for letting me camp in his pasture and feeding me breakfast. Jan Dassinger and Jack Hoban for letting me camp at the Kenesaw arena. Gene Hunt for letting me camp in the powder magazine at Fort Kearny. Joe and Dianne Jeffrey for letting me camp in their yard and taking me to Medo's for dinner. Frank Pride for letting me camp in his yard when he wasn't home. Dan Seaburger for being the first cowboy that I met on my journey and for bringing me breakfast from Burger King. Angie Blagdon for letting me camp at an empty house outside North

ACKNOWLEDGMENTS

Platte. Steve, Holly, Dylan, and Shyann Sward for letting me rest Badger at their barn. Nadine Bishop for showing me the most beautiful grasslands on the North American continent. Mary Cone for letting me camp in her pasture. Marcia Mays for letting me camp in her pasture. Linda Dolezal for cutting my hair and finding a pasture for my horses. Gordy Wilkins for cooking me dinner and showing me the museum. Ray Robinson for helping me understand the golden days of the over-the-road trucker. Dawn and Terry Adamson for cooking the Mormon backpacker and me dinner. Bill Frakes for taking photos and bringing me groceries. Kelly Davies for cooking me red chile enchiladas and giving me a saddle pad for Badger. Tim Sussex for stopping by to say howdy and for teaching me how to be quiet with horses. Roy Dougherty and his wife, Mary, for letting me camp in their yard. Bill Sinnard for a quiet afternoon of conversation on Roy and Mary's back deck. Larry Chamberlain for letting me camp at the site of the La Prelle Pony Express station. Les Bennington for riding a day with me, putting up my horses for several days, and feeding me for just as long. Matt Wold for securing permission for me to camp at his family ranch west of Casper. Matt Hoobler for telling me about ranching with sage grouse. Nate Bressler for taking photographs and bringing dinner. Laurie Redland for her hospitality. Scott Zimmerman for riding over the Continental Divide with me. Andy and Melissa Misner for their optimism and hospitality. Pastor Joe Reynolds for getting me through southeast Wyoming. Jane and Terry Siegismund for letting me camp in their barn and feeding me dinner. Robert Douglas for his help finding camp-sites and for holding my horses in the parking lot of a grocery store while I reprovisioned. Jeff Young of Ensign Ranches for allowing me to camp on the ranch and for showing me the way toward Salt Lake City. Trever Carpenter for hauling my horses around the city. Zane Dansie for putting up my horses for a week of rest. Nate Unkefer and Kate Stirling for letting me camp in their yard and borrow a car. Nathan Carpenter for caching hay and water for me in the West Desert. Don and Beth Anderson for letting me rest a day at their ranch. The Bateman Family for their hospitality. Brent Gardner for letting me camp in the ranch yard. Hank Vogler for letting me camp at the Need More Sheep Company. Leonet and his *sobrino* for dinner and coffee at the ranch. Tony Zamora for his maps and information. Tom Fowlks for taking photo-graphs and bringing food, alfalfa cubes, and water. Martin Etcheverry for letting me camp at the Roberts Creek Ranch. Omar and Javier for their hospitality. Mark Damele for his advice. Tom Damele for helping me understand the wild nature of the Pony Express. Kay Knudtsen for dinner and letting me camp in her yard. Susan Williams for letting me camp in her yard and looking after my horses. My brother, Newell, and my mother and father for renting an RV and saving my hide after I became sick. My sisters, Margaret and Caroline, for their continued support and tolerance of the project. Billy Gandolfo for helping move my horses. The nice people at Middlegate Station. Arthur Chapman for brining me hay, water, and cantaloupes. Bill and Starr Schwoerer for bringing me hay, water, and dinner south of Fallon. Jake Gabris of the US Navy for brining me hay, water, and whiskey. John Ehrenfeld for chasing me down to take photos. Megan Miller for meeting Claire and I in Sacramento. And Joe Nardone for sharing his insight and knowledge of the Pony Express.

Notes

CHAPTER 1

1   Entwistle, P.G., A.M. DeBolt, J.H. Kaltenecker, and K. Steenhof, compilers. Proceedings: Sagebrush Steppe Ecosystems Symposium, 2000. Bureau of Land Management Publication No. BLMIIDIPT-001001+I150, Boise, ID.

2   U.S. Department of Agriculture, *Atlas of American Agriculture*, by O.E. Baker, Washington, DC: U.S. Government Printing Office, 1936.

3   Sanford, Ward E., and David L. Selnick, "Estimation of Evapotranspiration Across the Conterminous United States Using a Regression with Climate and Land-Cover Data," *Journal of the American Water Resources Association*, 49 (2012), 217–30.

4   U.S. Department of the Interior, U.S. Geological Survey, *Report on the Lands of the Arid Region of the United States with a More Detailed Account of the Land of Utah with Maps*, by J.W. Powell, Washington, DC: U.S. Government Printing Office, 1879.

5   Webb, Walter Prescott, *The Great Plains* (Waltham, MA: Blaisdell Publishing Company, 1931), 8.

6   Turner, Frederick Jackson, "The Significance of the Frontier in American History." *Annual Report of the American Historical Association* (Madison: State Historical Society of Wisconsin, 1893), 197–227.

7   Neider, Charles, *The Great West: A Treasure of Firsthand Accounts*, (New York: Coward-McCann, Inc., 1958), 11.

8   Dobie, Frank J., *The Mustangs* (Edison, NJ: Castle Books, 1952), 22–24.

9   Ambrose, Stephen E., *Undaunted Courage: Meriwether Lewis, Thomas Jefferson, and the Opening of the American West* (New York: Simon and Schuster, 1996), 102.

10   Ibid., 397.

11   Parkman, Francis, *The Oregon Trail: Sketches of Prairie and Rocky-Mountain Life* (Compass Circle, 2020), 2.

12   Unruh, John David, *The Plains Across: The Overland Emigrants and the Trans-Mississippi West, 1840–60* (Chicago: University of Illinois Press, 1993), 119–20.

13   Mayer, Frank H., and Charles B. Roth, *The Buffalo Harvest* (Denver, CO: Sage Books, 1958), 15.

14   Ibid., 93.

15   Abbott, E. C., and Helena Huntington Smith, *We Pointed Them North: Recollections of a Cowpuncher* (New York: Farrar & Rinehart, 1939), 32.

16   Ibid., 34.

17   Chrisman, Harry E., *The Ladder of Rivers: The Story of I.P. (Print) Olive* (Lincoln, NE: Dawson County Historical Society, 2004), 247–51.

18   Abbot, 35.

19   Bradley, Glenn D., *The Story of the Pony Express* (Chicago: A.C. McClurg and Co., 1913), 59.

20   A timeline in the National Pony Express Museum in St. Joseph, Missouri, includes Herodotus's report.

21   Ramsay, A. M., "The Speed of the Roman Imperial Post." *Journal of Roman Studies* 15, no. 1 (1925): 60–74. doi:10.2307/295601.

22   This information comes from the author's personal experience in Mongolia, as well as personal correspondence with William Taylor, an assistant professor of archeology at the University of Colorado, who worked in Mongolia.

23   Banning, William, and George Hugh Banning, *Six Horses* (New York: The Century Company, 1930), 235.

24   These figures are the results of correspondence between the author and Joe Nardone, who was perhaps the only expert on the Pony Express before he died in 2021.

25   Burton, Richard F., *The City of the Saints: Among the Mormons and Across the Rocky Mountains to California* (Torrington, WY: The Narrative Press, 2003), 336, 361, 342.

26   Frajola, Richard C., George K. Kramer, and Steven C. Walske, *The Pony Express: A Postal History* (New York: The Philatelic Foundation, 2005), 3, 28–29, 103.

27   Frajola, Kramer, and Walske wrote about this incident for Siegel Auctions: https://siegelauctions.com/2013/1038/Platte.pdf.

28   Lewin, Jacqueline, and Marilyn Taylor, *On the Winds of Destiny: A Biographical Look at Pony Express Rider* (St. Joseph, MO: Platte Purchase Publishers, 2002), 63.

     Godfrey, Anthony, *Historic Resource Study: Pony Express National Historic Trail* (Washington DC: U.S. Department of the Interior, National Park Service, 1994).

29   Visscher, William Lightfoot, *A Thrilling and Truthful History of the Pony Express* (Chicago: Rand, McNally, and Co., 1908), 42.
30   Lewin and Taylor, 125.
31   Biographical information on Pridham is from the Pony Express National Museum in St. Joseph, MO.
32   *New-York Tribune*, 30 April 1860.
33   Bradley, 72.
34   Ellis, John M., and Robert E. Stowers, "The Nevada Uprising of 1860 as Seen by Private Charles A. Scott," *Arizona and the West* (Tucson, AZ: The University of Arizona Press, 1961), 358.
35   Clampitt, John W., *Echoes from the Rocky Mountains* (Chicago: The National Book Concern, 1888), 42.
36   https://www.ponyexpress.org/historical-timeline.
37   Banning and Banning, 215.
38   Banning and Banning, 225.

CHAPTER 2

1   Greeley, Horace, *An Overland Journey, From New York to San Francisco, in the Summer of 1859* (New York: C.M. Saxton, Barker & Co., 1860), 177.
2   Buck, Rinker, *The Oregon Trail: A New American Journey* (New York: Simon and Schuster, 2013), 246.
3   Wallacker, B.E., and R.I. Meserve, "The emperor of China and the hobbled horse of the Xiongnu," *Central Asiatic Journal* 49, no. 2 (January 2005): 284–302.
4   https://www.newyorker.com/tech/annals-of-technology/instagram-mules-follow-the-leader.
5   https://www.newspressnow.com/news/local_news/business/transport-360-doubles-its-capacity/article_22fc4d9c-ddb2-11ec-9411-83081afa6796.html.

CHAPTER 3

1   https://pubs.usgs.gov/unnumbered/70039437/report.pdf.
2   https://www.census.gov/library/publications/1864/dec/1860a.html.
3   Root, Frank A., and William Elsey Connelly, *The Overland Stage to California: Personal Reminiscences and Authentic History of the Great Overland Stage Line and Pony Express from the Missouri River to the Pacific Ocean* (Topeka, KS: Crane & Co., 1901), 39.

4   Loving, Mabel, *The Pony Express Rides On!* (St. Joseph, MO: Robidoux Printing Company, Inc., 1961), 66.

5   National Agriculture Statistics Service, February 2021. [AU: Can you provide a more specific source? A particular report?] YES HERE IS SUMMARY OF DATA: https://extension.umn.edu/dairy-news/dairy-industry-50-years

6   MacDonald, James M., Jonathan Law, and Roberto Mosheim. *Consolidation in U.S. Dairy Farming*, USDA ERR-274, July 2020.

7   Personal correspondence with Roy Winkler, who has worked as a pig farmer.

8   Slack, Tim, and Leif Jensen. "The Changing Demography of Rural and Small-Town America." *Population Research and Policy Review* 39, 775–83 (2020). https://doi.org/10.1007/s11113-020-09608-5.

9   https://www.ktik-nsn.gov/history.

10 Burton, Richard F., *The City of the Saints: Among the Mormons and Across the Rocky Mountains to California* (Torrington, WY: The Narrative Press, 2003), 24.

11 Greeley, Horace, *An Overland Journey, From New York to San Francisco, in the Summer of 1859* (New York: C.M. Saxton, Barker & Co., 1860), 53.

12 Root, 190–91.

13 http://amishamerica.com/amish-technology-friendliness.

Chapter 4

1   Gensini, V. A., D. Gold, J.T. Allen, and B.S. Barrett. "Extended U.S. Tornado Outbreak During Late May 2019: A Forecast of Opportunity," *Geophysical Research Letters* 46, issue 16 (27 August 2019): 10150–158. https://doi.org/10.1029/2019GL084470.

2   https://www.nass.usda.gov/Newsroom/2022/01-12-2022.php.

3   Chengane, S., C.L. Beseler, E.G. Duysen, R.H. Rautiainen. Occupational stress among farm and ranch operators in the midwestern United States. *BMC Public Health* 21 (12 Nov. 2021): 2076. https://doi.org/10.1186/s12889-021-12053-4.

4   https://americanhistory.si.edu/tractor.

5   https://cropwatch.unl.edu/fertilizer-history-p3.

6   https://www.osha.gov/sites/default/files/publications/grainstorage-FACTSHEET.pdf.

7   https://extension.entm.purdue.edu/grainlab/content/pdf/US_GrainEntrapments.pdf.

8   Buck, Rinker, *The Oregon Trail* (New York: Simon and Schuster, 2015), 14, 274, 287, 281, 316–317.

CHAPTER 5

1   Roger C. Anderson. "Evolution and origin of the Central Grassland of North America: climate, fire, and mammalian grazers," *The Journal of the Torrey Botanical Society*, 133 no. 4 (1 October 2006): 626–47.

2   https://databasin.org/datasets/110a8b7e238444e2ad95b7c17e889b66.

3   Scholtz, R., & Twidwell, D. (2022). The last continuous grasslands on Earth: Identification and conservation importance. *Conservation Science and Practice*, 4(3), e626. https://doi.org/10.1111/csp2.626.

1   Muhs, Daniel R., and James R. Budahn, "New geochemical evidence for the origin of North America's largest dune field, the Nebraska Sand Hills, central Great Plains, USA," *Geomorphology* 332 (1 May 2019) 188–212. https://doi.org/10.1016/j.geomorph.2019.02.023.

2   Schmeisser McKean, Rebecca, David Loope, and David Wedin. "Clues to the Medieval destabilization of the Nebraska Sand Hills, USA, from ancient pocket gopher burrows," Palaios. 24 no. 12 (2019) 809–17. https://doi.org/10.2110/palo.2009.p09-037r.

3   Hayford, Barbara, and Debbie Baker. "Lakes of the Nebraska Sandhills." *Lakeline* 31 (2012): 26–30.

4   https://ne.water.usgs.gov/ogw/hpwlms/images/dtw2000.jpg.

5   Burton, Richard F., *The City of the Saints: Among the Mormons and Across the Rocky Mountains to California* (Torrington, WY: The Narrative Press, 2003), 45–99.

6   Brodie, Fawn F., *The Devil Drives: A Life of Sir Richard Burton* (New York: W.W. Norton and Co., 1967), 52–53.

7   Chapman, Arthur, *The Pony Express: The Record of a Romantic Adventure in Business* (New York: G. P. Putnam's Sons, 1932), 229–30.

8   Burton, 338.

CHAPTER 6

1   Frink, Maurice, W. Turrentine Jackson, and Agnes Wright Spring, *When Grass was King* (Boulder, CO: University of Colorado Press, 1956), 138.

2   Sandoz, Mari, *The Cattlemen: From the Rio Grande Across the Far Marias* (New York: Hastings House, 1958), 235, 257.

3   Frink, Jackson, and Spring, 139.

4   Sandoz, 237.

5   Ibid., 267.

6   Abbott, E. C., and Helena Huntington Smith, *We Pointed Them North: Recol-*

lections of a Cowpuncher (New York: Farrar & Rinehart, 1939), 184–85.

7   https://obamawhitehouse.archives.gov/blog/2015/09/22/unprece-dented-collaboration-save-sage-grouse-largest-wildlife-conservation-effort-us.

8   https://pma.westernenergyalliance.org/press-room/western-energy-alliance-challenging-federal-sage-grouse-land-use-plans.

9   https://www.doi.gov/sites/doi.gov/files/uploads/so_3353.pdf.

10 https://www.energy.gov/sites/default/files/2018/05/f51/NWCC-Sage-Grouse-Fact-Sheet.pdf.

11 Bagley, Will, *South Pass: Gateway to a Continent* (Norman, Oklahoma: University of Oklahoma Press, 2014) 15.

Chapter 7

1   Deonna, W. "The Crab and the Butterfly: A Study in Animal Symbolism." *Journal of the Warburg and Courtauld Institutes* 17, no. 1/2 (1954): 47–86. https://doi.org/10.2307/750132.

2   https://alkali.genesisenergy.com/our-business/plant-operations.

3   https://worldpopulationreview.com/state-rankings/largest-landowners-by-state

4   https://www.sltrib.com/religion/2022/04/05/new-database-gives-widest.

5   https://www.churchofjesuschrist.org/study/general-conference/1991/04/the-state-of-the-church?lang=eng.

6   https://www.cbsnews.com/news/massive-mormon-deseret-ranch-plan-orlando-florida.

7   https://www.churchofjesuschrist.org/study/scriptures/bofm/ether/2?lang=eng.

8   https://blogs.loc.gov/maps/2016/04/the-state-formerly-known-as-deseret.

9   https://www.churchofjesuschrist.org/church/news/viewpoint-lesson-of-the-bees?lang=eng.

10 https://www.nbcnews.com/id/wbna8928524.

11 https://enrollment.byu.edu/financial-aid/cost-of-attendance.

12 https://www.weather.gov/slc/CliPlot.

Chapter 8

1   https://www.pewtrusts.org/en/research-and-analysis/articles/2015/03/19/nevadas-basin-and-range-a-classic-western-landscape.

2   https://www.nps.gov/grba/planyourvisit/the-great-basin.htm.

3   https://pubs.usgs.gov/pp/0257a/report.pdf.

4   Durham, Michael S., *Desert Between the Mountains: Mormons, Miners, Padres, Mountain Men, and the Opening of the Great Basin 1772–1869* (Norman, OK: University of Oklahoma Press, 1997), 81–82.

5   https://www.blm.gov/programs/wild-horse-and-burro/herd-management/herd-management-areas/utah/onaqui-mountain.

6   https://www.doi.gov/ocl/wild-horses-and-burros-0.

7   Simpson, George Gaylord, *Horses: The Story of the Horse Family in the Modern World and Through Sixty Million Years of History* (New York: Oxford University Press, 1951), 145–47.

8   https://www.mustangmonument.com.

9   https://psmag.com/environment/western-cattlemen-square-off-against-60000-mustangs.

10 Davies, K. W., G. Collins, and C. S. Boyd. "Effects of feral free-roaming horses on semi-arid rangeland ecosystems: an example from the sagebrush steppe." *Ecosphere* 5 no. 10 (2014): 127. http://dx.doi.org/10.1890/ES14-00171.1.

11 https://awionline.org/content/wild-horses-native-north-american-wildlife.

12 Burton, Richard F., *The City of the Saints: Among the Mormons and Across the Rocky Mountains to California* (Torrington, WY: The Narrative Press, 2003), 336.

13 Ibid., 336.

14 Greeley, 262.

15 Ibid., 338.

16 https://www.fws.gov/refuge/fish-springs/about-us.

17 Harrill, J.R., and D. Prudic. *Aquifer Systems in the Great Basin Region of Nevada, Utah, and Adjacent States—Summary Report* (Washington, DC: USGS, 1998), A1–A66.

18 Begay, David, Dennis Defa, Clifford Duncan, Ronald Holt, Nancy Maryboy, Robert S. McPherson, Mae Parry, Gary Tom, and Mary Jane Yazzie. *History Of Utah's American Indians.* Edited by Forrest S. Cuch. (Boulder, CO: University Press of Colorado, 2000). https://doi.org/10.2307/j.ctt46nwms.

19 https://indian.utah.gov/confederated-tribes-of-the-goshutes.

20 https://utahindians.org/archives/goshute/history.html.

21 https://utahindians.org/archives/goshute/history.html.

22 https://www.outsideonline.com/outdoor-adventure/environment/valley-shadow.

23 https://www.cityweekly.net/utah/last-stand/Content?oid=2161323.

NOTES

CHAPTER 9

1 https://worldpopulationreview.com/states/new-jersey-population.
2 https://statesummaries.ncics.org/chapter/nv.
3 Burton, Richard F., *The City of the Saints: Among the Mormons and Across the Rocky Mountains to California* (Torrington, WY: The Narrative Press, 2003) 342.
4 https://www.uscis.gov/working-in-the-united-states/temporary-workers/h-2a-temporary-agricultural-workers.
5 https://www.dol.gov/agencies/eta/foreign-labor/programs/h-2a/herding.
6 https://www.reviewjournal.com/local/local-nevada/southern-nevada-water-agencys-money-losing-sideline-ranching-farming.
7 http://zimmer.csufresno.edu/~johnca/humanities/Sheep.htm.
8 https://www.britannica.com/topic/Basque-language.
9 https://www.mcewenmining.com/operations/gold-bar-project/default.aspx.
10 Settle, Raymond W. and Mary Lund Settle, *Saddles and Spurs: The Pony Express Saga* (Lincoln, NE: University of Nebraska Press, 1955) 156.

CHAPTER 10

1 Frajola, Richard C., George K. Kramer, and Steven C. Walske, *The Pony Express: A Postal History* (New York: The Philatelic Foundation, 2005) 87–88, 96.
2 Greeley, Horace, *An Overland Journey, From New York to San Francisco, in the Summer of 1859* (New York: C.M. Saxton, Barker & Co., 1860), 281–82.
3 Twain, Mark, *Roughing It* (San Francisco: American Publishing Company, 1872), 152–53.

Index

INDEX

Will Grant currently lives in Santa Fe, New Mexico, where he's a writer for *Outside* magazine. His work has also appeared in *Bloomberg Businessweek*, and he was previously the Action Sports editor at *VICE*. Since graduating college, he has broken in horses at a Colorado ranch, apprenticed under legendary horse trainer Jack Brainard, cowboyed in Texas, raced the Mongol Derby, a nearly 900-mile horse race in Mongolia, and ridden horses on every continent but Antarctica.